The Dione Lucas
Meat and Poultry Cook Book

THE DIONE LUCAS
Meat and Poultry Cook Book

BY

Dione Lucas and Ann Roe Robbins

Drawings by Phoebe Nicol

GRAMERCY PUBLISHING COMPANY • NEW YORK

This edition published by Gramercy Publishing Co.,
a division of Crown Publishers, Inc.,
by arrangement with Little, Brown & Company
c   d   e   f   g   h

PRINTED IN THE UNITED STATES OF AMERICA

CONTENTS

CONTENTS

Lamb

CONTENTS

Ham and Pork

CONTENTS   *xiii*

Turkey

CONTENTS

INTRODUCTION

As the title of this book explains, the book is concerned primarily with meat — beef, veal, lamb, ham and pork — and with what we have broadly called poultry — chicken, capon, turkey, duck, goose, squab and guinea hen. The recipes are of varied origins. Many of them are French, since it is quite generally agreed that French cooking is the finest in the world. But they are not limited to France by any means, since other countries also produce many fine and interesting dishes. Incidentally, this does not claim to be a complete meat and poultry cook book, which would be almost an impossibility anyway, since there are hundreds if not thousands of recipes.

When thinking of French food, many people have a mistaken notion that it is always painstakingly elaborate and rich, far beyond the scope of the ordinary cook. Of course that is true of some French dishes. The so-called *haute cuisine* is the cooking of chefs and very experienced cooks who have had years of training, and who produce miracles in the form of complicated dishes which take hours and great skill to prepare. But obviously everyone in France is not equipped with these techniques, and the important factor in French cooking is not the fancy chef's techniques. They are excellent and you will be able to produce similar results with some of the recipes in this book. But the real keynote to French cooking — and for that matter all good cooking — is a loving attitude towards food. Care is taken in every detail of cooking. For example, if potatoes are to be diced, each piece is the same size. Carrots and turnips in casseroles or ragouts are not merely sliced but are cut into small olive shapes resembling the original shape of the vegetable. Meats are cooked until just the right state of tenderness, not left to get dry and tough or to lose their flavor. Much attention is paid to the serving of all food. Entrées are arranged on attractive-looking serving dishes, and usually garnished with complementary and appetizing-looking foods. Care is taken to contrast color and texture.

To accentuate flavor, there is a judicious use of wine, herbs and spices. One reason this is either looked down upon or feared by many people is that it is not correctly understood or is over-done. Wine has an alcoholic content, but since alcohol has a low boiling point, it evaporates quickly, leaving behind only a tantalizing flavor. A wise use of herbs gives an indefinable flavor to food; a lavish use overpowers all other flavors and can ruin a dish. So use both wine and herbs in moderation, and see how exciting the results will be.

We have taken into account the fact that most people are too busy to have unlimited time for cooking. There are many recipes which take a minimum of time and effort to prepare. There are also certain simplifications. Few people can take hours to make a fine brown sauce, so the basis of brown sauces in this book is concentrated meat glaze such as Bovril or B–V. Although really fresh vegetables are without any doubt better than either canned or frozen ones, the latter are timesaving and convenient. So their use is acceptable at times, especially when there are not garden-fresh vegetables available. Stock is an integral part of most sauces and gravies, so ideally we would all have beef, veal and chicken stock on hand at all times, especially since they can be frozen. But many of us do not. So beef stock can be made with meat glaze or bouillon cubes, and chicken concentrates or canned chicken soup make an adequate chicken stock.

Although we have tried to make the recipes very explicit, we have presumed elementary common sense. For instance, onions are always peeled, so we do not specify this every time an onion is used, which is often. The same is true of garlic. Fresh peas are always shelled and so on.

General Instructions: To make cooking as easy as possible and for your own peace of mind, cultivate orderly work habits. Line up all the ingredients before you start any dish. Clean up as you go along by putting used bowls and pans in the sink, and wiping up the work space with a damp cloth. Always keep a wet and dry cloth near you for this purpose. Pare vegetables over a piece of waxed paper which can be quickly disposed of with no mess. When working at the stove, have a plate handy for wet utensils so that the top of the stove stays clean and uncluttered.

Since it is best to have meat at room temperature when you cook it, take it out of the refrigerator at least an hour ahead of time.

It is not necessary to wash meat unless it is bloody. Heat is sterilizing, as we all know, and while water may be cleansing, it can also wash away a lot of flavor. If you do wash it, do it quickly and then dry the meat on paper towels. Never soak meat except for a few quite bloody parts like the brains, head and sweetbreads.

Do not pierce meat with a fork to see if it is done. The inside juices will just follow the fork out of the meat, drying it out and taking along some of the flavor.

It is best to let roasts stand for 10 to 15 minutes after they are cooked and before they are carved. They will become firmer and therefore easier to carve, and there will be less loss of juices. To keep them warm, put them in the oven with the heat off and the door open.

If you are planning to serve a cooked roast cold for a second meal, the flavor will be much better if it is not put in the refrigerator. If the weather is unseasonably warm or humid, the meat has to be refrigerated. But normally it is perfectly safe to keep it at room temperature for at least 24 hours.

If a roast is recooked, the flavor is either altered or lost — and the altering is never for the better. So if you wish to serve a cooked roast hot for a second meal, just heat it up, do not cook it for any length of time.

The French seldom thicken gravy with a lot of flour the way Americans and the English do. A little flour or potato flour may be used occasionally, but the usual practice is to thicken gravy only by boiling it down a little, and it makes a very pleasant gravy when you get used to it.

Seasoning with a little carrot, onion and celery has a decided influence on the flavor of some dishes, so always have them on hand for ready use.

Mushrooms are used with some frequency in these recipes.

Choose firm white mushrooms and leave the skins on, since they are full of flavor. Mushrooms that have started to turn brown must be skinned, but since they are old and tired, they are a poor buy and should be avoided. The stems are usually removed; sometimes they are cut off level with the caps; sometimes the whole stem is removed. The stems of fresh mushrooms have a good flavor and can be chopped for many uses; they have a rather woody taste in older mushrooms, so should be discarded. The stems and any peelings can be simmered in boiling salted water for 10 to 15 minutes to make a nice stock for sauces and gravies.

Hollandaise sauce for some reason is considered difficult to make and to keep. Instead of making it in a double boiler, which is often recommended, use a small china or glass mixing bowl placed in a skillet with an inch or so of simmering water in the bottom. Beat the sauce with a small wire whisk. After it is made, it can stand indefinitely. Cover the bowl with waxed paper or aluminum foil to prevent a skin forming on the top — in fact, this should be done with any sauce that is to stand. Add enough cold water to the water in the skillet to make it lukewarm; this keeps the sauce warm without cooking it any more. Then forget about it, except to check if the water is warm if the sauce stands for hours. If it thickens a little, it can be thinned with a little cream.

To flame foods, heat the liquor in a small pan but do not let it boil. It must be warm to flame, but boiling evaporates the alcohol, which is what burns.

Serving: One of the distinguishing phases in fine cooking is the way food is served. A little attention to what might seem like small details can make a world of difference. In the first place you need suitable and attractive serving dishes. For the meat and poultry we are concerned with that means platters. Oval platters are the most useful, although one large round dish is good for recipes involving ring molds. They may be made of china, and the design should be simple enough not to compete with the food. Copper and silver platters are ideal, and preferably you should have both. Oval copper dishes with two handles are stunning-looking and show off many meats to fine advantage.

(Copper used to be a nuisance to clean, but there is a cleansing product on the market now which is very quick and leaves the copper beautifully shiny.) Silver platters, of course, are always handsome and in good taste.

The French bone many roasts to make carving easier. Then instead of serving the roast whole and carving it at the table, a frequent practice is to cut off as many slices as are needed for one meal and to arrange them slightly overlapping on the platter with the uncut piece at one end. More slices can always be cut off at the table, if needed, and if the uncut piece is left for another meal, it retains its juiciness and flavor far better than it would if the whole roast were cut.

When the meat is to be covered with gravy or sauce, with a large, rather shallow spoon make an even layer over the meat, rather than just dumping it anywhere.

Plan elaborate garnishes and arrange them neatly. Garnishing meat with potatoes and other vegetables often means that the whole meal can be served on one dish, which both saves time and satisfies the eye.

Serve hot food on hot serving dishes and plates, cold food on cold plates. This is not a new idea, but is worth repeating. Heating serving dishes used to be simple enough when stoves had warming sections and the stoves themselves got so much hotter than they do now. One way to warm them is to leave them in an oven which has been in use, with the heat off and the door open. Or you can run very hot water over them. A more elaborate way is to have an electric plate warmer enclosed in a section of the kitchen. Cold dishes are easier — just leave them in the refrigerator for an hour or two.

GLOSSARY

This is not a complete glossary of cooking terms, but merely a short description of some of the terms used in this book. One word in general about methods of cooking meat. All meat is cooked in one of two ways, either by dry heat or by moist heat. Tender meat, with soft connective tissue, can be cooked by dry heat; that is, roasting, broiling and pan-broiling or frying (sometimes called sautéing). Moist heat is a long, slow cooking process using some liquid, needed to tenderize cuts of meat with tough muscles and connective tissue. Moist cooking methods are braising, stewing and simmering.

Acidulated water. Water to which an acid has been added: usually vinegar or lemon juice in the proportion of 1 tablespoon to 2 to 3 cups of water.

Bake. To bake is to cook food in the oven, at an even temperature, with dry heat. The term applies to all foods except meat; cooking all meat (except ham) in the oven is called roasting rather than baking.

Baste. To keep food moistened by spooning liquid or fat over the surface when it is cooking. If meat is continually basted with fat, it will become well browned and have an excellent flavor even if the inside of the meat is still rare. Baste with a meat baster (see page 15) or a large spoon; meat basters are better because they can reach the liquid in the bottom of a roasting pan more easily. Meats covered with a layer of fat are self-basting and do not require any attention.

Beef extract. See meat glaze.

Blanch. This word comes from the French *blanche,* which means white, so to blanch literally means to whiten. In cooking, to blanch means to put food into a saucepan with cold water, bring slowly to a boil, then drain.

Boil. To cook in a liquid which is boiling. At sea level, the boiling point is 212° F. and it decreases about 1° for every 500 feet of elevation, so that at 1000 feet, it is 210° F. and so forth. When liquid boils, it is full of bubbles which break on the surface, so that it is a simple enough matter to tell when the boiling point is reached. Slow boiling is just as effective as rapid boiling, so after the boiling point is reached, the heat can be lowered and just kept high enough so that the water is in constant motion.

Bouquet garni. A bunch of mixed herbs used for seasoning. They may be tied together or put in a small cheesecloth bag for easy removal. Herbs most frequently used are parsley, thyme, tarragon, chives, bay leaf. Marjoram and summer savory are nice but are not as readily available. Dill and rosemary have very definite characteristic flavors, which are fine when properly used.

Braise. To cook food, usually meat, by first browning it on all sides in a small amount of fat, then adding a little liquid and cooking covered at a low temperature, either in the oven or on top of the stove.

Bread crumbs. There are two types of bread crumbs, soft and dry. Soft bread crumbs are made from fresh white bread, preferably a little stale, with the crusts removed. Dry bread crumbs, also called cracker dust, are very fine. They can be purchased in packages, or, better still, make your own. Keep all scraps and bits of leftover bread, including crusts, in a paper bag. Put pieces on a cookie sheet in a slow oven at 325° until dried out and lightly browned. Remove, roll with a rolling pin and sift. These will keep indefinitely in a screw-top jar. In this book when bread crumbs are specified, it means dry bread crumbs unless they are called soft bread crumbs.

Brochette. *Brochette* is a French word meaning skewer, so any food *en brochette* is cooked on a skewer. The same type of food is also called shashlik or shish kabob.

Broil. To broil is to cook food with heat applied directly on it. This means that it is cooked either under the heat of a broiler or over hot coals. Most stoves have a broiler unit with overhead heat; the food is placed a few inches below the fire and the top surface is cooked by direct heat.

Browning meat. Meat is browned to add flavor, give it a nice appearance and seal in the juices. It should be done at high heat in a large, preheated, heavy pan with a little very hot fat. Also the meat should be dry and only enough meat should be in the pan at one time as will fit in a single layer. If the meat is cubed, the pieces should not touch each other. A slow heat, too much fat, or crowding results in steaming rather than browning, and the meat just gets gray and loses juices.

Chop. To chop is to cut food into small pieces. This is best done with a large chopping knife (see page 16) on a wooden surface.

Crouton. The French word for crust. Croutons are small cubes or triangles of bread which are either fried in butter or toasted until golden brown.

Deglaze. To add a little liquid to a pan in which meat has been cooked and then bring to a boil to dissolve all the fine-flavored brown bits in the pan. When meat browns, whether on top of the stove or when roasted, the meat juices and fats slowly form a brown substance, called glaze, which is the essence of meat flavor and should never be wasted. To preserve it all, it must be dissolved in a little liquid.

Dot. To cover the surface of food with small bits of fat, usually butter. The pieces of fat should be about the size of a pea and be placed ¾ to 1 inch apart each way; then when the fat melts in cooking, it will spread over the entire top.

Drippings. The same as glaze; that is, the fat and juices which are rendered from meat and poultry when they are cooked.

Fry. To cook food in fat on top of the stove. If the food is cooked in a small amount of fat, the method is often called sautéing or pan-frying. If the fat is deep enough to cover the food entirely, it is called deep-fat or French frying.

Glaze (verb). To give cooked foods an even brown top. It is done under the broiler. Incidentally, foods may be glazed on a silver platter, since it will not melt when it is under the heat of a broiler for only a short time.

Julienne. To cut food into very thin, long, matchlike sticks. The name comes from the chef, Jean Julienne, who invented a clear soup containing vegetables cut in this fashion.

Lard (verb). To add fat to lean meat, either by placing pieces of fat on the surface, or by inserting pieces of fat (usually bacon or salt pork) right through the meat with a larding needle (see page 17).

Marinade. A well-seasoned liquid, usually made with an oil and acid mixture, in which food is marinated.

Marinate. To soak for a period of time in a liquid mixture, often a French dressing or a wine mixture. There should be enough liquid to entirely cover the meat, which is left for several hours to several days. The marinade helps both to flavor and to tenderize the meat.

Meat glaze. Meat glaze, or glace de viande, is concentrated essence of beef made with both bone and meat. True glace de viande as made by chefs is prepared by first browning beef bones with meat on them, then making stock with them which is finally reduced to about one tenth of the original quantity. This is an expensive and time-consuming process, which is why the prepared meat glazes such as Bovril and B–V (which is what most of us use) are rather costly. However, since the flavor is so concentrated, a little is potent.

Pan-broil. To cook food such as meat in a hot pan with no additional fat, or with just enough to keep the food from sticking, so that the cooking somewhat resembles broiling. The pan should be very hot and the fat poured off as it accumulates, so that the cooking will be more like broiling than frying.

Parboil. Parboiling is preliminary to other cooking. It means to boil for a short time, not long enough to completely cook the food.

Pilaff. A Turkish way of cooking rice which is also used in other Central European countries. It may be plain rice or rice cooked with other foods such as meat and/or vegetables.

Poach. To cook in liquid which is below the boiling point. It is really the same as simmering, except that poaching is usually applied to solid foods such as eggs, fish and fruit which are cooked gently to preserve their shape intact, and simmering is a more general term.

Potato flour. Sometimes called potato starch. A thickening agent, used in place of flour because it will make a clear rather than a cloudy gravy. Flour may be used to replace potato flour in any recipe if the latter is not obtainable; just remember, though, that they are not used in equal amounts but that 1 teaspoon of potato flour is equivalent to 1 tablespoon of flour.

Preheat. To heat a pan, an oven or a broiling unit to the desired temperature before putting in the food to be cooked.

Purée. The word means strained, and refers to food which is cooked until soft and then pressed through a strainer or a rotary food mill.

Ragout. The French word for a thick, well-seasoned stew.

Render. To remove fat from meat by cooking it slowly in a heavy pan or double boiler until the fat melts and can be drained off. Also, to melt down pieces of meat fat for cooking.

Roast. Originally to roast was to cook meat on a turning spit before or over an open fire. Now it generally means to cook in the oven and the term is usually applied to meat (other oven cooking is called baking). The slight difference in meaning between roasting and baking lies in the fact that baking is cooking in dry heat, while roasted meat does draw juices and fat so that there is some moistness in the cooking. Roasted meats should never be covered, since they will then steam rather than roast.

Roux. A blended mixture of cooked fat and flour, usually in equal proportions, used to thicken liquids such as gravy, sauce, stews and soup. A white roux is cooked gently for a short time, just until the raw taste is gone from the flour but not long enough for the flour to change color. A pale roux is cooked just until the flour begins to turn color, a dark roux long enough to brown the flour.

Sauté. *Sauté* is a French word meaning tossed in a pan or lightly fried. It is really synonymous with frying, but sautéing is gently frying in a small amount of fat, while frying is a hotter method using either deep or shallow fat.

Score. To cut gashes or narrow grooves in the surface of food, usually in the fat surrounding meat, to prevent the meat from curling up or for decoration.

Sear. To brown the surface of meat at a high temperature, either in the oven or on top of the stove in a little fat. This is supposed to seal the outside surface and keep the juices in. Searing roasts is in some disfavor now because tests by qualified experts have proved that steady cooking at a lower temperature will produce the same browned surface with much less shrinkage.

Shashlik. A dish originated by nomad tribes in the Caucasus. Water was scarce and the meat was cooked over an open fire; the meat was cut in cubes and strung on a sword, then roasted over the fire. The dish as served now consists of cubes of meat or fish, often alternated with vegetables, and skewers do service more often than swords, perhaps unfortunately from the dramatic standpoint.

Shred. To cut food into thin strips, usually with a sharp knife, although vegetables are sometimes shredded on a special cutter.

Simmer. To cook in liquid which is below the boiling point. It is not actually bubbling, but the bubbles form slowly and break just below the surface so that the liquid is barely trembling.

Stew (verb). To cook food in a small amount of liquid, usually just enough to barely cover the food, at a gentle heat often below the actual boiling point. When meat is stewed, some of the meat juices are extracted and added to the liquid, so there will be more liquid at the end of the cooking period than at the beginning; in other words, if the liquid doesn't quite cover the meat to begin with, there should be an ample amount when the cooking period is over. Too much liquid just results in a watery stew.

Stock. The broth in which food has been cooked; it may be meat, poultry, fish or vegetables.

Truffle. A type of fungus, something like a mushroom, with an exceptionally good flavor. Truffles grow mostly in France, in clusters beneath the ground around the roots of oak trees. Pigs are specially trained to root them out. Truffles from Périgord are considered among the finest.

Truss. To tie up a chicken or any other meat so that it will keep its shape while it is cooking.

Try out. Means the same as to render.

EQUIPMENT

You cannot cook properly without the right tools. With a large, sharp chopping knife a big onion can be finely chopped in about two minutes; it may take half an hour with a dull knife, and then it won't be done correctly. The basic equipment for good cooking is not extensive. If necessary, you can get along with good knives, a few large heavy saucepans, a wooden spoon or two and some serving dishes. Even fully equipping a kitchen does not mean a large outlay of money if you stick to really useful items and don't get carried away by frivolous gadgets. Some of the functional as well as beautiful items like copper pans and casseroles are relatively expensive, but can be bought piece by piece or given as presents, and they last a lifetime. Since cooking equipment is used daily and for years, it is an economy to buy heavy, substantial utensils rather than cheap light ones which inevitably have a short life. A heavy, sturdy egg beater, for example, may cost a dollar or two more than a light one, but you will have it forever, and since it will be faster than a light one, will save time as well as money.

The following is a list of the equipment needed for meat and poultry cooking, as well as the other miscellaneous cooking included in this book. Actually, the only items left out are cake pans and other equipment needed for pastry making and general desserts.

Although we do strongly recommend having the best possible quality for the main items, the dime stores can supply some of the things that are not used often.

Apple corer. This is an item to buy in the dime store. When you want to core an apple, it is difficult to do it with anything else, so it is worth buying even if you only use it once or twice a month.

Basters. These are like huge eye droppers and much easier for basting meat than a spoon.

Bread (or loaf) pans. In glass, aluminum or tin. The glass ones are easy to keep clean and good for the uses in this book. Metal pans are better for bread, because they give it a nice brown crust.

Cake rack. Included here because meats to be coated with aspic are placed on cake racks so that the excess aspic can run off.

Can opener. If you have any available wall space, by all means have a wall can opener; all you have to do is turn a handle and the top of any size or shape tin can is open. Hand can openers will do, but are not nearly as efficient.

Casseroles. Casseroles are indispensable since they can be used for both cooking and serving. It is best to have at least two, one small family size and a large one for parties; individual ones are nice, too. The usual materials are glass, earthenware pottery, copper and enamel-glazed cast iron. The last two are the best; they can be used for top-of-the-stove cooking as well as in the oven, conduct and hold heat well, and are handsome-looking.

Chopping or pastry board. Made of wood and the use is obvious and constant. Small ones are handy for chopping vegetables and such; large ones are needed for pastry, unless you have a marble slab.

Colander. Colanders are large strainers with legs or a base, made of a solid material with perforated holes. Very useful, since the colander can sit on its legs and food can drain without any attention from you.

Cookie sheet. Large, flat, metal baking sheets, used for cookies and many other things.

Corkscrew. Although there are inexpensive corkscrews, they are difficult to use, while imported stainless-steel or brass ones are foolproof. For opening any kind of bottle in existence, there is a product called "Open-All" which is infallible.

Cutters. These aren't essential but are useful. Two sets, plain and fluted, which are made of aluminum and come in varying sizes. There can be as many as twenty in one small container.

Double boiler. Available in glass, enamel and aluminum. If you only have one, the best buy is heavy aluminum. If you have two, enamel is easy to clean and is good for egg dishes and cereals, foods that stick to the pan. In general, enamel isn't as satisfactory as aluminum because eventually it chips and it doesn't conduct heat as well.

Electric mixer. Expensive but worth it because of the time and effort saved, and the results. You certainly can cook without one, but it makes cooking anything that requires much beating considerably easier. Extra equipment for some mixers includes fruit-juice extractors, automatic sieves and meat grinders.

Fork for carving.

Frying basket. The best way to handle food that is being fried in deep fat, unless you have one of the excellent, electric, thermostatically controlled deep-fat fryers. With a basket all the food can be removed at once, the second it is done, rather than having to fish out each piece separately.

Frying pans. These must be made of a heavy material or they will not conduct heat well and therefore burn food and are useless. Good materials are copper, cast iron and enamel-glazed cast iron. At least two sizes are needed, one small and one large, and if you do much cooking, you will want a medium-size one also.

Garlic press. Crushes garlic evenly, finely, and eliminates any risk of unpleasant lumps.

Graters. Two graters are useful. A small rotary grater for cheese and the like, and a large four-sided grater which on three sides grates food to varying degrees and shreds it on the fourth side.

Kitchen shears. For any use that scissors are needed for, as well as being heavy enough to cut many bones with.

Knives. Knives are the keystone of good cooking. Buy the best French knives you can get, which are made of tempered steel which can be sharpened as often as is needed to keep them like razors. Stainless-steel knives are not sound buys because they cannot be sharpened. You should have three sizes: a large one for chopping; a medium size for carving, boning and so on; and a small paring size. An electric knife sharpener saves the nuisance of sending the knives out to be sharpened.

Ladle. Stainless steel is best, but enamel will do. Used for soup, stews, gravy, jam and pickle making. The long handle and deep, full cup greatly facilitate getting reasonable amounts out of a deep pan full of boiling hot food.

Larding needle. To lard meat by inserting fat through it. One end is pointed, the other open. Place a thin strip of fat several inches longer than the meat in the open end. Run the needle through the meat at right angles to the grain, revolving it as you push to make it go through more evenly. Trim off the ends of fat flush with the meat.

Mallet. A light wooden mallet for beating meat to make it thinner and more tender. Use for scallopini, beef birds, chicken breasts and so on.

Marble slab. Marble slabs provide a fine cool surface for making pastry, and can often be picked up for very little at secondhand stores.

Measuring spoons and cups. So many recipes use standard measurements that you must have standard measuring cups and spoons to follow them accurately. Standard cups hold ½ pint (8 ounces) or 1 pint (16 ounces); the ½-pint cup is marked to show ¼, ⅓, ½, ⅔ and ¾ cup; the 1-pint cup is marked accordingly. There are also nests of small measuring cups, each holding ¼, ½, ¾ and 1 cup, which are good for measuring small quantities because you can level off the top and be sure the measurement is accurate. Measuring spoons come in sets of four, with the capacity of ¼ teaspoon, ½ teaspoon, 1 teaspoon and 1 tablespoon.

Meat grinder or chopper. For grinding meat or any other food. There usually are two cutters, one fine and one coarse, and for most recipes the fine cutter is the prescribed one. Meat grinders are now available with a self-supporting base so that they do not have to be screwed to a table or working space.

Mixing bowls. You need mixing bowls of all sizes, and they are available in nests, which make them easy to store. China and glass are good, and so is aluminum which is light and unbreakable.

Pastry bags and tubes. Have two or three pastry bags on hand, and the large ones are the easiest to use. You will also want several tubes, including a large and small rose tube and a large and small plain tube. Pastry bags give food a professional look, save time and are easy to use with a little practice.

Pastry brush. Soft brush to use whenever a surface needs to be covered with a liquid substance such as melted butter and beaten egg.

Pepper grinder and shaker. Whole peppercorns are used in the pepper grinder, while ground pepper is put in the shaker. They both are in daily use.

Plank. A piece of heavy wood for cooking various planked dishes such as planked steak (see page 33).

Potato baller. A dime-store item for noisette potatoes, plain potato balls, melon balls and so on.

Ring mold. A ring mold is not essential but is nice for rice rings, meat mousses, some desserts, tomato aspic and such.

Roasting pans and rack. Two roasting pans are really needed, a large roasting pan with a cover for turkeys and any big roast, and a small shallow roasting pan for small roasts, preferably of aluminum since glass may break. Some large roasting pans have racks; or you can get separate adjustable racks which will fit any pan.

Rotary or Dover egg beater. Preferably the largest and strongest one available, for durability and to save time and energy.

Rubber scrapers. These cost very little so have at least two or three; the life expectancy isn't too long since they chip. But they are a must, since they are the only utensil which completely removes every particle of food from saucepans or mixing bowls. They also should be used for handling food when an electric mixer is in action, since metal spoons might damage the beaters.

Salt grinder and shaker. Salt grinders use special coarse salt with a more pronounced flavor than ordinary table salt and so it is well liked by salt lovers. Salt shakers use ordinary table salt and are best for general seasoning.

Saucepans. Every kitchen has to have these. Buy heavy aluminum, copper, or enamel-glazed cast-iron pans. Light pans do not conduct heat well or evenly and burn everything but water. One enamel pan is good just for boiling water for eggs, tea and so forth, because it is easy to clean and boiling water stains aluminum pans. But only for that. You will need several sizes, including large deep pans which are the most useful of all.

Serving dishes. These are discussed on pages 6 and 7.

Skewers and soft twine. Small stainless-steel skewers for closing vents in stuffed poultry, available at dime stores. Soft twine for lacing the skewers together and also for tying up poultry.

Soufflé dish. French soufflé dishes are made of china and have straight sides. A piece of greased waxed paper is tied around the top of the outside of the dish; then the dish is filled almost full with the soufflé mixture which rises up into the waxed paper. Just before serving, the waxed paper is removed, and the soufflé stands well above the dish. You don't have to use a special soufflé dish; heatproof glass baking dishes do very well. But soufflé dishes are the correct thing.

Spatula. Spatulas are in steady use. They are made of stainless steel and the best kind is the English "Cook's Friend," which is broader than the American ones, and tapered. But this kind is not easy to get, and American ones will do.

Spoons. A variety of spoons is needed. A few teaspoons and table-spoons. A large slotted spoon for removing foods that should be drained. A large spoon for covering meat with sauce or gravy. And several sizes of wooden spoons. Wood does not hold heat so can be left in pans while food is cooking. The smooth thick surface is also good for stirring sauces and such.

Strainers. Several sizes from very small to a large one.

Thermometer for meat. The most accurate way to determine when a roast is sufficiently cooked. Insert the thermometer in the thickest part of the meat, making sure it does not touch any bone.

Timer. Easiest way to keep a record of time without any mental wear and tear. One of the few pieces of nonessential equipment that is invaluable.

Tongs. Good for turning meat or removing it from pans, since they do not pierce the meat the way a fork does.

Vegetable brush. For scrubbing vegetables like potatoes and carrots; and use it only for vegetables so that it will not be tainted with other odors.

Vegetable peelers. Cost about ten cents each and are in constant use; they make paring vegetables a matter of seconds and keep the parings down to a minimum.

Wire whisks. Small and large. The small ones guarantee smooth sauces. The large ones are used for beating egg whites for soufflés, for making aspic and so on.

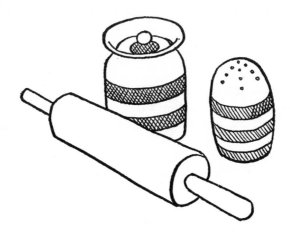

BEEF

In the United States beef is used far more extensively than it is in Europe. In France, because there isn't enough pasture for large herds of beef cattle, calves are often slaughtered when young, and veal rather than beef is a staple item in daily menus. Since beef is very expensive there, the manner of serving it typifies some of the basic differences between French and American cooking.

Sirloin and porterhouse steaks are favorites with the majority of Americans, certainly of American men, and the larger and thicker the steak, the happier everyone is. In France the tendency is to serve small individual steaks, called tournedos and entrecôtes, with a sauce or garnish. Other cuts of beef are always treated to bring out the flavor. In French stews or ragouts the meat and vegetables are first browned in butter, and there is some wine or brandy in the gravy. Large pieces of beef for braising are often marinated before cooking to sharpen the taste and help tenderize the meat, or are larded with a larding needle to insert fat through the meat for flavor and juiciness — or both. A roast of beef is usually boned to facilitate carving. Chopped beef or "hamburger" is primarily an American dish, and you will have a hard time finding it as an entrée on a restaurant menu in France. There it is served only as part of more complicated dishes and not too often at that. But in this instance France's loss is our gain, and you will find a good selection of chopped-beef recipes in this beef section.

There is a great diversity of beef cuts and prices, from the expensive filet down to the economical flank steak. Although a filet of beef is admittedly an extravagance, when you have one it is worthy of the time it takes to prepare attractive garnishes. To get back to the subject of French cooking for a minute, it is true that in a good French cook book you will find more recipes for filet of beef than for rib roasts. But the garnish will be elaborate enough to require only moderate servings of the meat. And it is both more appetizing and appealing to have small amounts of several complementary foods on a plate than an enormous slab of beef with only one small potato.

Beef specialty meats such as the brains, tongue and tail make fine inexpensive dishes. Beef liver and kidneys are too strong in flavor for most people, and the more delicate calves' or lambs' liver and kidneys are preferable. Therefore there are no recipes in this beef section for kidneys or liver; if you do use them, they should be soaked for several hours or overnight in acidulated water or diluted red wine.

It is important to buy good beef and the first consideration is the grade. The United States government grades all beef sold in retail stores as *prime, choice, good, commercial* and *utility. Prime* is the highest quality; only a very small percentage of beef meets the requirements set up for this grade, and most of this is purchased by clubs and restaurants, who pay more for it at wholesale prices than the other grades cost retail. *Choice* is the best quality generally available in retail markets, and is excellent. *Good* beef is not as tender but can be used, especially if subjected to the slower moist forms of cooking such as braising and stewing. For quick dry cooking such as broiling and roasting it is wise to have a top grade. *Commercial* and *utility* are not recommended. For the best results and often the most economical ones, get fine grades of good cuts. Less expensive cuts are often so full of waste in the form of bone and tough tissue that they aren't any bargain in the long run.

In judging beef from looks, two tests are the color of the fat and the marbling. Marbling is the appearance caused by small streaks of fat running through the meat itself. Good marbling guarantees tender, juicy meat, so look for it particularly in steaks and roasts. Beef also often has fat surrounding it and this should be white or creamy white. A little fat is always advantageous, although in France they trim off far more of the fat than in America. A third test is supposed to be the color of the flesh, but this can be unreliable. All beef is hung before it is sold and this tends to darken the color. The first rib in a rib roast may be almost black and yet be deliciously tender.

For practical purposes the safest gauge for most people buying beef is a reliable butcher.

ROAST BEEF WITH YORKSHIRE PUDDING

sirloin or rib roast, boned	*1½ cups red wine*
piece of suet	*1½ cups boiling water*
salt, pepper	

YORKSHIRE PUDDING

1 cup flour	*3 small eggs*
1 teaspoon salt	*1 cup creamy milk*

Trim the meat neatly. Cover with a layer of suet and tie it with several pieces of string; the butcher will do this for you, if you wish. Season with salt and pepper. Put into a roasting pan, preferably on a rack. Pour ½ cup of red wine into the pan. Roast in a moderate oven at 350°. Allow about 18 to 20 minutes to the pound for rare meat (or a meat thermometer will register 140°), 23 to 25 minutes for medium rare (160°), 27 to 30 minutes (170°) for well done. Meat with the bone in takes less time to cook, since the bone helps conduct heat. Baste often, first with a little wine, using 1½ cups in all, then with the pan juices. While the meat is cooking, make the Yorkshire pudding.

Yorkshire Pudding: Sift 1 cup of flour and 1 teaspoon of salt into a large mixing bowl. Beat 3 small eggs for a minute or so with a rotary beater, add 1 cup of milk and stir until blended. Pour over the flour and beat for 2 to 3 minutes. If possible, let stand for ½ hour to 1 hour in the refrigerator. Preheat the oven to 450°. Heat a large baking pan about 9 × 12 inches. Put about ½ inch of beef fat or shortening into the pan and let that get hot. Pour in the batter. Bake for 15 minutes at 450°, then reduce the heat to 350° and cook another 10 to 15 minutes. Remove and serve at once.

To Serve: Cut as many slices of beef as are needed for one meal and arrange them slightly overlapping on a hot serving dish. Place the uncut piece at one end. Reheat the roasting pan and deglaze it with 1½ cups of boiling water. Taste for seasoning.

Spoon a little of the gravy over the meat and serve the rest in a gravy bowl. Surround the meat with squares of Yorkshire pudding. The Yorkshire pudding will serve 6 people.

COLD ROAST BEEF WITH VEGETABLE GARNISH

12 *thin slices cold roast beef*	2 *tablespoons sour cream*
6 *firm ripe tomatoes*	¼ *cup creamed butter*
2 *cups cooked peas*	1 *tablespoon chopped chives*
2 *3-ounce packages cream*	1 *bunch carrots*
cheese	1 *bunch asparagus*

FRENCH DRESSING

2 *tablespoons tarragon vinegar*	*salt*
¾ *cup salad oil*	*freshly cracked black pepper*
½ *teaspoon French mustard*	

Cut the roast beef into very thin slices and arrange them slightly overlapping on a cold serving dish. Garnish with the following vegetables. Skin 6 tomatoes and cut them in half. Scoop out half of them and fill with cold cooked peas which have been mixed with a little French dressing. Blend together thoroughly 2 3-ounce packages of cream cheese, 2 tablespoons of sour cream, ¼ cup of creamed butter and 1 tablespoon of finely chopped chives. Put into a pastry bag with a large rose tube and pipe on top of the rest of the tomatoes. Scrape a bunch of carrots, cut into small julienne strips and cook until just tender. Drain well, mix with a little French dressing and chill. Cook the asparagus tips, drain, mix with French dressing and chill also. This will serve 6.

French Dressing: Put 2 tablespoons of tarragon vinegar, ¾ cup salad oil — at least part olive oil for flavor — salt, freshly cracked black pepper and ½ teaspoon French mustard in a small screw-top jar. Shake well and chill in the refrigerator. Shake thoroughly again before using.

FILET OF BEEF

Filet (or tenderloin) of beef is the tenderest and most expensive cut of beef. It should always be cooked rare to retain the maximum flavor, and since it is such a tender cut requires very little cooking, at high heat. It should be well trimmed of fat and connective tissue, and then is either surrounded with a thin layer of beef suet or pork fat, or is larded with a larding needle. A whole filet weighs 6 to 8 pounds before it is trimmed, and can be roasted or braised.

ROAST FILET OF BEEF

½ filet of beef, 3 to 4 pounds
salt, pepper
½ cup dry white wine
¾ pound mushrooms, sliced
3 tablespoons butter

1 shallot or small white onion
1 teaspoon meat glaze
1 teaspoon tomato paste
2 teaspoons potato flour
1 cup stock or water

½ cup Madeira

Remove the fat and connective tissue from the meat. Surround it with a thin layer of fat, preferably beef suet, and tie it with string at 1½-inch intervals. Season with salt and pepper. Place in a shallow roasting pan and roast in a hot oven at 450° for 10 to 12 minutes to the pound, or until a meat thermometer registers 140°. Remove the meat, pour ½ cup of dry white wine over it and keep it warm while the sauce is prepared. Meanwhile sauté ¾ pound of sliced mushrooms in 3 tablespoons of butter.

Remove all but 2 tablespoons of fat from the pan the meat was cooked in. Sauté 1 finely chopped shallot or small white onion until soft but not brown in this fat. Blend in, off the fire, 1 teaspoon of meat glaze, ½ teaspoon of tomato paste and 2 teaspoons of potato flour. Add 1 cup of stock or water and ½ cup of Madeira and stir over the fire until the mixture comes to a boil. Add the sautéed mushrooms, season and simmer for 4 to 5 minutes.

To Serve: Cut the strings off the meat and carve as many slices as are needed for one meal. Arrange them slightly overlapping on a hot serving dish and place the uncut piece at one end. Spoon a little of the sauce over the meat and serve the rest in a sauce bowl. To complete the meal and make the platter look attractive, garnish it with little mounds of cooked fresh vegetables such as carrots, green beans, peas, cauliflower, asparagus tips, and at one end have a pile of noisette potatoes (see page 122). Serves 6 to 8.

BRAISED FILET OF BEEF

½ filet of beef, about 3 pounds
1 tablespoon butter
1 medium-size onion, sliced
1 carrot, sliced
1 teaspoon meat glaze

½ teaspoon tomato paste
3 teaspoons potato flour
½ cup stock or water
½ cup Madeira or red wine
salt, pepper

GARNISH

6 large mushrooms
¼ pound mushrooms
6 small tomatoes
1 cup finely chopped onion
4 tablespoons butter
1 cup bread crumbs

3 hard-boiled eggs
salt, pepper
3 to 4 tablespoons sour cream
1 teaspoon chopped parsley
6 artichoke bottoms, cooked
¾ cup grated Parmesan cheese

Remove the fat and connective tissue from the beef. Surround it with a thin layer of fat, preferably beef suet, and tie it with string at 1½-inch intervals. Brown it all over in 1 tablespoon of hot butter in a heavy deep saucepan. Remove the beef. Lightly brown 1 thinly sliced medium-size onion and 1 sliced carrot in the same pan. Stir in, off the fire, 1 teaspoon of meat glaze, ½ teaspoon of tomato paste and 3 teaspoons of potato flour. Pour on ½ cup of stock or water and ½ cup of Madeira or red wine. Stir over the fire until the mixture comes to a boil and season with salt and pepper. Put the meat back, cover and simmer for 15 minutes to the pound. Meanwhile prepare the following garnish.

Stuffed Mushrooms, Tomatoes and Artichoke Bottoms: Remove the stems from 6 large mushrooms and chop the stems and ¼ pound of mushrooms very finely. Cut the tops off 6 small tomatoes and scoop out the seedy pulp. Sauté 1 cup of finely chopped onion and the chopped mushrooms in 3 tablespoons of butter until soft but not brown. Add 1 cup of bread crumbs, 3 chopped hard-boiled eggs, salt and pepper, and cook about 1 minute. Remove from the fire and blend in 3 to 4 tablespoons of sour cream and 1 teaspoon of finely chopped parsley. Fill the mushroom caps, tomatoes and 6 artichoke bottoms. Place on a cookie sheet and sprinkle with about ¾ cup of grated Parmesan cheese and 1 tablespoon of melted butter. Broil until nicely browned. Have the cookie sheet at least 3 inches away from the fire so that the vegetables can become heated through as well as browned.

To Serve: Remove the meat, cut off the strings and carve as many slices as are needed for one meal. Arrange them slightly overlapping on a hot serving dish with the uncut piece at one end. Strain a little of the gravy over the meat and serve the rest in a sauce bowl. Surround with the garnish. Serves 6.

BOEUF STROGANOFF

1½ pounds filet of beef
3 tablespoons butter
1 large yellow onion, finely chopped
½ pound mushrooms, sliced
½ teaspoon meat glaze
½ teaspoon tomato paste
2 tablespoons flour
1 cup stock
salt, pepper
1 cup sour cream
2 teaspoons finely chopped dill

Trim the beef of all fat and sinew. Cut into small strips, about 2 inches long and ½ inch thick, against the grain. Brown very quickly all over in 1 tablespoon of hot butter in a large skillet. Remove the beef from the pan when it is browned.

Peel and finely chop 1 large yellow onion and slice ½ pound of mushrooms. Melt the remaining 2 tablespoons of butter in the same pan and cook the onion and mushrooms over a moderate fire until the onion is soft but not brown. Stir in, off the fire, ½ teaspoon of meat glaze, ½ teaspoon of tomato paste and 2 tablespoons of flour. Blend in 1 cup of stock and stir over the fire until the sauce comes to a boil. Season with salt and pepper. Add 1 cup of sour cream, a little at a time, using a small wire whisk and starting in the center of the sauce. Put back the beef with 1 teaspoon of chopped dill. Cook just until the meat is heated through.

Serve in a casserole and sprinkle the remaining teaspoon of dill over the top. Serves 4.

Note: Round of beef may be used instead of the filet. It is not as tender and therefore requires longer cooking, so instead of just heating the meat in the sauce, allow it to simmer for 20 to 30 minutes.

Although dill gives the dish an excellent flavor, it may be omitted.

BEEF WITH PEPPERS

1½ pounds filet of beef	1½ cups chicken stock
3 tablespoons butter	3 tablespoons vinegar
2 green peppers	1 to 2 teaspoons sugar
½ pound mushrooms, sliced	salt
3 teaspoons potato flour	about ⅛ teaspoon powdered ginger

Trim 1½ pounds filet of beef of any sinew and most of the fat. Cut into strips about ½ inch thick and 2 inches long, against the grain. Heat 1 tablespoon of butter in a heavy skillet and when it is on the point of turning color, quickly brown the meat all over. Remove the meat from the pan. Core and seed 2 green peppers and cut them into strips the same size as the meat. Slice ½ pound of mushrooms. Heat another 2 tablespoons of butter in the same pan the meat was browned in and sauté the peppers and mushrooms until lightly browned. Blend in 3 teaspoons of potato flour, off the fire. Pour on 1½ cups of chicken stock and stir over the fire until the mixture comes to a boil. Add 3 tablespoons of vinegar and 1 to 2 teaspoons of sugar; the sauce should be sour-sweet and the only way to get the proportions right is by tasting. Season with salt and a generous pinch of powdered ginger. Simmer for about 10 minutes to cook the peppers a little. Put back the beef and cook just until the beef is thoroughly heated; filet of beef is so tender it needs almost no cooking.

Serve in a casserole with plainly boiled rice. Serves 4.

BROILED STEAK

Sirloin or porterhouse steaks are the cuts generally used for broiled steaks large enough to serve 2 or more people. It is diffi-cult to give precise cooking times for steak, since so much depends on the thickness and quality of the meat, the distance it is from the fire and the heat of the fire. The most accurate test for doneness is to insert a small knife close to the bone and see for yourself how the steak looks in the middle.

Always preheat the broiler unit and broiler pan. For rare steak the meat is placed 2 to 3 inches from the fire throughout the cooking period. Medium-rare and well-done steak is browned close to the fire and then placed 3 to 4 inches away to finish cooking, or the heat of the fire can be reduced.

Plain broiled steak is usually seasoned after it is cooked. There is a theory that salting the steak before cooking will draw out some of the blood, although it is doubtful that anyone has proved it. But seasoning will only penetrate the surface, so nothing much is gained by seasoning beforehand. The steak should also be spread generously with softened butter before serving. Pieces of garlic may be inserted in small slits in the surface before cooking; try to remove them before serving so that no one gets a piece. Steaks may be boned before cooking to facilitate carving.

Some variations of broiled steak follow. Also any of the sauces or garnishes given later for tournedos or entrecôtes may be used for broiled steak.

BROILED STEAK WITH DRAWN BUTTER SAUCE

3 to 3½ pound steak	½ cup dry white wine
6 tablespoons butter	½ cup water
2 tablespoons flour	salt, white pepper
1 to 2 teaspoons finely chopped parsley	

Serve broiled steak with the following drawn butter sauce. Melt 3 tablespoons of butter in a small saucepan. Blend in 2 tablespoons of flour, off the fire. Add ½ cup of dry white wine, ½ cup of water, salt and white pepper. Stir over the fire until the mixture comes to a boil. Beat in the remaining 3 tablespoons of butter, bit by bit. Just before serving add 1 to 2 teaspoons of finely chopped parsley. This will serve 4 to 6 people.

BROILED STEAK WITH ROQUEFORT CHEESE

Blend together until soft and smooth, preferably in an electric mixer, 2 ounces of Roquefort cheese, 3 ounces of cream cheese, 1 to 2 tablespoons of cream, ¼ teaspoon of meat glaze, salt and a little cayenne pepper. After the steak has been broiled on one side, turn it over and spread the uncooked side with this mixture. Continue cooking until well browned and serve very hot.

BROILED STEAK PARMIGIANA

3 to 3½ pound sirloin or por-	*1 cup grated Parmesan cheese*
terhouse steak	*½ cup bread crumbs*
2 cloves crushed garlic	*salt, pepper*
½ cup olive oil	*½ teaspoon dried oregano*
¼ teaspoon chopped rosemary	

Put the steak in a flat shallow dish. Add 2 cloves of crushed garlic to ½ cup of olive oil and pour over the steak. Let stand for 1 hour, turning the steak every 15 minutes. Make a mixture of 1 cup of grated Parmesan cheese, ½ cup of bread crumbs, salt, pepper, ½ teaspoon of dried oregano and ¼ teaspoon finely chopped rosemary. Put the steak on a preheated broiler pan. Cover one side evenly with half the cheese mixture and broil on one side. Turn, brush the other side with a little of the garlic oil and coat with the rest of the cheese mixture. Broil until browned and the steak is done. Serve on a hot platter and carefully pour any remaining garlic oil over the top. Serves 4 to 6.

BROILED STEAK MIRABEAU

(Broiled Steak with Anchovies and Olives)

Before broiling the steak, rub each side with melted butter blended with a little anchovy paste. After the steak is cooked and placed on a hot platter, garnish the top with thin strips of anchovy arranged in a lattice fashion. Surround the steak with pitted green olives.

BROILED STEAK WITH GARLIC BUTTER

Instead of inserting garlic into the steak, either of the following garlic butters may be used. Plainly broil a steak in the usual manner. Coarsely chop 2 or 3 cloves of garlic. Put into a saucepan with ¼ pound of butter and heat very slowly until the butter is melted. Keep over a slow fire about 5 minutes, then strain. Place the steak on a hot platter and pour the garlic butter over the top.

Or add 1 large clove of crushed garlic to ¼ pound of well-creamed butter and spread over the steak just before serving.

PLANKED STEAK

2½ to 3 pound porterhouse steak	4 sautéed chopped chicken livers
2 cloves garlic, crushed	½ pound cooked ham, ground
7 tablespoons butter	1 teaspoon chopped parsley
salt and pepper	3 tablespoons sour cream
4 tomatoes	2 tablespoons grated Parmesan cheese
8 large mushrooms	
1 cup finely chopped onion	6 medium-size old potatoes
	2 eggs
about ½ cup hot creamy milk	

Rub the steak with 1 clove of crushed garlic, brush with 2 table-spoons of melted butter and season with salt and pepper. Broil on one side only. Place on a large wooden plank which has been rubbed with oil, uncooked side up. Prepare the following stuffing for the tomatoes and mushroom caps. Chop the mushroom stems and sauté in 1 tablespoon of butter with 1 cup of finely chopped onion until soft and lightly browned. Blend with 4 sautéed chopped chicken livers, ½ pound of ground cooked ham, a teaspoon of chopped parsley, 3 tablespoons of sour cream, salt and pepper. Cut the tops off 4 tomatoes and scoop out the seedy pulp with a spoon. Fill with the stuffing, top with 2 tablespoons of grated Parmesan cheese and 2 tablespoons of melted butter. Fill 4 mushroom caps with the same mixture, cover with the other 4 caps and sprinkle with 2 tablespoons of melted butter.

Meanwhile peel 6 potatoes and cook for about 20 minutes in boiling salted water, or until tender. Drain and dry for a minute or so over a slow fire. Put through a ricer or strainer, beat in 1 egg, about ½ cup of hot creamy milk, salt and pepper.

Place the mushrooms and tomatoes alternately around the steak. Pipe the potatoes all around the edge, using a pastry bag with a large rose tube. Brush the potatoes with a slightly beaten egg. Place under the broiler, at least 3 to 4 inches away from the flame, for 8 to 10 minutes. Serve on the plank. Serves 4.

Note: Four filets mignon may be used instead of a porterhouse steak to simplify the carving situation. Or the steak may be boned before it is cooked for the same reason.

ENTRECÔTE

An entrecôte is a steak which is cut from the ribs. It may be cut 1½ to 2 inches thick and large enough to serve about 4 people. In France this is a popular cut, but in this country either a porterhouse (T-bone) or sirloin steak is generally used for large steaks. Here entrecôtes are usually cut a little more than ½ inch thick, weigh about 7 to 10 ounces and make 1 generous or 2 small servings. They are called club steaks or delmonico steaks, and as a rule they are boneless.

Large entrecôtes are first brushed with butter and then broiled, following the directions for steak on page 30. Individual entrecôtes are usually sautéed. Put 1 tablespoon of butter into a hot skillet and when it is on the point of turning color, put in the entrecôte and lower the fire to medium heat. Cook about 2 to 3 minutes until nicely browned on one side. Put another tablespoon of butter in the pan and brown the other side. Place on a hot serving dish. Season with salt and pepper and put a good spoonful of softened butter on the top. Pour over any pan juices if you wish. And the pan may be deglazed with a little stock or red wine and this glaze poured over the meat. Serve with fresh watercress or parsley, and straw potatoes are excellent with it.

As well as the following entrecôte recipes, any of the preceding recipes for broiled steak and tournedos may be used.

ENTRECÔTES À LA FORESTIÈRE
(Entrecôtes with Sautéed Potatoes and Mushrooms)

4 *individual entrecôtes*	½ *pound small white mushrooms*
2 *pounds old potatoes*	1 *teaspoon lemon juice*
6 *tablespoons butter*	¼ *pound sliced Canadian bacon*
salt, pepper	½ *cup white wine*

1 to 2 *tablespoons finely chopped parsley*

Sautéed entrecôtes in this recipe are garnished with rissolé potatoes, sautéed mushrooms and Canadian bacon. Canadian bacon may not sound particularly French, but it is more like French bacon than the American bacon with its large proportion of fat.

Pare 2 pounds of old potatoes and cut them into neat ¾-inch cubes. Let stand for ½ hour in cold water to cover, then drain and dry. Melt 3 tablespoons of butter in a skillet. When it is foaming put in the potatoes. Cook over a moderate fire until nicely browned all over; shake the pan occasionally and turn the potatoes so that they will brown evenly. They will take about 20 to 25 minutes to cook. Season with salt and pepper just before serving.

Cut the stems off ½ pound of small white mushrooms and sauté the caps in 2 tablespoons of butter with 1 teaspoon of lemon juice, salt and pepper. Cook ¼ pound of sliced Canadian bacon in 1 tablespoon of butter until lightly browned.

To Serve: Arrange the sautéed entrecôtes on a hot serving dish, slightly overlapping. Add ½ cup of white wine to the pan they were cooked in, bring it to a boil and pour this pan gravy over the meat. Surround the steaks with small alternate piles of rissolé potatoes, mushrooms and bacon. Sprinkle the potatoes and mushrooms with 1 to 2 tablespoons of finely chopped parsley. Serves 4.

ENTRECÔTES À LA BORDELAISE

4 *individual entrecôtes*	1 *cup red wine*
2 *shallots or 1 small white onion*	½ *cup beef stock*
2 *tablespoons butter*	*cooked marrow*

1 *tablespoon finely chopped parsley*

Serve sautéed entrecôtes with the following sauce. Finely chop 2 shallots or 1 small white onion. Sauté in 1 tablespoon of butter until soft but not brown. Add 1 cup of red wine and ½ cup of beef stock and simmer until it is reduced to about 1 cup. Add another tablespoon of butter, bit by bit, beating it in with a small wire whisk. Dice a few pieces of cooked marrow and add them to the sauce. Taste for seasoning.

Arrange the cooked entrecôtes on a hot platter, slightly overlapping. Pour the sauce over them and sprinkle with a tablespoon of finely chopped parsley. If possible, garnish with slices of cooked marrow. Serves 4.

ENTRECÔTES MAÎTRE D'HÔTEL

4 individual entrecôtes	*1 tablespoon finely chopped parsley*
4 tablespoons butter	*salt, white pepper*
	few drops lemon juice

Serve sautéed entrecôtes with the following maître d'hôtel butter. Let 4 tablespoons of butter soften at room temperature for half an hour or so in a small mixing bowl. Cream it until it is fluffy. Add 1 tablespoon of finely chopped parsley, a little salt and white pepper and a few drops of lemon juice. Mix until well blended. Form into small round cakes about ¼ inch thick and as big around as a silver dollar. Chill until firm in the refrigerator. Place one piece on each entrecôte when it is cooked and ready to be served. The heat of the steak will melt and spread it. Serves 4.

CUBE STEAKS WITH SAUCE BERCY

4 cube steaks	*1 or more tablespoons butter*

SAUCE BERCY

4 tablespoons butter	*1 cup chicken stock*
2 tablespoons finely chopped onion	*salt, pepper*
2 tablespoons finely chopped shallot	*2 tablespoons flour*
1 cup white wine	*1 teaspoon finely chopped parsley*

Cube steaks are individual steaks cut from the round of beef. They are put through a special machine which scores the meat, breaking down tendons and therefore tenderizing the meat. Since they take only a few minutes to cook, the sauce should be started first.

Sauce Bercy: Melt 2 tablespoons of butter in a saucepan. Put in 2 tablespoons of finely chopped onion and 2 tablespoons of finely chopped shallot and cook very slowly until they are soft but not browned. Add 1 cup of dry white wine and 1 cup of chicken stock, season and cook gently for 5 minutes. Blend 2 tablespoons of flour and 2 tablespoons of butter and add bit by bit to the sauce, stirring all the while. When the flour and butter mixture is all incorporated and the sauce is smooth, let it simmer for about 15 minutes. Just before serving, strain, and add 1 teaspoon of finely chopped parsley.

Cube Steaks: Heat a large heavy skillet. Put in 1 tablespoon of butter and when it is on the point of turning color, quickly brown the cube steaks on both sides, allowing 2 to 3 minutes for each side. Only 2 steaks will probably fit into the pan at one time and more butter may be needed to cook them all.

To Serve: Arrange the steaks on a hot serving dish. Serve the sauce in a separate bowl. Serves 4.

TOURNEDOS

Tournedos are a round cut of tender, boneless steak about 2 inches in diameter and 1 inch thick. They are cut from the thin end of the filet, trimmed and then surrounded with a thin layer of fat. *Filets mignon* are similar but cut from the slightly larger center section of the filet. Filet of beef is an expensive cut and an adequate substitute can be made by cutting a thick steak into rounds of solid meat and securing each round with a thin slice of beef suet, salt pork, or bacon. One tournedo is allowed for each serving.

Tournedos can be sautéed or broiled, with sautéing the preferred method. Season the meat lightly with salt and pepper and cook in a heavy skillet in plenty of butter over a moderate fire.

When the meat is browned on one side, lower the heat a little and cook for another 4 to 5 minutes on the other side. To broil, place on a preheated pan in a preheated broiling unit and cook 4 to 5 minutes on each side for rare meat, 7 to 8 minutes for medium rare. Tournedos should always be served either rare or medium rare, not well done.

Chateaubriand is cut from the thickest end of the filet. It weighs 1 to 2 pounds and since it is boneless will serve at least 2 to 4 people. It may be sautéed but is best broiled. Any of the preceding recipes for steak or any of the following recipes for tournedos and entrecôtes may be used for chateaubriand or filets mignon.

TOURNEDOS WITH MUSHROOM SAUCE

4 tournedos
salt, pepper
5 tablespoons butter
½ pound mushrooms, sliced

¼ cup brandy
¾ cup heavy cream
¼ teaspoon meat glaze
4 rounds of bread

1 tablespoon finely chopped parsley

Season 4 tournedos with salt and pepper and sauté in 2 tablespoons of butter. Remove them from the pan and keep them warm. Melt another 2 tablespoons of butter in the same pan and sauté ½ pound of sliced mushrooms until lightly browned. Add ¼ cup of brandy and cook 1 to 2 minutes. Stir in ¾ cup of heavy cream and ¼ teaspoon of meat glaze and simmer 3 to 4 minutes. Taste for seasoning. Meanwhile cut 4 rounds of white or French bread slightly larger than the tournedos and fry them in butter until golden brown on both sides.

To Serve: Place the bread rounds on a hot serving dish and put the tournedos on top of them. Spoon the sauce over the tournedos and sprinkle with 1 tablespoon of finely chopped parsley. Serves 4.

Note: A thin layer of pâté de foie gras or one of the good domestic pâtés may be spread over the tournedos after they are cooked.

TOURNEDOS À LA BÉARNAISE

4 tournedos
½ teaspoon crushed garlic
salt, pepper

5 to 6 teaspoons butter
4 large mushroom caps
4 small mushroom caps

4 rounds of bread

BÉARNAISE SAUCE

¼ cup vinegar
¼ cup white wine
1 teaspoon chopped shallot
or onion
salt, peppercorns
pinch of thyme
1 small bay leaf

2 large egg yolks
1 tablespoon cream
¼ pound butter
1 teaspoon chopped tarragon
½ teaspoon chopped parsley
few drops lemon juice
watercress or parsley for garnish

Season 4 tournedos with a little crushed garlic, salt and pepper. Sauté in 2 tablespoons of hot butter. Remove the tournedos and keep them warm. Melt another 2 tablespoons of butter in the same pan and sauté 4 large and 4 small mushroom caps. Remove them. Again in the same pan fry 4 rounds of white bread which are slightly larger than the tournedos until golden brown on both sides, adding more butter as needed. Meanwhile make the following Béarnaise sauce.

Béarnaise Sauce: Put ¼ cup of vinegar, ¼ cup of dry white wine, 1 teaspoon of finely chopped shallot or onion, a pinch of salt, 3 or 4 peppercorns, a pinch of thyme and a small crushed bay leaf into a small saucepan. Cook over a gentle fire until reduced to 2 tablespoons. Cool a little and strain into a small bowl. Add 2 large egg yolks and a tablespoon of cream and beat until smooth with a small wire whisk. Put the bowl into a skillet with about an inch of simmering water in the bottom and beat over a slow fire until the mixture begins to thicken. Then beat in ¼ pound of butter, bit by bit. Just before serving add a teaspoon of finely chopped tarragon, ½ teaspoon of finely chopped parsley and a few drops of lemon juice.

To Serve: Place the bread rounds on a hot serving dish and top with the tournedos. Put a large mushroom cap, stem side up, on each tournedo and fill the caps with Béarnaise sauce, letting some sauce spill over and cover the meat. Top with the small mushroom caps. Garnish with watercress or parsley and serve immediately while the bread is still crisp. Serves 4.

TOURNEDOS WITH SAUCE CHORON

Place 4 sautéed tournedos on 4 rounds of white bread which have been fried in butter until golden brown on both sides. Serve with sauce Choron either spooned over the top or in a separate bowl. Sauce Choron is made by combining equal amounts of Béarnaise sauce (preceding recipe) and well-reduced tomato sauce. Omit the finely chopped tarragon and parsley in the Béarnaise sauce.

TOURNEDOS HENRY VI

This recipe is similar to Tournedos Béarnaise with 4 large artichoke hearts substituted for the large mushroom caps. Reheat the artichoke hearts in a little butter and place them on the sautéed tournedos. Fill with Béarnaise sauce and top with a small mushroom cap. Fresh artichoke hearts should be used in preference to canned ones because they are cup-shaped and will hold the sauce better.

FLANK STEAK WITH MUSHROOM SAUCE

1 flank steak, 1½ to 2 pounds

MUSHROOM SAUCE

½ pound mushrooms, sliced	*1½ cups stock*
3 tablespoons butter	*salt, pepper*
1 teaspoon meat glaze	*1 to 2 teaspoons lemon juice or*
2 teaspoons potato flour	*sherry*

Flank steaks are inexpensive and if properly cooked and carved are very tender and good. If the steak is to be broiled, as in this recipe, just be sure it is a top grade of meat.

Preheat the broiler. Broil the steak for 8 minutes on one side and 5 minutes on the other side. The steak will be long and thin before it is cooked but contracts during cooking so that it is shorter and thicker when it is done. This cooking time is for rare meat; add another 2 minutes on each side for medium rare.

Put the steak on a wooden board. With a long sharp knife cut it into slices about ½ inch thick, across the grain and not straight down but at a 45-degree angle. Straight cutting gives tough meat; cut at an angle, it is tender. Arrange the slices slightly overlapping on a hot serving dish and pour over the following mushroom sauce.

Mushroom Sauce: Sauté ½ pound of sliced mushrooms briskly in 2 tablespoons of butter until lightly browned. Add another tablespoon of butter. Blend in, off the fire, 1 teaspoon of meat glaze and 2 teaspoons of potato flour. Pour on 1½ cups of stock and stir over the fire until the mixture comes to a boil. Season with salt and pepper and simmer for at least 5 minutes. Just before serving add 1 to 2 teaspoons of lemon juice or sherry. Serves 4.

STUFFED FLANK STEAK

1 flank steak	*1 cup cooked rice*
1 cup finely chopped onion	*1 egg*
½ cup finely chopped carrot	*1 small clove garlic, crushed*
½ cup finely chopped celery	*salt, pepper*
4 tablespoons butter	*½ cup red wine*

Spread the steak out flat and cut off any excess lumps of fat. Cook 1 cup of finely chopped onion, ½ cup of finely chopped carrot and ½ cup of finely chopped celery slowly in 3 tablespoons of butter in a deep heavy saucepan until soft but not browned. Put 1 cup of cooked rice in a large mixing bowl. Add the cooked vegetables, 1 egg, 1 small clove of crushed garlic, salt and pepper. Blend thoroughly. Spread about half the stuffing on the steak, leaving a 1-inch margin all around. Roll up lengthwise and tie with string at 2-inch intervals.

Heat 1 tablespoon of butter in the same pan the vegetables were cooked in and when it is on the point of turning color, quickly brown the meat all over. Put the rest of the vegetables in the pan and lightly brown them. Add ½ cup of red wine. Cook covered in a moderate oven at 350° for 2 hours.

To Serve: Remove the meat, cut off the strings and cut the steak into slices. Arrange them slightly overlapping on a hot serving dish and surround with the vegetables. Serves 4 to 6.

SPICED BEEF

1 flank steak	*½ teaspoon pepper*
1 large yellow onion, finely	*½ teaspoon ground ginger*
chopped	*¼ teaspoon saltpeter*
1 teaspoon salt	*1 cup coarse salt*
½ cup brown sugar	

This is a traditional Norwegian Christmas Eve dish but is also good any other time of the year. Lay the flank steak out flat. Peel and finely chop a large yellow onion and blend with 1 teaspoon of salt, ½ teaspoon of pepper, ½ teaspoon of ground ginger and ⅛ teaspoon of saltpeter. Spread evenly on the steak, leaving a 1-inch margin all around. Roll up and tie securely with string at 1½-inch intervals.

Bring 3 quarts of water to a boil with 1 cup of coarse salt, ½ cup of brown sugar and ⅛ teaspoon of saltpeter. Boil for a few minutes, then cool. Pour this brine over the rolled meat and let stand for 6 days. Put a weight on to keep the meat under the brine.

After 6 days remove the meat. Put into a pan with cold water to cover, bring to a boil and simmer for 3 hours. Remove and press for several hours between 2 plates with a weight on the top plate. Serve cold, cut into thin slices. Serves 8 to 10.

BOEUF EN CASSEROLE

1½ pounds top sirloin or round beef	*½ teaspoon tomato paste*
12 small white onions	*1 teaspoon meat glaze*
6 small carrots	*3 teaspoons potato flour*
6 small white turnips	*or 3 tablespoons flour*
1 celery heart	*1½ cups stock or water*
4 large mushrooms	*¼ cup red wine*
3 tablespoons butter	*salt and pepper*
¼ cup brandy or sherry	*1 bay leaf*
2 tablespoons chopped parsley	

Trim most of the fat from the meat and cut into 1-inch squares. Skin 12 small white onions. Peel 6 small carrots, cut them in half, then trim each piece so that it is olive-shaped — this is done primarily for appearance and is not essential. Do the same with 6 small white turnips. Quarter a celery heart and 4 large mushrooms.

Heat 1 tablespoon of butter in a heavy saucepan and brown the meat quickly all over in very hot butter. When all the meat is browned, heat ¼ cup brandy or sherry in a small pan, ignite and pour over the meat. Remove the meat from the pan. Put another 2 tablespoons of butter into the pan and quickly brown the onions, carrots, turnips and celery. Add the mushrooms and cook another minute or so. Blend in, off the fire, ½ teaspoon of tomato paste, 1 teaspoon of meat glaze and 3 teaspoons of potato flour or 3 tablespoons of flour. Pour on 1½ cups of stock or water and stir over the fire until the mixture comes to a boil. Put back the meat with any juices and a bay leaf. Cover with waxed paper and a lid and simmer for 1 to 1½ hours, or until the meat is tender; top sirloin requires less time than round beef.

Serve in a casserole and sprinkle with 2 tablespoons of finely chopped parsley. A copper casserole or any good-looking one that is suitable for serving may be used for cooking this dish and can also come to the table. Serves 4 to 6.

VINTNERS BEEF

2 pounds top round of beef	salt, peppercorns
2 cups red wine	3 tablespoons butter
½ teaspoon dried thyme	1 clove garlic, crushed
1 bay leaf	3 tablespoons flour
2 sprigs parsley	½ cup stock
1 small onion, sliced	¼ pound bacon, diced
1 small carrot, sliced	12 baby white onions

Cut the beef into 1-inch cubes. Marinate it for 24 hours in a bowl with 2 cups of red wine, ½ teaspoon of dried thyme, 1 bay leaf, 2 sprigs of parsley, a small sliced onion, a small sliced carrot, salt and a few peppercorns.

Remove the meat from the marinade and dry it with a cloth. Brown all over in a heavy pan in 2 tablespoons of very hot butter. Remove the beef from the pan. Put another tablespoon of butter into the pan and a clove of crushed garlic, and cook for 1 minute. Blend in 3 tablespoons of flour and let it brown slowly. Pour on the strained marinade and ½ cup of stock and stir over the fire until the mixture comes to a boil. Put back the beef. In another pan lightly sauté the diced bacon, add the bacon to the beef. Brown 12 baby white onions in the bacon fat, then put them in with the beef also. Cover and simmer for 1 to 1½ hours, or until the meat is tender. Meat that has been marinated usually gets tender more quickly than ordinary meat. Serve in a casserole; it may be cooked and served in the same dish. Serves 4 to 6.

STEAK AND KIDNEY PIE

1½ pounds round beef	3 tablespoons flour
4 to 6 lamb kidneys	½ teaspoon tomato paste
4 tablespoons butter	1½ cups stock
2 teaspoons vinegar	salt, pepper

QUICK PUFF PASTRY

2 cups flour	1 teaspoon salt
1½ sticks butter (¼ pound each)	about ¼ cup ice water
1 egg	

Cut the beef into 1-inch cubes and trim off any large pieces of fat. Remove outer membrane of kidneys, cut them in half and remove the white center cores. Brown the beef all over in 1 tablespoon of hot butter in a heavy deep saucepan. Remove the beef. Put another tablespoon of butter in the pan and brown the kidneys over a hot fire, cut side down at first to seal in the juices. Pour 2 teaspoons of vinegar in the pan, then remove the kidneys. Melt the remaining 2 tablespoons of butter in the pan. Blend in, off the fire, 3 tablespoons of flour and ½ teaspoon of tomato paste. Add 1½ cups of stock and stir over the fire until the mixture comes to a boil. Season with salt and pepper, put back the beef and kidneys, and simmer covered for 1 hour, or until the beef is tender. Meanwhile make the pastry.

Quick Puff Pastry: Put 2 cups of flour on a pastry board or marble slab. Make a well in the center and in it put 1½ sticks of butter, 1 teaspoon of salt and ¼ cup of ice water. Work the center ingredients to a smooth paste. Then work in the flour with the heel of your hand. Knead lightly. Form into a ball, wrap in waxed paper and place in the refrigerator to chill for at least ½ hour before rolling out.

Place the steak and kidney mixture in a pie dish or shallow baking dish. Brush the edge of the dish with beaten egg to prevent the pastry from shrinking. Cover with pastry rolled about ½ inch thick and decorate. Brush with beaten egg. Make a few slits for steam to escape or use a pie bird. If time allows, chill in the refrigerator for at least ½ hour. Place on a cookie sheet and bake in a hot oven at 400° for 20 to 30 minutes, until golden brown. Serve in the baking dish. Serves 4 to 6.

Note: Ideally the filling should cool before it is covered with crust; the pastry should chill before it is rolled out; and the uncooked pie should chill before it is baked; but none of this is essential.

STEAK AND KIDNEY PUDDING

2 pounds round of beef	3 tablespoons flour
6 to 8 lamb kidneys	salt, pepper
about 1½ cups boiling water	

SUET CRUST

2 cups flour	1 teaspoon salt
1 teaspoon baking powder	8 ounces beef suet
½ to ¾ cup tepid water	

The crust is the first step in this famous English dish. Sift together into a large mixing bowl 2 cups of flour, 1 teaspoon of baking powder and 1 teaspoon of salt. Add 8 ounces of ground or very finely chopped beef suet; most butchers are obliging enough to grind it for you. Work with your fingers or a pastry blender until well blended. Then work in enough tepid water to make a dough that is stiff but manageable, ½ to ¾ cup. Roll out ¾ of the dough on a lightly floured board. Line a 2-quart pudding basin if you have one, otherwise any sort of baking dish that has a good rim. English pudding basins are shaped like flowerpots, and the narrower and deeper the dish the better, since the idea is to have as little top surface as possible.

Cut the beef into rather small ¾-inch cubes. Halve 6 to 8 kidneys, remove the white center core and cut each piece in half. Place the beef and kidneys in layers in the crust, sprinkling each layer with a little flour and seasoning with salt and pepper. Pour in enough boiling water to come within an inch of the top. Roll out the rest of the dough and cover the top, tucking it in well. Put several layers of waxed paper over the top and tie it on firmly. Place the dish on a rack in a large pan and pour in enough boiling water to come ¾ of the way up the dish. Cover and steam for 4 hours. Add more water occasionally as the water boils away.

To Serve: Remove the paper and cut a few gashes in the top for the steam to escape. Serve either turned out on a hot serving dish or in the baking dish. Serves 6.

BOEUF BOURGUIGNON
(Beef Ragout with Burgundy)

2 pounds round beef	½ teaspoon tomato paste
3 tablespoons butter	1 cup stock or water
3 tablespoons brandy	1 cup burgundy
24 small white onions	salt
12 small white mushrooms	freshly cracked black pepper
3 tablespoons flour	1 bay leaf
1 teaspoon meat glaze	1 tablespoon finely chopped parsley or chives

Cut the meat into 1-inch cubes and brown them quickly all over in 1 tablespoon of hot butter. Heat 3 tablespoons of brandy in a small pan, ignite and pour over the beef. Remove the beef. Add the remaining 2 tablespoons of butter to the pan and quickly brown 24 small white onions. Cut 12 small white mushrooms in half and cook them about 2 minutes. Blend in, off the fire, 3 tablespoons of flour, 1 teaspoon of meat glaze and ½ teaspoon of tomato paste. Pour on 1 cup of stock or water and 1 cup of Burgundy and stir over the fire until the mixture comes to a boil. Season with salt and freshly cracked black pepper. Put back the meat with a bay leaf. Cover and simmer for 1¼ to 1½ hours, or until the meat is tender.

Serve in a casserole — in fact, the whole dish can be cooked and served in the same casserole. Remove the bay leaf and sprinkle with 1 tablespoon of finely chopped parsley or chives. Serves 4 to 6.

Note: This is an excellent informal-party dish because it can be kept waiting as long as you wish over a very low fire. It can also be made ahead of time and reheated, and if anything, this improves the flavor.

BOEUF EN DAUBE
(Beef Stew with Mushrooms and Olives)

2 pounds top round of beef	3 tablespoons flour
4 tablespoons butter	1½ cups stock
3 tablespoons brandy	½ cup claret
12 small mushrooms	1 tablespoon red currant jelly
24 pitted green olives	1 bay leaf
½ teaspoon tomato paste	3 tomatoes, peeled and thinly
½ teaspoon meat glaze	sliced

½ cup grated Swiss cheese

DUCHESS POTATOES

6 medium-size old potatoes	1 egg
¼ cup top milk	2 tablespoons butter

Cut beef in ½-inch cubes and brown them quickly all over in 2 tablespoons of hot butter. Heat 3 tablespoons of brandy in a small pan, ignite and pour over the beef. Remove the meat. Put another tablespoon of butter in the pan and 12 small mushrooms and cook for 3 to 4 minutes, or until the mushrooms are lightly browned. Add 24 pitted green olives and cook another minute or so. Blend in, off the fire, ½ teaspoon of tomato paste, ½ teaspoon of meat glaze and 3 tablespoons of flour. Pour on 1½ cups of stock and stir over the fire until the mixture comes to a boil. Add ½ cup of claret, 1 tablespoon of red currant jelly and a bay leaf. Season with salt and pepper. Return the meat to the pan, cover and simmer until the meat is tender, about 30 to 40 minutes. Meanwhile prepare the Duchess potatoes.

Duchess Potatoes: Cook 6 old peeled potatoes in boiling salted water until tender. Drain and dry out for a minute or so over a very low fire. Put through a ricer. Heat ¼ cup top milk with 2 tablespoons of butter and beat into the potatoes with 1 egg, salt and pepper.

To Serve: Place the meat and gravy on a hot ovenproof serving dish. Cover them with 3 thinly sliced peeled tomatoes. Sprinkle with ½ cup grated Swiss cheese and dot with 1 tablespoon of butter. Put the potatoes into a pastry bag with a large rose tube and pipe around the edge of the dish. Brown lightly under the broiler and serve immediately. Serves 4 to 6.

POT ROAST

4 to 5 pounds bottom round of beef	*2 thin slices lemon*
1 tablespoon butter	*1 cup water or red wine*
1 large can tomatoes	*salt, pepper*
1 bay leaf	*2 tablespoons flour or 2 teaspoons potato flour*
1 sprig parsley	*¼ cup cold water*
2 large yellow onions, thinly sliced	*½ teaspoon dried thyme*
	½ teaspoon celery salt
¼ cup sherry	

Brown the beef all over in 1 tablespoon of hot butter, using a deep heavy saucepan. Add 1 large can of tomatoes, 1 bay leaf, a sprig of fresh parsley, 2 large thinly sliced yellow onions and 2 thin slices of lemon. Cover and let simmer over a very low fire. The total cooking time is 50 minutes for each pound of meat. Add 1 cup of water or red wine, a little at a time, and turn the meat several times to ensure even cooking. When it has cooked for 2 hours, season with salt and pepper.

When the meat is done, take it out of the pan. Cut as many slices as are needed for one serving and arrange them slightly overlapping on a hot serving dish. Place the uncut piece at one end of the dish. Blend 2 tablespoons of flour or 2 teaspoons of potato flour with ¼ cup of cold water. Stir it into the gravy and continue stirring until the gravy is thickened. Add ½ teaspoon of dried thyme, ½ teaspoon of celery salt and ¼ cup of sherry. Simmer for 2 to 3 minutes. Spoon some of the gravy over the meat and serve the rest in a gravy bowl. This will serve 6 people.

BEEF IN RED WINE

3½ to 4 pounds pot roast of beef	½ cup red wine
3 tablespoons butter	¼ cup Marsala
1 clove garlic, crushed	3 tablespoons sherry
1 teaspoon meat glaze	3 tablespoons brandy
3 teaspoons potato flour	salt
1 cup stock	freshly cracked black pepper
½ teaspoon dried thyme	

A pot roast should be covered with a thin layer of fat, which most butchers usually do automatically. Brown the meat all over in 1 tablespoon of hot butter, using a deep heavy saucepan. Remove the beef. To the pan add another 2 tablespoons of butter and a crushed clove of garlic and cook for ½ minute. Blend in, off the fire, 1 teaspoon of meat glaze and 3 teaspoons of potato flour. Pour on 1 cup of stock, ½ cup of red wine, ¼ cup Marsala, 3 tablespoons of sherry and 3 tablespoons of brandy. Season with salt, freshly cracked black pepper and ½ teaspoon of dried thyme. Stir over the fire until the mixture comes to a boil. Put back the meat and cook covered in a moderate oven at 350° for 50 minutes to the pound, turning the meat 2 to 3 times. Serve in an earthen-ware dish and pour over the sauce. Serves 4 to 6.

SAUERBRATEN

4 to 5 pounds round or rump of beef	*4 cloves*
	6 whole allspice
2 onions, sliced	*½ teaspoon dried thyme*
1 carrot, sliced	*1 sprig parsley*
1 stalk celery, sliced	*4 tablespoons butter*
2 cups red wine vinegar	*3 tablespoons flour*
1 tablespoon salt	*1 tablespoon red currant jelly*
12 peppercorns	*4 or 5 gingersnaps*

2 tablespoons Madeira or claret

Place the meat in a crock or glass bowl which has a cover. Combine the following ingredients and pour over the meat: 2 sliced onions, 1 sliced carrot, 1 sliced stalk of celery, 2 cups of red wine vinegar, 1 tablespoon of salt, 12 peppercorns, 4 cloves, 6 whole allspice, ½ teaspoon of dried thyme and 1 sprig of parsley. Cover and leave in a cold place for 3 to 4 days. Turn the meat twice a day.

Remove the meat from the marinade and dry it. Heat 1 table-spoon of butter in a heavy deep saucepan and brown the meat all over. Remove the meat from the pan. Melt another 3 tablespoons of butter in the pan. Blend in 3 tablespoons of flour. Add the strained marinade and bring to a boil, stirring constantly. Put back the meat, cover and simmer for about 2½ hours; by then the meat should be very tender.

Take the meat out of the pan and cut into slices, as many as are needed for one meal. Arrange on a hot serving dish with the uncut piece at one end. To make the gravy sour-sweet, add 1 tablespoon of red currant jelly, 4 or 5 crumbled gingersnaps and 2 tablespoons of Madeira or claret. Spoon some of the gravy over the meat and serve the rest in a gravy bowl. Serve with potato pancakes or noodles; and red cabbage is often served with sauer-braten. This will serve 6 to 8 people.

BOEUF BRAISÉ À LA FRANCFORT
(Braised Beef with Tomatoes and Carrots)

*3 pounds top sirloin of beef,
   rolled*
salt and pepper
3 small onions
2 cloves garlic, crushed
1 bay leaf
½ cup red wine
4 tablespoons sherry
6 tablespoons butter

2 small carrots
2 mushrooms
1 tablespoon flour
½ cup stock
2 teaspoons tomato paste
6 small firm tomatoes
1 tablespoon chopped chives
1 bunch small carrots
1 teaspoon lemon juice

The beef should be prepared with a covering of thin suet or bacon which is tied on with thin string. Season it well with salt and pepper. Put it into a mixing bowl. Over the top scatter 1 sliced onion, a crushed clove of garlic and a crushed bay leaf. Pour over ½ cup of red wine and 2 tablespoons of sherry and marinate for an hour, turning the meat over every 15 minutes. Remove the meat and dry it thoroughly. Brown all over in 2 tablespoons of hot butter in a deep heavy saucepan. Heat 2 tablespoons of sherry in a small pan, ignite and pour over the beef. Remove the beef. Put another 2 tablespoons of butter into the pan, then 2 small sliced onions, 2 small sliced carrots and 2 sliced mushrooms. Cook until lightly browned. Blend in 1 tablespoon of flour. Strain on the marinade and add ½ cup of stock. Stir until the mixture comes to a boil. Put back the beef. Cook covered in a moderate oven at 375° for 1½ hours, or until the beef is tender. Half an hour before the meat is done, prepare the following vegetables.

Tomatoes: Melt 1 tablespoon of butter in a skillet. Add 1 clove of crushed garlic, 2 teaspoons of tomato paste, 6 tomatoes which have been skinned and cut into thick slices, salt and pepper. Cook over a moderate fire for about 15 minutes. Add 1 tablespoon of finely chopped chives.

Carrots: Scrape a bunch of small carrots and cut them into fourths lengthwise. Cook in boiling salted water with 1 teaspoon of lemon juice until just tender. Drain, then heat again with 1 tablespoon of melted butter.

To Serve: Make a bed of the tomatoes on a hot serving dish. Cut as many slices of beef as are needed for one serving and arrange them slightly overlapping on the tomatoes. Put the uncut piece at one end. Reduce the sauce a little and strain it over the meat. Pile the carrots at the other end of the dish. Serves 6.

BEEF À LA MODE
(French Pot Roast)

3 to 4 pounds boneless pot roast	*bouquet garni (bay leaf, parsley, thyme)*
¼ pound salt pork	*½ calf's foot or 1 veal knuckle*
2 tablespoons butter	*salt, pepper*
3 tablespoons brandy	*24 small white onions*
1 cup dry white wine	
6 large carrots	

Lard the beef, or have the butcher do it, with thin strips of salt pork and a larding needle (see page 17 for instructions). Heat 2 tablespoons of butter in a deep heavy pan. When it is on the point of turning color, quickly brown the beef all over. Heat 3 tablespoons of brandy in a small pan, ignite and pour over the meat. Add 1 cup of dry white wine and enough water to almost cover the meat. Bring slowly to a boil and skim. Add a bouquet garni consisting of a bay leaf, 2 or 3 sprigs of parsley and a sprig of thyme. Also add half a calf's foot or a cracked knuckle of veal. Season with salt and pepper. Cover and cook in a moderate oven at 350° for 1½ hours. Put 24 small peeled white onions and 6 large carrots cut into small olive shapes into the pan and cook another 1½ hours.

To Serve: Place the beef on a hot serving dish. If a calf's foot was used, chop the meat; discard a veal knuckle. Surround the meat with the vegetables and the calf's foot meat, if any. Remove the fat that rises to the top of the gravy and strain it. Serve in a separate gravy bowl. Serves 6 to 8.

BOEUF BRAISÉ DUBARRY
(Braised Beef with Cauliflower)

3 to 4 pounds round of beef	3 tablespoons flour
½ pound salt pork	1½ cups stock
5 tablespoons butter	½ cup red wine
3 tablespoons sherry	salt
1 teaspoon tomato paste	freshly cracked black pepper
1 teaspoon meat glaze	1 bay leaf
	1 large cauliflower

½ to 1 cup grated Parmesan or Cheddar cheese

Cut the salt pork into long thin strips and lard the beef with a larding needle (see page 17 for instructions on larding). Brown quickly all over in 1 tablespoon of hot butter in a heavy deep saucepan. Heat 3 tablespoons of sherry in a small pan, ignite and pour over the meat. Remove the meat from the pan. Melt another 2 tablespoons of butter in the same pan. Blend in, off the fire, 1 teaspoon of tomato paste, 1 teaspoon of meat glaze and 3 tablespoons of flour. Add 1½ cups of stock and stir over the fire until the mixture comes to a boil. Add ½ cup of red wine, salt, freshly cracked black pepper and a bay leaf. Put back the beef, cover and either simmer on top of the stove or cook in a moderate oven at 350° for 2 to 2½ hours, until the meat is tender. Meanwhile prepare the cauliflower garnish.

Cauliflower: Separate a large cauliflower into flowerets and cook them in boiling salted water until just soft. Drain and dry on a cloth. Place on a cookie sheet. Sprinkle with ½ to 1 cup grated cheese and 2 tablespoons of melted butter and brown under the broiler.

To Serve: Cut as many thin slices of beef as are needed for one meal and arrange them slightly overlapping on a hot serving dish. Place the uncut piece at one end. Strain the gravy and pour a little of it over the meat; serve the rest in a gravy bowl. Garnish with the cauliflower flowerets. Serves 6.

BRAISED BEEF WITH FRENCH FRIED POTATOES

1½ pounds top sirloin of beef	1½ cups stock
3 tablespoons butter	1 bay leaf
3 tablespoons sherry	1 sprig tarragon
1 clove garlic, crushed	4 or 5 old potatoes
1 teaspoon meat glaze	vegetable shortening or salad oil for deep-fat frying
3 teaspoons potato flour	salt, pepper

Trim most of the fat off the meat. Brown quickly on both sides in 1 tablespoon of hot butter. Heat 3 tablespoons of sherry in a small pan, ignite and pour over the meat. Remove the meat from the pan. To the pan add a clove of crushed garlic and the remaining 2 tablespoons of butter and cook about 1 minute. Blend in, off the fire, 1 teaspoon of meat glaze and 3 teaspoons of potato flour. Pour on 1½ cups of stock and stir over the fire until the mixture comes to a boil. Put back the meat with a bay leaf and a sprig of tarragon. Season well. Cover and simmer for 1 to 1¼ hours, or until the meat is tender. Remove and serve cut into slices with the gravy strained over it. Garnish with French fried potatoes.

French Fried Potatoes: Peel 4 or 5 large old potatoes and cut them into long thin fingers; there are special cutters for French fried potatoes which are timesaving if you have these potatoes often, and very inexpensive. Soak the cut potatoes for ½ hour in cold water. Drain and dry thoroughly on a cloth. Cook until soft and lightly browned in deep hot fat at 370°. Drain on absorbent paper. Just before serving brown quickly in very hot fat at 390°. Drain again, sprinkle with salt and serve immediately. This double frying ensures complete cooking and crisp potatoes; with just one frying they may be half raw and limp. Serves 4.

LARDED BRAISED BEEF

3 to 4 pounds top round of
    beef
½ pound salt pork for larding
5 tablespoons butter
3 tablespoons sherry or brandy
1 teaspoon tomato paste
3 tablespoons flour
½ cup stock

salt
freshly cracked pepper
6 large tomatoes
½ pound mushrooms
1 pound small new potatoes
½ cup bread crumbs
½ cup grated Parmesan
    cheese

2 pounds peas, cooked

Marinate the beef for 24 hours in a marinade crue (see page 72 for recipe). Remove from the marinade and dry. Cut the salt pork into long thin strips and lard the beef with a larding needle (see page 17 for instructions on larding). Heat 1 tablespoon of butter in a heavy deep saucepan. Brown the meat quickly all over. Heat 3 tablespoons of sherry or brandy in a small pan, ignite and pour over the meat. Remove the meat from the pan. Melt another tablespoon of butter in the pan. Blend in, off the fire, 1 teaspoon of tomato paste and 3 tablespoons of flour. Stir in the strained marinade and ½ cup of stock. Season with salt and freshly cracked pepper and stir over the fire until the mixture comes to a boil. Put back the meat and simmer for 2 to 2½ hours, until the meat is tender. Since marinating helps tenderize meat, 2 hours will probably be long enough.

To Serve: Cut enough beef for one meal into thin slices and arrange them slightly overlapping on a hot serving dish. Strain the gravy and spoon a little over the meat; place the rest in a gravy bowl. Garnish with tomatoes, sautéed mushroom caps and sautéed new potatoes. To prepare the tomatoes cut them in half. Sprinkle 6 of the halves with ½ cup of bread crumbs, ½ cup of grated Parmesan cheese and dot with 2 tablespoons of butter. Broil until nicely browned. Scoop out the centers of the other 6 halves, put a small piece of butter in each and broil until golden brown; then fill with cooked peas. Serves 6.

BEEF IN BEER

2 pounds round beef in 1 piece	1½ cups beer
2 tablespoons flour	½ cup water
salt, pepper	1 sprig parsley
3 tablespoons butter	1 sprig thyme
1 large clove garlic, crushed	1 stalk celery
1 large yellow onion, sliced	1 bay leaf

Pound 2 tablespoons of seasoned flour into both sides of the beef with a wooden mallet. Heat 1 tablespoon of butter in a heavy skillet and brown the meat quickly on both sides. Remove the meat. Put another 2 tablespoons of butter into the pan and sauté 1 large clove of garlic and 1 large thinly sliced yellow onion until lightly browned. Pour 1½ cups of beer and ½ cup of water into the pan and bring to a boil. Replace the meat and lower the heat to simmering. Put 1 sprig of parsley, a sprig of thyme, a stalk of celery and a bay leaf in the pan. Simmer covered for about 1¼ hours, until the meat is tender. Remove the meat and cut into serving pieces. Arrange on a hot platter and strain the sauce over it. Serves 4 to 6.

BEEF OLIVES

3 or 4 dried mushrooms	1 teaspoon tomato paste
1½ pounds top round of beef	1 teaspoon meat glaze
1 cup buckwheat groats, cooked	3 teaspoons potato flour or 3
4 tablespoons butter	tablespoons flour
1 medium-size yellow onion,	1½ cups stock
chopped	½ pound broad noodles
½ pound fresh mushrooms,	¼ pound cooked ham,
sliced	shredded
12 pitted green olives	¼ cup melted butter

Soak 3 or 4 dried mushrooms for 1 to 2 hours in cold water to cover. Drain and finely chop.

Cut the meat into thin slices, as for scallopini. Put the slices between 2 pieces of waxed paper and beat with a wooden mallet until very thin. Spread each slice with a generous tablespoon of the cooked buckwheat groats. Roll up and tie each end with string. Heat 2 tablespoons of butter in a large skillet and when it is on the point of turning color, put in the beef rolls and brown them quickly all over. Remove the beef rolls. Put another 2 tablespoons of butter into the pan and lightly brown 1 finely chopped medium-size onion, the chopped dried mushrooms, half a pound of sliced fresh mushrooms and 12 pitted green olives. Blend in, off the fire, 1 teaspoon of tomato paste, 1 teaspoon of meat glaze and 3 teaspoons of potato flour (or 3 tablespoons flour). When smooth add 1½ cups of stock. Stir over the fire until the mixture comes to a boil. Taste for seasoning. Put back the beef rolls and simmer covered for 30 to 40 minutes.

While the beef rolls are simmering cook ½ pound of broad noodles in plenty of boiling salted water until tender. Drain thoroughly and blend with ¼ pound shredded ham and ¼ cup of melted butter.

To Serve: Spread the noodles on a hot serving dish. Arrange the beef rolls on top and strain the sauce over all. Serves 4.

BEEF BIRDS WITH PEA PURÉE

8 *thin slices round of beef*	3 *tablespoons brandy*
6 *chicken livers*	1 *teaspoon meat glaze*
3 *tablespoons butter*	½ *teaspoon tomato paste*
¼ *pound mushrooms, sliced*	2 *teaspoons potato flour*
salt, pepper	1¼ *cups stock*
8 *thin slices cooked ham or*	¼ *cup red wine*
tongue	1 *bay leaf*

PEA PURÉE

3 *cups fresh or frozen peas*	2 *tablespoons butter*
salt, pepper	2 *tablespoons flour*
3 *tablespoons sour cream*	

Put the slices of beef between 2 pieces of waxed paper and beat until very thin with a wooden mallet. Brown 6 chicken livers quickly in 1 tablespoon of hot butter. Remove them from the pan. Put another tablespoon of butter into the pan and sauté ¼ pound sliced mushrooms until lightly browned. Shred the chicken livers and mix with the mushrooms, salt and pepper. Put a thin slice of ham or tongue on each piece of beef with a spoonful of the mushroom mixture on top. Press down carefully. Roll each slice of beef and fasten each end with string. Brown these beef birds quickly all over in 1 tablespoon of hot butter. Heat 3 table-spoons of brandy in a small pan, ignite and pour over the beef birds. Remove them from the pan.

Blend in, off the fire, 1 teaspoon of meat glaze, ½ teaspoon of tomato paste and 2 teaspoons of potato flour. Pour on 1¼ cups of stock and ¼ cup of red wine and stir over the fire until the mixture comes to a boil. Taste for seasoning. Put back the beef birds with a bay leaf. Cover with waxed paper and a lid and cook gently until the beef is tender, about 45 minutes. While the beef is simmering prepare a pea purée.

Pea Purée: Cook 3 cups of shelled fresh or frozen peas in boiling salted water until very tender. Drain well and put through a strainer. Melt 2 tablespoons of butter in a small pan. Stir in 2 tablespoons of flour, salt and pepper, and brown very slowly. Add the strained peas, 3 tablespoons of sour cream and a little more seasoning. Keep warm in a double boiler until ready for use.

To Serve: Make a bed of pea purée on a hot serving dish. Re-move the beef birds, cut off the strings and arrange the beef birds on top of the pea purée. Strain the sauce over all. Allow 1 or 2 for each serving.

BEEF AND RICE CASSEROLE

4 tablespoons butter	*1½ pounds ground round beef*
1 green pepper, diced	*salt, pepper*
1 large yellow onion, thinly sliced	*1 teaspoon meat glaze*
1 cup finely chopped celery	*3 cups boiling water*
1½ cups raw rice	*½ cup grated Parmesan cheese*
	2 tablespoons chopped parsley

Melt 3 tablespoons of butter in a large skillet. Put in a diced green pepper, 1 large thinly sliced yellow onion, 1 cup of finely chopped celery and 1½ cups of rice. Cook over a moderate fire for 7 to 8 minutes, stirring frequently. Add 1½ pounds of round beef ground and cook over a brisk fire for 3 to 4 minutes, until the meat is lightly browned. Season with salt and pepper. Put into a casserole. Dissolve 1 teaspoon of meat glaze in 3 cups of boiling water and pour into the casserole. Bake covered in a moderate oven at 350°. Remove the cover, sprinkle the top with ½ cup of grated Parmesan cheese and 2 tablespoons of finely chopped parsley, and dot with 1 tablespoon of butter. Cook another 15 minutes or so, uncovered, until the top is lightly browned. Serve in the casserole. This will serve 5 or 6 people.

BISCUIT BEEF ROLL

BISCUIT DOUGH

1½ cups flour	*3 tablespoons shortening*
3 teaspoons baking powder	*¼ cup milk*
½ teaspoon salt	*¼ cup water*

STUFFING

¼ cup finely chopped onion	*1 tomato*
½ diced green pepper	*1 pound ground round beef*
1 tablespoon butter	*½ cup chopped celery*
2 eggs	

watercress or parsley for garnish

Biscuit Dough: Sift together into a large bowl 1½ cups flour, 3 teaspoons of baking powder and ½ teaspoon of salt. Cut in 3 tablespoons of vegetable shortening. Combine ¼ cup of milk and ¼ cup of water. Make a hole in the center of the dry ingredients, pour in the liquid and stir quickly just until well mixed. Roll out a rectangle ¼ inch thick on a marble slab or pastry board.

Stuffing: Sauté ¼ cup of chopped onion and ½ diced green pepper in 1 tablespoon of butter until soft but not brown. Peel 1 tomato, cut into quarters, remove the seedy pulp and chop the rest. Blend together 1 pound of ground round beef, the sautéed onion and pepper, ½ cup finely chopped celery, the tomato, 1 egg, salt and pepper.

Spread the stuffing evenly on top of the dough, leaving a 2-inch margin all around. Fold the margin over the meat on opposite long sides to hold in the stuffing. Then roll up like a jelly roll, pressing in the end. Place on a cookie sheet and brush with a beaten egg. Bake in a hot oven at 425° for about 30 minutes, until the top is a nice brown. Remove carefully to a hot platter and garnish with parsley or watercress. A garlic tomato sauce (page 183) or a mushroom sauce (page 40) may be served separately. Serves 5 or 6.

CHOPPED BEEF CASSEROLE

10 slices bacon	*2 eggs*
2 pounds ground round beef	*salt, pepper*
1 cup finely chopped onion	*about ½ teaspoon dried oregano*
2 tablespoons butter	*1 pound mushrooms, sliced*
½ cup bread crumbs	*2 10½-ounce cans mushroom*
1 small clove garlic, crushed	*soup*
1 cup red wine	

Cook 10 slices of bacon in a large skillet until brown and crisp. Remove and drain on absorbent paper. Put 2 pounds of ground beef in a large mixing bowl. Cook 1 cup of finely chopped onion in 2 tablespoons of butter until soft but not brown. Remove the onion and add to the beef. Lightly brown ½ cup of bread crumbs (dry) and 1 small clove of crushed garlic in the same pan, adding a little more butter if needed. Put this in with the beef and also add 2 eggs, salt, pepper and about ½ teaspoon of dried oregano. Work until thoroughly blended, preferably with your hands. Form into small balls, brown them in the bacon fat and put them into a greased casserole. Sauté 1 pound of sliced mushrooms in the same pan. Blend in 2 cups of condensed mushroom soup and 1 cup of red wine. Taste for seasoning and pour this sauce over the meat. Crumble the bacon and sprinkle it over the top.

Cover and bake in a moderate oven at 350° for 45 minutes, or until ready to serve. Serve in the casserole. Serves 6 to 8.

STUFFED FRENCH BREAD

1 long loaf French bread	3 tablespoons sour cream
4 tablespoons butter	salt
1 small clove garlic, crushed	freshly cracked black pepper
¾ pound ground round beef	2 tablespoons grated onion
2 eggs	2 teaspoons chopped chives
1 tablespoon brandy	

Cut a long loaf of French bread in half lengthwise. Scoop out all the soft insides. Blend together 4 tablespoons of softened butter and a small clove of crushed garlic, and spread it on the bread. Bake in a moderate oven at 350° for 8 to 10 minutes, until lightly browned. Mix together ¾ pound of ground beef, 2 eggs, 3 table-spoons of sour cream, plenty of salt and freshly cracked black pepper, 2 tablespoons of grated onion, 2 teaspoons of finely chopped chives and 1 tablespoon of brandy. Fill the bread with this mixture, reshape, roll in waxed paper and place in the re-frigerator for at least 1 hour. Slice and serve as a luncheon dish or an hors d'oeuvre. Makes 15 to 20 slices.

MEAT SAUCE FOR SPAGHETTI

3 tablespoons butter	1 tablespoon tomato paste
1 cup finely chopped onion	2 tablespoons flour
½ cup finely chopped mush-rooms	1 cup stock
1 large clove garlic, crushed	1 tablespoon red currant jelly
salt and pepper	2 tablespoons chopped parsley
½ pound ground beef	3 skinned, seeded, chopped to-matoes
1 teaspoon meat glaze	2 tablespoons red wine

Heat 3 tablespoons of butter in a heavy skillet. Add 1 cup of finely chopped onions and cook very slowly until golden brown. Add ½ cup of finely chopped mushrooms and a large clove of crushed garlic and cook slowly for about 5 minutes. Season with salt and pepper. Add ½ pound of chopped beef and cook for 5 to 6 minutes, stirring occasionally. Blend in, off the fire, 1 teaspoon of meat glaze, 1 tablespoon of tomato paste and 2 tablespoons of flour. Pour on 1 cup of stock and stir over the fire until the mixture comes to a boil. Add 1 tablespoon of red currant jelly, 2 tablespoons of finely chopped parsley, 3 skinned, seeded, chopped tomatoes and 2 tablespoons of red wine. Taste for seasoning. Simmer for 10 to 15 minutes. Serve with spaghetti. Serves 4 to 6.

MEAT LOAF I

1½ pounds lean ground beef	*½ teaspoon dried thyme*
½ pound sausage meat	*salt*
1 clove garlic, crushed	*1 large yellow onion, chopped*
2 eggs	*1 tablespoon butter*
1 tablespoon chopped parsley	*2 hard-boiled eggs*
	½ cup red or white wine

TOMATO SAUCE

3 tablespoons butter	*2 tablespoons tomato paste*
1½ teaspoons potato flour or	*1 small clove garlic, crushed*
* 1½ tablespoons flour*	*2 tomatoes, skinned and sliced*
salt, cayenne	*1½ cups water*

Mix together in a large bowl 1½ pounds of ground beef, ½ pound of sausage meat, 1 clove of crushed garlic, 2 eggs, 1 tablespoon of finely chopped parsley, ½ teaspoon of dried thyme and a little salt. Sauté a large finely chopped yellow onion in 1 tablespoon of butter over a moderate fire until lightly browned. Add to the rest of the ingredients. When well blended roll out into a rectangle about ¾ inch thick on waxed paper. Place 2 hard-boiled eggs down the center, the long way of the meat. Fold the two long sides over the eggs and pat into an even shape. Place in a baking dish and pour ½ cup of red or white wine around it. Bake for 50 to 60 minutes in a moderate oven at 350°, basting several times with the pan juices. Meanwhile prepare the following tomato sauce.

Tomato Sauce: Melt 2 tablespoons of butter. Blend in, off the fire, 1½ teaspoons of potato flour or 1½ tablespoons of flour, salt and cayenne pepper, 2 tablespoons of tomato paste and 1 small clove of crushed garlic. Add 2 skinned and sliced tomatoes and 1½ cups of water. Stir over the fire until the sauce comes to a boil, then simmer for 10 to 15 minutes. Just before serving add the remaining tablespoon of butter, bit by bit.

To Serve: Remove the meat loaf from the pan and cut into slices. Arrange them slightly overlapping on a hot serving dish. Spoon a little of the tomato sauce over the meat and serve the rest in a sauce bowl. Serves 5 or 6.

MEAT LOAF II

1 medium-size yellow onion	*1 pound ground round beef*
1 green pepper	*1 pound ground lean pork*
2 tablespoons butter or bacon fat	*1 egg*
3 thin slices white bread	*salt, pepper*
½ pint light cream	*¼ teaspoon oregano*
1 large can tomatoes	

Peel 1 medium-size yellow onion and chop it finely. Core and seed 1 green pepper and chop that finely also. Sauté until soft but not brown in 2 tablespoons of butter or bacon fat. Meanwhile cut the crust off 3 slices of thinly sliced white bread and put them into a mixing bowl. Cover with ½ pint of light cream and let stand for about 5 minutes. Add 1 pound of ground round of beef, 1 pound of ground lean pork, 1 egg, salt, pepper and ¼ teaspoon of oregano. Work with one hand until thoroughly blended, adding about ¼ cup of the liquid from the canned tomatoes. Place in a buttered loaf pan, forming the meat so that there is a little space on each side. Pour the canned tomatoes and the rest of the juice over the top and sides. Bake uncovered in a moderate oven at 350° for 1 hour, basting several times. Serve hot or cold. Serves 5 or 6.

LASAGNA

½ pound wide lasagna noodles	1 egg
2 tablespoons salad oil	3 tablespoons sour cream
salt, pepper	1 cup grated Parmesan cheese
1 pound ricotta or cottage cheese	2 tablespoons chopped chives
6 ounces cream cheese	1 Mozzarella cheese, thinly sliced

TOMATO MEAT SAUCE

3 tablespoons butter or olive oil	4 tomatoes, peeled and sliced
1 clove garlic, crushed	salt, pepper
1 large onion, finely chopped	½ cup stock
3 tablespoons tomato paste	½ pound ground beef

Bring 2 to 3 quarts of water to a boil with 2 tablespoons of oil and 2 to 3 tablespoons of salt. Put in the lasagna, one by one, and cook for 15 to 20 minutes, until tender. Drain carefully and put on a cloth to dry; place the noodles so that they are not touching.

Mix together 1 pound of ricotta or cottage cheese and 6 ounces of cream cheese. When quite smooth add 1 egg, 3 tablespoons of sour cream, ¼ cup of grated Parmesan cheese and 2 tablespoons of finely chopped chives, salt and pepper. Beat until thoroughly blended. Spread a generous spoonful of this mixture on each noodle, smooth with a spatula and roll up. Place the rolled noodles in a large shallow baking dish, pour tomato meat sauce over them and top with thin slices of Mozzarella cheese. Sprinkle with ¾ cup of grated Parmesan cheese and bake in a moderate oven at 375° for 10 to 15 minutes, until thoroughly heated.

Tomato Meat Sauce: Heat 3 tablespoons of butter or olive oil in a skillet and lightly brown 1 clove of crushed garlic and 1 large finely chopped yellow onion. Add 3 tablespoons of tomato paste, 4 skinned and sliced tomatoes, ½ cup of stock, salt and pepper, and simmer for 10 minutes. Add ½ pound of raw ground beef and cook another 5 to 10 minutes, or until ready to use.

To Serve: Serve in the baking dish. Serves 6 to 8.

STUFFED CABBAGE

1 medium-size green cabbage
salt and pepper
1 cup finely chopped onion
1 tablespoon olive oil
½ cup chopped mushrooms
½ pound ground beef
½ cup diced cooked ham or tongue

¼ cup chopped olives
1 small clove garlic, crushed
1 tablespoon chopped chives
1 egg white, unbeaten
2 tablespoons sour cream
1 tablespoon butter
6 slices bacon
½ cup stock

BROWN SAUCE

1½ tablespoons butter
2 chicken livers
½ teaspoon tomato paste
1 teaspoon meat glaze

3 teaspoons potato flour
1½ cups water
½ cup red wine
salt, pepper

Put the cabbage in a deep heavy saucepan, cover with cold water, season with salt and pepper and bring slowly to a boil. Remove and cut off the bottom stalk. Separate the leaves carefully from the center of the cabbage, folding back all the outside leaves but leaving the heart whole. Sauté 1 cup of finely chopped onion in 1 tablespoon of olive oil until lightly browned. Add ½ cup of chopped mushrooms and ½ pound of ground beef and cook over a brisk fire for 3 to 4 minutes. Add ½ cup diced cooked ham or tongue, ¼ cup chopped olives, 1 small clove crushed garlic and 1 tablespoon finely chopped chives. Remove from the fire and blend in 1 unbeaten egg white, 2 tablespoons of sour cream and 1 tablespoon of butter. Taste for seasoning because it should be highly seasoned. Spread the stuffing inside the cabbage leaves, folding each leaf back into place so that the head looks about the same as it did in the first place. Tie with heavy string and cover with 6 strips of bacon. Put into a baking dish which has a cover, sprinkle with salt and pepper and put ½ cup of stock into the pan. Cook covered in a moderate oven at 375° for about 1 hour, basting occasionally. Serve on a hot platter covered with the following brown sauce.

Brown Sauce: Heat ½ tablespoon of butter and quickly brown 2 chicken livers. Remove them from the pan. Add another tablespoon of butter. Blend in, off the fire, ½ teaspoon of tomato paste, 1 teaspoon of meat glaze and 3 teaspoons of potato flour. Pour on 1½ cups of water and ½ cup of red wine and stir over the fire until the sauce comes to a boil. Cut the chicken livers into thin slices and add to the sauce. Season and let simmer for at least 5 minutes. Serves 4 to 6.

DOLMAS DE CHOUX
(Stuffed Cabbage Leaves)

1 medium-size green cabbage	1 cup cooked rice
1 medium-size yellow onion	2 hard-boiled eggs, chopped
4 tablespoons butter	1 tablespoon finely chopped
1 clove garlic, crushed	parsley
¼ pound mushrooms, sliced	salt, pepper
½ pound ground beef	2 tablespoons sour cream

TOMATO SAUCE

3 tablespoons butter	1½ cups water or cabbage stock
3 tablespoons flour	2 tomatoes
2 tablespoons tomato paste	salt, pepper
1 clove garlic, crushed	1 tablespoon sour cream

Put the cabbage into a saucepan with 4 cups of cold salted water. Bring slowly to a boil and simmer for 3 to 4 minutes. Drain well, saving the cooking water. Carefully remove 8 of the large outer leaves; if you work from the core end, the leaves should not break. Cut off the tip end of the stalks. Place a generous spoonful of the following stuffing in the center of each leaf and fold the leaf around the filling. Place in a shallow ovenproof serving dish or casserole, folded side down, and cover with tomato sauce. Bake covered in a moderate oven at 350° for 20 to 30 minutes.

Stuffing: Peel and finely chop a yellow onion. Cook slowly in 2 tablespoons of butter until soft but not brown. Add another 2 tablespoons of butter, a clove of crushed garlic and ¼ pound sliced mushrooms and cook for 3 to 4 minutes. Add ½ pound ground beef, 1 cup of cooked rice, 2 chopped hard-boiled eggs, 1 table-spoon of finely chopped parsley, salt and pepper. Turn up the heat and cook briskly for 2 to 3 minutes. Off the fire blend in 2 tablespoons of sour cream.

Tomato Sauce: Melt 3 tablespoons of butter. Blend in, off the fire, 3 tablespoons of flour, 2 tablespoons of tomato paste and a crushed clove of garlic. Add 1½ cups of water or the cabbage stock and stir over the fire until the sauce comes to a boil; let simmer about 5 minutes. Peel 2 tomatoes, cut them into small pieces and add to the sauce with salt and pepper; the seedy pulp can be discarded or strained and added to the sauce. Blend in 1 tablespoon of sour cream.

To Serve: Serve in the baking dish. Serves 4.

RAVIOLI

2 *pounds ravioli dough*	2 *tablespoons chopped chives*
6 *ounces ground beef*	*or parsley*
1 *medium-size yellow onion,*	1 *small clove garlic, crushed*
chopped	*salt, pepper*
½ *pound raw spinach, ground*	¼ *cup water*
or minced	1 *egg yolk*
½ *cup grated Parmesan cheese*	

TOMATO SAUCE

5 *tablespoons butter*	2 *cups water*
3 *tablespoons flour*	1 *small clove garlic, crushed*
2 *tablespoons tomato paste*	3 *tomatoes, skinned and sliced*
salt, pepper	

Ravioli dough can be either purchased from Italian specialty stores or made at home (instructions follow this recipe). Spread half the dough on a flat surface to dry out a little. Into a large mixing bowl put 6 ounces of ground beef, a finely chopped medium-size yellow onion, ½ pound ground or minced raw spinach, 2 table-spoons of chopped chives or parsley, a small clove of crushed garlic, salt and pepper. Add ¼ cup of water and blend well. Form into small balls the size of a large marble and place them on the ravioli dough about 3 inches apart. Brush the dough with an egg yolk which has been lightly beaten with a tablespoon of water. Cover with the rest of the ravioli dough. Cut around each meat ball with a fluted cutter or cut into squares with a pastry wheel. Press again in the center right around the meat ball with a small plain cutter to push out all the air, but do not cut through the dough. Simmer for 5 minutes in a large pan of salted water; do not let the water boil or the ravioli may disintegrate. Meanwhile prepare the following tomato sauce.

Tomato Sauce: Melt 3 tablespoons of butter. Blend in, off the fire, 3 tablespoons of flour and 2 tablespoons of tomato paste. Add 2 cups of water and bring to a boil with constant stirring. Simmer for at least 5 minutes. Lightly brown 2 tablespoons of butter in a small skillet. Add a small clove of crushed garlic and 3 skinned and sliced tomatoes and cook briskly for 2 to 3 minutes. Add to the rest of the sauce and season with salt and pepper.

To Serve: Remove the ravioli with a slotted spoon and put on a dry cloth to drain thoroughly. Place them on a hot serving dish. Cover with tomato sauce, sprinkle with at least ½ cup of grated Parmesan cheese and serve immediately. Serves 6.

RAVIOLI DOUGH

2 cups flour	*½ teaspoon salt*
2 small eggs, beaten	*2 to 3 tablespoons cold water*

Put 2 cups of flour on a pastry board or marble slab. Make a well in the center and in it put 2 beaten eggs, ½ teaspoon of salt and 2 to 3 tablespoons of cold water. Work the flour into the center ingredients. Knead for about 5 minutes. Let stand for 10 minutes, then roll out very thin on a floured board. Keep turning the dough when rolling it out, because one usually rolls more heavily with one hand than the other, which will make the dough thinner on one side if it isn't turned. Wrap in a dry cloth and then in a wet one and place in the refrigerator until ready to use.

SWEDISH MEAT BALLS

1 pound beef, ground twice	*½ teaspoon pepper*
3 slices white bread	*2 tablespoons chopped chives*
½ cup cream	*½ teaspoon tomato paste*
¾ cup chopped onion	*1 teaspoon meat glaze*
4 tablespoons butter	*2 tablespoons flour*
2 eggs	*1 cup stock*
1 small clove garlic, crushed	*1 cup sour cream*
½ teaspoon ground nutmeg	*1 pound broad noodles*
1 teaspoon salt	*½ cup melted butter*

¼ cup grated Parmesan cheese

Cut the crusts off 3 slices of white bread and soak the bread in ½ cup of cream for about 5 minutes. Cook ¾ cup finely chopped onion in 1 tablespoon of butter over a slow fire until soft but not brown. Put 1 pound of ground beef into a large mixing bowl with 2 slightly beaten eggs, 1 small clove of crushed garlic, ½ teaspoon of ground nutmeg, 1 teaspoon of salt, ½ teaspoon of pepper, the sautéed onions and the soaked bread and 1 tablespoon of finely chopped chives. Work with one hand until well blended and light. Form the mixture into small balls the size of a walnut, using your hands and dipping them occasionally into cold water. Heat 3 tablespoons of butter in a large skillet and cook the meat balls until golden brown all over. Cook only a single layer at a time and do not have the meat balls touching. Remove the meat balls and make the sauce in the skillet. Blend in, off the fire, ½ teaspoon of tomato paste, 1 teaspoon of meat glaze and 2 tablespoons of flour. Add 1 cup of stock and stir over the fire until the sauce comes to a boil. Beat in 1 cup of sour cream a little at a time, using a wire whisk and starting in the center. Taste for seasoning. Put back the meat balls and heat thoroughly over a slow fire.

Meanwhile cook 1 pound of noodles in 2 to 3 quarts of boiling salted water until tender, usually about 10 to 12 minutes. Drain thoroughly and blend with ½ cup of melted butter and ¼ cup grated Parmesan cheese.

To Serve: Make a bed of the noodles on a hot serving dish. Place the meat balls on top and spoon the sauce over all. Sprinkle with 1 tablespoon of chopped chives. This will serve 6 to 8 people. *Note:* Part veal or lean pork may be used instead of all beef.

MINCEMEAT

3 *pounds lean round beef, ground*
2 *pounds suet, ground*
3 *quarts apples, cored, finely chopped*
3 *pounds seeded raisins, ground*
2 *pounds currants*
1 *pound citron, chopped*
½ *cup candied orange peel, chopped*
½ *cup candied lemon peel, chopped*
½ *cup lemon juice*
¼ *cup orange juice*
2 *tablespoons salt*
4 *cups sugar*
1 *cup coffee*
2 *cups cider (not too new)*
1 *teaspoon ground cloves*
1 *teaspoon ground allspice*
2 *teaspoons cinnamon*
1 *cup red currant jelly*
3 *cups brandy*
1 *cup sherry*

Put all of the ingredients except the brandy and sherry into a large heavy saucepan. Stir well, bring slowly to a boil and cook over a gentle fire for 2 hours, giving it an occasional stir. When cool but not cold add 3 cups of brandy and 1 cup of sherry. Place in an earthenware crock and let ripen for at least a week before using it. It will keep for several months in a cool place. This makes enough for at least a dozen large pies.

MOUSSAKA À LA TURQUE
(Stuffed Eggplant Turkish Style)

1 *large eggplant*
about ½ *cup salad oil*
1 *cup chopped onion*
2 *cloves garlic, crushed*
2 *cups ground cooked beef or 1 pound ground raw beef*
4 *tomatoes, skinned and sliced*
¾ *cup grated Parmesan cheese*
1 *tablespoon butter*

TOMATO SAUCE

3 *tablespoons butter*
2 *tablespoons tomato paste*
2 *teaspoons potato flour*
1 *clove garlic, crushed*
1½ *cups water*
1 *tomato, skinned and chopped*
salt, pepper

Cut the eggplant into thin slices without removing the skin. Fry in hot salad oil until golden brown on both sides. Remove the eggplant. Lightly brown 1 cup of finely chopped onion and 2 cloves of crushed garlic in the same pan. Meanwhile make the following tomato sauce.

Tomato Sauce: Melt 3 tablespoons of butter. Blend in, off the fire, 2 tablespoons of tomato paste, 2 teaspoons of potato flour and a clove of crushed garlic. Add 1½ cups of water and stir over the fire until the mixture comes to a boil. Add a skinned chopped tomato, salt and pepper, and simmer for at least 5 minutes.

Place half the browned eggplant in a casserole. Cover with half of the meat, onions and garlic, sliced tomatoes and sauce. Repeat all the layers once again. Top with ¾ cup grated Parmesan cheese and dot with 1 tablespoon of butter. Bake uncovered in a moderate oven at 350° for 10 to 15 minutes if the meat is cooked, for 20 to 25 minutes if it is raw. Then brown the top under the broiler. Serves 5 or 6.

PETITE MARMITE

1 pound beef bones, cut in 3 or 4 pieces	*bouquet garni: 1 sprig parsley, 1 sprig thyme, 1 bay leaf*
2 pounds round or brisket of beef	*1 large onion*
neck and gizzard of 1 chicken	*3 carrots*
salt	*1 stalk celery*
peppercorns	*2 leeks*
	2 small white turnips, optional
French bread	*grated Parmesan cheese*

Petite marmite is a classic French dish which supplies a wonderful nourishing soup, meat which can be used for a main course and leftover soup which can be used as a base for other soups or as stock in innumerable dishes.

Put the beef bones, piece of beef and the neck and gizzard of a chicken into a large deep saucepan, preferably earthenware. If you are feeling extravagant, use a small whole chicken or part of one; the meat can always be used for hash or other dishes.

Cover with 3 quarts of cold water and bring slowly to a boil.
Skim several times until all the scum is gone. Season with salt,
peppercorns and a bouquet garni consisting of a sprig of parsley,
a sprig of thyme and a bay leaf. Cover and let simmer about 2
hours. Then add the following vegetables cut into small neat
slices: 1 onion, 3 carrots, 1 stalk of celery, 2 leeks and 2 small
white turnips if you can get ones that aren't bitter — that seems
to be easier to do in France than it is here. Simmer another 1½ to
2 hours, tasting occasionally for seasoning.

To Serve: Strain the soup and discard the bones and bouquet
garni. Place the piece of beef on a platter and keep warm. Let the
soup stand for a few minutes and then remove any fat that rises to
the top. Reheat enough soup for one meal. Serve it in individual
bowls garnished with a few pieces of vegetables and a little diced
beef. Cut thin slices of French bread, 1 for each serving, sprinkle
with grated Parmesan cheese and brown under the broiler. Put
on top of the soup and serve immediately.

The beef is then served as the main course. Although the remaining vegetables may be served with it, most of their flavor
has gone into the soup and they'll be a bit tired. A good horse-
radish or mustard sauce is better, with some coarse salt and a green
salad. Store the remaining soup in the refrigerator and bring to
a boil every 2 or 3 days. Serves 4.

MARINADE CRUE

salt, pepper
1 large yellow onion, thinly sliced
2 large carrots, sliced
2 cloves
1 bay leaf
1 clove garlic, chopped

10 peppercorns
4 sprigs parsley
1 sprig thyme or ¼ teaspoon dried thyme
1½ cups red or white wine
½ cup oil
¼ cup wine vinegar

Season the meat to be marinated. Lay in an earthenware dish. Into the dish put the following ingredients: 1 large thinly sliced yellow onion, 2 large sliced carrots, 2 cloves, 1 bay leaf, 1 chopped clove of garlic, 10 peppercorns, 4 sprigs of parsley and 1 sprig of fresh thyme or ¼ teaspoon of dried thyme. Blend together 1½ cups of red or white wine, ½ cup of salad oil (at least part olive oil preferably) and ¼ cup of wine vinegar. Pour this mixture over the meat. Leave the meat in the marinade for 1 or 2 days, basting and turning it several times a day.

BEEF STOCK

1 large knuckle veal, cracked
1 to 2 pounds beef bones
2 pounds brisket of beef
4 quarts water
1 large onion, thinly sliced
1 large carrot, thinly sliced

1 large leek, thinly sliced
1 stalk celery, thinly sliced
1 tablespoon tomato paste
mushroom peelings
bouquet fresh herbs
peppercorns, salt

Cover the knuckle of veal and beef bones with 4 quarts of cold water. The best utensil to use when making stock is an earthenware marmite with an asbestos mat placed over the heat for slow cooking, or a deep-well cooker. Bring slowly to a boil. Skim carefully. Add the brisket of beef, 1 large sliced onion, 1 large sliced carrot, 1 large sliced leek, a sliced stalk of celery, 1 tablespoon of tomato paste, a few mushroom peelings, a bouquet of fresh herbs such as parsley, chives and thyme, and a few peppercorns. Simmer slowly for at least 3 hours, adding salt after the stock has cooked for 1 hour.

Strain the stock, cool and lift off any grease that rises to the top. Stock will keep for at least a week in the refrigerator; during the summer it should be boiled up once or twice. It can also be frozen, preferably in small containers rather than one large one, just enough for an individual recipe.

Note: If you wish really dark, flavorful stock, first brown the bones in a hot oven at 400° for 30 to 40 minutes.

POIVRADE
(Pepper Sauce)

2 ounces green beans	1 teaspoon meat glaze
2 small white turnips	½ cup red wine
2 carrots	2 cups stock
2 mushrooms	2 chicken gizzards
8 tablespoons butter	2 chicken livers
salt, pepper	2 chicken hearts
½ cup water	¼ cup brandy
1 small onion	1 cup Madeira
1 stalk celery	12 whole black pepper-
2 tablespoons flour	corns, coarsely crushed
1 teaspoon tomato paste	2 tablespoons red cur-
	rant jelly

Occasionally it is fun to make an exceptionally good sauce, even if it does take time. Poivrade is a worthy accompaniment to your best broiled beef or venison.

Dice 2 ounces green beans, 2 small white turnips, 2 carrots and 2 mushrooms. Put into a small thick pan with 2 tablespoons of melted butter and a little salt and pepper. Cook slowly for 4 minutes. Add ½ cup of water, cover with waxed paper and a lid, and cook slowly for 25 minutes or until soft. Meanwhile slice 1 small onion and 1 stalk of celery and brown them slowly in 2 tablespoons of butter. Add 2 tablespoons of flour and cook slowly until dark brown. Stir in, off the fire, 1 teaspoon of tomato paste and 1 teaspoon of meat glaze. Pour on ½ cup of red wine and 2 cups of stock. Stir over the fire until the sauce comes to a boil. Simmer for 1 hour.

While the brown sauce is cooking, quickly brown 2 chicken gizzards, 2 chicken livers and 2 chicken hearts in 1 tablespoon of hot butter. Flame with ¼ cup of warm brandy. Remove and cut into very small dice. Put into the same pan with the cooked vegetables (beans, turnips, carrots and mushrooms) with any juice left in the pan. Add 1 cup of Madeira and cook until reduced one half. Then pour into the brown sauce and add 12 coarsely cracked black peppercorns and 2 tablespoons of red currant jelly. Simmer about 5 minutes. Strain, reheat and at the last moment add 2 tablespoons of butter bit by bit.

OEUFS SUR LE PLAT FLAMENCO
(Baked Eggs with Frankfurters)

3 medium-size potatoes	2 pieces pimento, diced
4 tablespoons butter	3 tomatoes
3 frankfurters, skinned and sliced	2 tablespoons chopped parsley
	4 eggs
salt, pepper	freshly cracked black pepper
1 cup cooked peas	2 tablespoons cream
	cayenne pepper

Peel 3 medium-size potatoes, place in a saucepan, cover with cold water and bring slowly to a boil. Drain and dry on a cloth. Cut in small even cubes and put in a skillet with 4 tablespoons of melted butter and 3 skinned and sliced frankfurters. Cook over a moderate fire until the potatoes begin to brown, shaking the pan occasionally. Add salt, pepper, 1 cup of cooked peas and 2 diced pimentos and cook another 2 to 3 minutes. Skin 3 tomatoes, quarter them, discard the seedy pulp and cut the rest into shreds. Put into the pan with 2 tablespoons of finely chopped parsley and cook until well heated.

Place in a flat, ovenproof, earthenware serving dish, break 4 eggs on the top and season them with salt and freshly cracked black pepper. Bake in a moderate oven at 350° until the eggs are set, about 10 minutes. Pour over 2 tablespoons of cream and sprinkle with a very little cayenne pepper. Serve at once. Serves 4.

BEEF TONGUE

1 3-pound beef tongue	3 to 4 tablespoons butter
12 small white onions	2 tomatoes, skinned and sliced
1 cup diced carrots	salt, pepper
½ cup diced celery	1 to 2 tablespoons chopped parsley
¼ pound mushrooms, sliced	2 tablespoons flour

Soak the tongue for several hours or overnight in cold water to cover. Drain and place in a deep saucepan. Add enough cold water to just cover the tongue and bring slowly to a boil. Skim, then simmer for 2 hours. Take the tongue out of the stock and remove the skin and the gristle and bones at the thick end.

Sauté 12 small white onions, 1 cup of diced carrots, ½ cup of diced celery and ¼ pound of sliced mushrooms in 3 tablespoons of butter until lightly browned. Remove the vegetables and place them on the bottom of a deep covered baking dish or casserole, just large enough to hold the tongue. Add 2 skinned and sliced tomatoes and season with salt and pepper. Lightly brown the tongue in the same pan the vegetables were cooked in, adding a little more butter if necessary. Put the tongue over the vegetables, with 1 cup of the tongue stock. Cover and cook in a moderate oven at 350° for about 1½ hours, until the tongue is tender.

To Serve: Place the tongue on a hot serving dish and sprinkle with 1 to 2 tablespoons of finely chopped parsley. Surround the tongue with the vegetables. Thicken the gravy with 2 tablespoons of flour which have been blended with ¼ cup of cold water, strain and serve in a gravy bowl. Serves 6.

BEEF TONGUE WITH CHICKEN LIVERS

1 beef tongue, 2½ to 3 pounds   *1 sprig fresh parsley*
1 bay leaf   *2 tablespoons butter*

CHICKEN LIVER SAUCE

½ pound chicken livers   *3 teaspoons potato flour or 3*
3 tablespoons butter   *tablespoons flour*
½ pound mushrooms,   *1½ cups chicken stock*
  sliced   *¼ cup red wine*
½ teaspoon tomato paste   *salt and pepper*
          ground nutmeg

Soak the tongue for several hours or overnight in cold water to cover. Drain and put into a large pan. Cover with cold water and bring slowly to a boil. Skim carefully. If the tongue is smoked, no seasoning is needed. If it is a fresh tongue, season the cooking water with a sliced onion, a bay leaf, about a tablespoon of salt and a few peppercorns. Cover and simmer until the tongue is easily pierced with a fork, about an hour to the pound. Remove, cool a little, then cut off the bones and gristle at the thick end and remove the skin. Cut 12 very thin slices and put them into the following sauce with a bay leaf and a sprig of parsley. Simmer covered for ½ hour.

Chicken Liver Sauce: Brown ½ pound of chicken livers quickly in 1 tablespoon of hot butter. Remove the livers. Add another 2 tablespoons of butter to the pan and cook ½ pound of sliced mushrooms briskly for 2 minutes. Blend in, off the fire, ½ teaspoon of tomato paste and 3 teaspoons of potato flour or 3 tablespoons of flour. Pour on 1½ cups of chicken stock and stir over the fire until the mixture comes to a boil. Add ¼ cup of red wine, salt, pepper and a pinch of ground nutmeg. Chop the chicken livers coarsely and add them to the sauce.

To Serve: Place the tongue and sauce on a hot ovenproof serving dish. Dot with 2 tablespoons of butter cut into small bits and glaze under the broiler. Serves 4.

TONGUE IN WINE SAUCE

12 slices cooked tongue	*1 cup tongue stock*
1 small onion, finely chopped	*½ cup red wine*
2 tablespoons butter	*1 teaspoon grated orange rind*
½ teaspoon meat glaze	*½ piece stick cinnamon*
½ teaspoon tomato paste	*bay leaf, cloves, peppercorns*
3 teaspoons potato flour	*1 tablespoon red currant jelly*

Cut 12 thin slices of cooked tongue, allowing 3 slices for each serving. Cook 1 finely chopped small onion in 2 tablespoons of butter until soft but not browned. Blend in, off the fire, ½ teaspoon of meat glaze, ½ teaspoon of tomato paste and 3 teaspoons of potato flour. Add 1 cup of tongue stock and ½ cup of red wine and stir over the fire until the mixture comes to a boil. Season with 1 teaspoon of grated orange rind, half a piece of stick cinnamon, a small bay leaf, 1 or 2 cloves and 3 or 4 peppercorns. Simmer for at least 15 to 20 minutes. Strain and add 1 tablespoon of red currant jelly. Bring to the simmering point and taste for seasoning; whether salt will be needed depends on the tongue stock. Put in the tongue and cook until it is thoroughly heated.

To Serve: Arrange the slices of tongue slightly overlapping on a hot serving dish and cover with the sauce. Serves 4.

TOMATOES STUFFED WITH TONGUE

4 large tomatoes	*1 cup finely chopped onion*
1 small clove garlic, crushed	*½ cup chopped mushrooms*
salt, pepper	*2 cups chopped cooked tongue*
4 chicken livers	*1 tablespoon chopped parsley*
4 tablespoons butter	*3 tablespoons sour cream*
½ cup grated Parmesan cheese	

Cut the tops off 4 large firm tomatoes and scoop out the pulp with a spoon. Season the bottoms with a crushed clove of garlic, salt and pepper. Brown 4 chicken livers quickly in 1 tablespoon of hot butter. Remove and slice. Add another tablespoon of butter to the pan and sauté 1 cup of finely chopped onion and ½ cup of chopped mushrooms until soft but not brown. Blend together 2 cups of chopped cooked tongue, the sliced chicken livers, sautéed onions and mushrooms, 1 tablespoon of finely chopped parsley and 3 tablespoons of sour cream. Taste for seasoning. Fill the tomatoes. Sprinkle the tops with ½ cup of grated Parmesan cheese and dot with 2 tablespoons of butter. Place under the broiler, about 3 inches away from the fire so that they won't cook too quickly. Broil until nicely browned. Serve on a hot platter and garnish with shoestring potatoes and fresh watercress. This makes a nice luncheon dish. Serves 4.

CERVELLES AU BEURRE NOIR
(Calves' Brains with Black Butter)

4 pairs calves' brains	*about 2 tablespoons flour*
1 tablespoon lemon juice	*2 tablespoons butter*
potatoes	

BEURRE NOIR

butter in pan and 3 more   1 tablespoon tarragon vinegar
   tablespoons   salt, black pepper
1 tablespoon lemon juice   ¼ cup capers

1 to 2 tablespoons finely chopped parsley

Soak the calves' brains in cold water to cover with 1 tablespoon of lemon juice for 1 to 2 hours. Drain and, using a small knife, remove skin and veins. Dry well on a cloth. Dust very lightly and evenly with flour. Heat 2 tablespoons of butter in a large skillet. When the butter is on the point of turning color, put in the brains, being careful not to let them touch each other. Brown on one side and then turn over and brown the other. Place them slightly overlapping on a hot serving dish and keep warm in a very slow oven while the black butter sauce is being prepared.

Beurre Noir (Black Butter): Put another 3 tablespoons of butter in the pan the brains were cooked in. Let it get dark very slowly — this may take 10 minutes. Then add 1 tablespoon of lemon juice, 1 tablespoon of tarragon vinegar, salt, pepper and ¼ cup of capers.

To Serve: Pour the sauce over the brains. Pile small new potatoes or sautéed potato balls at each end of the dish and sprinkle them with 1 to 2 tablespoons of finely chopped parsley. Serves 4.

SOUFFLÉ DE CERVELLES
(Brain Soufflé)

2 pairs calves' brains   3 tablespoons butter
lemon juice   3 tablespoons flour
1 cup chicken stock   ½ cup milk
½ cup mixed sliced onion,   4 egg yolks
   carrot and celery   ½ teaspoon French mustard
1 bay leaf   6 egg whites, stiffly beaten
5 or 6 peppercorns   about ½ cup bread crumbs
salt, cayenne   about ½ cup grated Parmesan cheese

Wash the brains well in a little lemon juice and water. Let them soak for 1 hour in cold water to cover. Drain and dry. Place in a shallow saucepan with 1 cup of chicken stock, ½ cup of mixed sliced onion, carrot and celery, 1 bay leaf, 5 or 6 peppercorns and a little salt. Bring slowly to a boil, cover and simmer for 10 minutes. Take the brains out of the stock with a slotted spoon and rub them through a fine strainer. Reduce the stock to ¼ cup.

Melt 3 tablespoons of butter. Stir in, off the fire, 3 tablespoons of flour, a little salt and cayenne. Add the ¼ cup of stock, strained, and ½ cup of milk. Stir over the fire until the mixture just comes to a boil. Remove from the fire and mix in the brain purée, 4 egg yolks, one at a time, and ½ teaspoon of French mustard. Lightly fold in 6 stiffly beaten egg whites.

Butter a porcelain soufflé dish and dust it out with bread crumbs and grated Parmesan cheese. Tie a band of buttered waxed paper around the outside. Fill with the soufflé mixture and sprinkle the top with a little grated cheese and bread crumbs. Bake in a moderate oven at 375° for 35 to 40 minutes. Carefully take off the paper. Tie a napkin around the outside and serve at once. Serves 4 to 6.

CALVES' BRAINS WITH SUPRÊME SAUCE

2 pairs calves' brains	1 sprig fresh tarragon
lemon juice	salt, peppercorns
1 cup chicken stock	8 large mushroom caps
¼ cup white wine	1 tablespoon butter
1 large truffle	

SUPRÊME SAUCE

4 tablespoons butter	2 egg yolks
1½ cups brain stock	½ cup cream
3 tablespoons flour	2 tablespoons dry sherry

Soak the calves' brains in cold water with 1 tablespoon of lemon juice for 1 to 2 hours. Remove, put into a saucepan with cold water to cover and 1 tablespoon of lemon juice, bring slowly to a boil and drain. Put immediately into a bowl of iced water for at least 5 to 10 minutes. Then carefully remove the skin and veins.

Place in a saucepan with 1 cup of chicken stock, ¼ cup of white wine, a sprig of fresh tarragon, a few peppercorns and a little salt. Bring slowly to a boil and simmer for 8 to 10 minutes.

Meanwhile stem 8 large mushroom caps and sauté them in 1 tablespoon of butter, salt and pepper, and a few drops of lemon juice. Arrange the caps, stem side up, on a hot serving dish. Take the brains out of the stock with a slotted spoon, drain well and cut in half. Place half a brain on each mushroom cap. Keep warm in a slow oven while the following sauce is prepared.

Suprême Sauce: Melt 3 tablespoons of butter in a small saucepan. Stir in, off the fire, 3 tablespoons of flour. Strain on 1½ cups of the brain stock and stir over the fire with a small wire whisk until the mixture comes to a boil. Simmer about 5 minutes. Beat in another tablespoon of butter, bit by bit. Blend 2 egg yolks with ½ cup of cream and stir into the sauce. Do not let the sauce boil after the egg yolks have been added. Lastly add 2 tablespoons of dry sherry and a few drops of lemon juice.

To Serve: Spoon the sauce over the brains and garnish each brain with a slice of truffle. Serves 4.

CLEAR OXTAIL SOUP

1 oxtail, about 2½ pounds	*pinch of mace*
salt	*a bouquet of herbs (parsley,*
2 quarts beef stock or water	*thyme, a bay leaf)*
½ onion	*2 tablespoons tomato paste*
1 carrot, sliced	*3 egg whites, stiffly beaten*
1 stalk celery	*2 teaspoons potato flour*
3 peppercorns	*½ cup dry sherry*
1 clove	*2 carrots, 1 white turnip, cut in*
	fancy shapes and cooked

The oxtail should be cut into short lengths. Cover with cold water and a little salt, bring to a boil and strain. Return the oxtail to a large heavy saucepan with 2 quarts of beef stock or water. Bring slowly to a boil and skim. Add half an onion, a sliced carrot, a stalk of celery, 3 peppercorns, 1 clove, a pinch of mace, salt and a bouquet of herbs (parsley, thyme and a bay leaf).

Simmer for 3 hours. Then strain the stock and let it get cold. Remove any fat that rises to the top. To clarify the soup, add to it 2 tablespoons of tomato paste and 3 stiffly beaten egg whites. Beat with a large wire whisk over a slow fire until it comes to a boil. Remove from the fire and let stand for 15 minutes. Strain through a large strainer covered with a dish cloth which has been wrung out in cold water. Blend 2 tablespoons of potato flour with a little cold water, add it to the soup and bring to a boil.

To Serve: Add ½ cup of dry sherry, the carrot and turnip garnish, and a little of the lean oxtail meat cut into fine shreds. Serves 8 to 10.

Note: The rest of the oxtail may be served with a vinaigrette or mustard sauce.

QUEUE DE BOEUF VINAIGRETTE
(Oxtail with Vinaigrette Sauce)

3 pounds oxtail, cut up	*4 cups stock or water*
1 cup mixed sliced onion,	*¼ cup white wine*
celery, carrot	*salt, black pepper*
a bouquet of herbs	*3 to 4 tablespoons chopped parsley*

VINAIGRETTE SAUCE

1 teaspoon salt	1 tablespoon chopped parsley
½ teaspoon cracked black pepper	1 tablespoon chopped green
¼ teaspoon dry mustard	olives
¼ teaspoon sugar	1¼ cups vegetable oil
1 hard-boiled egg	¼ cup olive oil
1 tablespoon chopped onion	¼ cup tarragon vinegar
few drops lemon juice	

Cover the oxtail with cold water, bring slowly to a boil and drain. Put into a deep saucepan with 1 cup of mixed sliced onion, celery and carrot, a bouquet of herbs (parsley, thyme and a bay leaf), 4 cups of stock or water, ¼ cup of dry white wine, salt and black pepper. Bring to a boil and simmer covered until the oxtail is very tender, about 2½ to 3 hours. Drain, dry well and then if you prefer the color and flavor of browned meat, brown the pieces quickly in 2 to 3 tablespoons of hot butter. Arrange on a hot serving dish and sprinkle well with 3 to 4 tablespoons of finely chopped parsley. Serve iced vinaigrette sauce in a separate sauce bowl.

Vinaigrette Sauce: Place the following ingredients in a 1-pint screw-top jar: 1 teaspoon of salt, ½ teaspoon freshly cracked black pepper, ¼ teaspoon of dry mustard, ¼ teaspoon sugar, 1 finely chopped hard-boiled egg, 1 tablespoon chopped raw onion, 1 tablespoon chopped parsley, 1 tablespoon chopped green olives, 1¼ cups vegetable oil, ¼ cup of olive oil, ¼ cup of tarragon vinegar and a few drop of lemon juice. Shake well and chill for at least a few hours before using. Shake again before using. Serves 4 to 6.

QUEUE DE BOEUF MOUTARDE
(Oxtail with Mustard Sauce)

3 pounds oxtail, cut up	*1 teaspoon meat glaze*
5 tablespoons butter	*2 teaspoons tomato paste*
¼ cup finely chopped onion	*2 cups stock*
¼ cup chopped dried mushrooms	*salt, cayenne*
2 teaspoons French mustard	*½ cup sour cream*
1 teaspoon dry mustard	*½ cup grated Parmesan*
3 tablespoons flour	*cheese*

2 tablespoons chopped chives

Heat 2 tablespoons of butter in a deep heavy saucepan and when the butter is very hot, quickly brown the cut-up oxtail. Remove from the pan. Put another 2 tablespoons of butter in the pan, then ¼ cup finely chopped onion and ¼ cup finely chopped dried mushrooms which have been previously soaked for an hour or so in cold water. Cook very slowly for 5 to 6 minutes. Blend in, off the fire, 2 teaspoons of French mustard, 1 teaspoon of dry mustard, 3 tablespoons of flour, 1 teaspoon of meat glaze and 2 teaspoons of tomato paste. Pour on 2 cups of stock and stir over the fire until the mixture comes to a boil. Season with salt and cayenne pepper. Put back the oxtails, cover and simmer until quite tender, about 3 to 3½ hours.

Remove the oxtails and arrange them in a shallow ovenproof

serving dish. Strain the sauce, boil it down a little, then slowly
beat in ½ cup of sour cream. Pour over the oxtails, sprinkle with
½ cup of grated Parmesan cheese, dot with 1 tablespoon of butter
and brown under the broiler. Serve at once. Serves 4 or 5.

OXTAIL RAGOUT

1 oxtail, 2½ to 3 pounds, cut up
5 to 6 tablespoons butter
12 baby white onions
1 bunch small carrots
1 heart of celery
1 small clove garlic, crushed
3 tablespoons flour
1½ cups stock
½ cup sherry
salt, pepper
1 sprig thyme or ¼ teaspoon
dried thyme
1 bay leaf

Heat 2 tablespoons of butter in a casserole. Brown the pieces of
oxtail all over. There will be more pieces than you can fit into
the pan in a single layer at one time, so add more butter as needed
to brown them all. When all the meat is browned, remove it
from the pan. Add another 2 tablespoons of butter to the pan
and brown 12 baby white onions, a bunch of carrots which have
been cut into small olive shapes and a sliced heart of celery.
When the vegetables are browned, add a clove of crushed garlic
and 3 tablespoons of flour and cook until the flour is browned.
Blend in 1½ cups of stock and ½ cup of sherry and stir over the
fire until the mixture comes to a boil. Season with salt and pepper,
a bay leaf and a sprig of fresh thyme or ¼ teaspoon of dried
thyme. Put back the meat, cover and simmer until the meat is
tender when pierced with a fork, about 3 hours. Serve in the
casserole. Serves 4 to 6.

TRIPE À LA MODE DE CAEN

4 pounds fresh tripe
1 pound white onions
3 large carrots
4 cloves
2 tablespoons butter
¼ pound beef suet
1 calf's foot, cut in half
bouquet garni: 1 leek, 1 sprig thyme,
* 1 sprig parsley, bay leaf*
2 cups dry white wine or cider
½ cup brandy
salt, pepper

Soak the tripe for 24 hours in cold water. Drain. Place in a saucepan, cover with cold water and bring slowly to a boil. Drain again and cut into 2-inch cubes. Slice 1 pound of white onions and 3 large carrots and stick 4 of the onion slices with 4 cloves. Sauté in 2 tablespoons of butter until soft but not brown. Cut ¼ pound of beef suet into small neat dice. Make alternate layers of the carrots and onions, the tripe and the beef suet in an earthenware casserole. In the center put the split calf's foot and a bouquet garni consisting of 1 leek, 1 sprig of thyme, 1 sprig of parsley and a bay leaf. Pour on 2 cups of dry white wine or cider, ½ cup of brandy and enough water to just cover the mixture. Season with salt and pepper.

The casserole should be kept covered during the entire cooking period and if possible it should be hermetically sealed with a paste made of flour and water. Bake in a slow oven at 250° for 6 to 8 hours, the longer the better. Remove the calf's foot and bouquet garni before serving. As far as the serving is concerned, here is what Escoffier has to say on the subject: "By virtue of its simplicity, tripe should be served in special *earthenware saucepans*, where the heat is best retained; and the cook should rather direct his attention to the serving of tripe as hot as possible, than to this or that fanciful method of dishing it up, which really has no reason for being in this case." Serves 8 to 10.

VEAL

Veal is the meat of a young calf, slaughtered when it is 1 to 2 months old and weighing 75 to 125 pounds. Because the animal is so young, veal has quite different characteristics from beef. It has more connective tissue, far less fat and is not as rich in the extractives which add flavor to meat. Therefore it is not as tender as high-quality, well-hung beef and requires long, slow cooking, often in moist heat and usually with plenty of additional fat. Veal is very seldom broiled. Some cuts are roasted, but the majority are braised. The aim in cooking veal is to develop flavor, soften the connective tissue and prevent the meat from drying out. The flavor is developed by browning the meat and adding fat and various vegetables, seasonings and wine. To soften the connective tissue, it is always thoroughly cooked. Unlike beef or even lamb, it is never served with any sign of pink. Since veal has so little fat, it has a tendency to dry out. To prevent this, do not cook the meat for any length of time at a high temperature and cook it with some fat or liquid.

The best United States government grades of veal are *prime, choice* and *good*. High-quality veal is light grayish pink; the grain is very fine; and the bones are small, red and soft. There is no marbling; what little fat there is should be white.

The number of veal recipes that follow may seem large, but veal can be so delicious that it is a shame it is not more popular in America. French cooking methods are admirably suited to veal, particularly the use of wine and seasonings, and in France its use is widespread.

Expensive veal cuts are chops and the legs. However, since the chops are larger than lamb chops, one is always ample for an individual serving. As with lamb, the best chop cuts are the loin and the rib. The leg has several uses. Although it is expensive per pound, the only waste is the small center bone. Whole slices of leg are used for veal cutlet and schnitzel. Scallopini and veal birds are cut from the sections of the leg that have solid rounds of meat, while the rest can be used for stew and casseroles. The size of these rounds can vary, according to the size of the animal and the way the rounds are cut. In most of the following scallopini recipes two slices have been allowed for each serving; if the pieces of meat are very small, you may want more. Whole legs are sometimes roasted, but they are usually a little large and the rump or round and rolled shoulder is more frequently used and costs less.

The shoulder and breast are inexpensive cuts. They both have some bones but plenty of good meat too. Because veal is so young, none of the meat is tough the way it can be in an older animal.

As for the veal specialty meats, they cannot be surpassed. Calves' liver, kidneys and sweetbreads are among the most delicate and delicious foods we have. Since it has been discovered how important liver is nutritionally, calves' liver has been in great demand and is therefore expensive. But it is all meat with no waste. Cook liver quickly, with only a little fat, to keep it tender and juicy. And there are several interesting recipes to avoid the everlasting liver and bacon. Sweetbreads are the thymus gland of a young calf, which disappears when the calf gets older so is found only in veal. Their consistency is so soft that they are usually parboiled, then soaked in ice water to stiffen them. They are popular and rather perishable so it used to be hard to get them everywhere. Luckily they are now obtainable frozen, which makes their distribution universal. Veal kidneys are not always easy to get either, but if you ask your butcher to save some for you, he probably will. Veal hearts, stuffed, make a very palatable dish, while the head produces the classic French tête de veau.

Because veal does need long, slow cooking, it lends itself well to informal entertaining, since many veal dishes can be prepared in advance and left to simmer while you are with your guests.

ROAST RUMP OF VEAL

piece of veal rump, about 8 pounds
1 large yellow onion
4 tablespoons butter
½ pound mushrooms, sliced
2 cups white bread crumbs
salt and pepper

2 tablespoons chopped parsley
½ teaspoon grated lemon rind
½ pound salt pork or fresh fat back
1½ cups dry white wine
3 tablespoons flour
1 tablespoon tomato paste

1½ cups stock

Have the butcher remove enough bone to leave a pocket for the stuffing. Finely chop a large yellow onion and cook over a moderate fire in 2 tablespoons of butter until soft. Add another 2 tablespoons of butter, ½ pound of sliced mushrooms and 2 cups of bread crumbs made by coarsely crumbling white bread at least a day old. Turn up the heat and cook briskly until lightly browned. Season with salt and pepper. Blend in 2 tablespoons of finely chopped parsley and ½ teaspoon of grated lemon rind. Fill the pocket of the veal. Close together with skewers laced with string.

Cover the top of the veal with thin slices of salt pork or fresh fat back. Place in a roasting pan and pour 1 cup of dry white wine into the pan. Cook uncovered in a moderate oven at 350° about 25 minutes to the pound; a meat thermometer will register 180° when the veal is done. Baste every 10 to 15 minutes, first with the remaining ½ cup of wine and then with the pan juices. Remove the veal.

The gravy can be made in two ways. A cup of stock can be mixed with the pan juices and the whole brought to a boil, the usual French method. Or it can be thickened, a more typical American gravy. Blend 3 tablespoons of flour and 1 tablespoon of tomato paste into the pan juices, off the fire. Add 1½ cups of stock and stir over the fire until the mixture comes to a boil. Taste for seasoning.

Serve the veal on a hot platter with the gravy in a separate sauce bowl. This will serve at least 8 people.

ROAST STUFFED VEAL

breast of veal, 3 to 4 pounds
2 egg whites, unbeaten
1 pound lean veal, ground
1½ cups light cream
salt, pepper
2 cloves garlic, crushed
4 ounces tongue or ham, shredded

about ¼ pound sliced bacon
1 cup dry white wine
3 tablespoons butter
2 tablespoons tomato paste
1 tablespoon flour
1½ cups water
4 tomatoes, skinned and sliced
2 tablespoons finely chopped parsley

Bone the veal or have the butcher do it. Mix 2 unbeaten egg whites into the ground veal. Then slowly beat in 1½ cups of light cream, salt and pepper. Season the boned veal with salt, pepper and 1 clove of crushed garlic. Spread with the veal stuffing, leaving a margin of an inch all around the outside edge. Put the strips of ham or tongue on top of the stuffing. Roll up. Cover the entire top with slices of bacon and tie the meat tightly with string at 1½-inch intervals. Place in a roasting pan with a cup of dry white wine. Roast for 30 minutes to the pound in a moderately slow oven at 325 to 350°, basting frequently.

Half an hour or so before the roast is done, start making the tomato sauce. Melt 1½ tablespoons of butter. Blend in, off the fire, 2 tablespoons of tomato paste and 1 tablespoon of flour. Pour on 1½ cups of water and stir over the fire until the mixture comes to a boil. Season with salt, pepper and 1 clove of crushed garlic. Add 4 skinned and sliced tomatoes and let simmer for 15 to 20 minutes. Beat in the remaining 1½ tablespoons of butter, bit by bit. The pan juices from the veal may also be added.

To Serve: Remove the veal from the roasting pan and let stand for a few minutes before carving. Cut off the strings. Cut as many slices as will be needed for one meal and arrange them slightly overlapping on a hot serving dish. Place the uncut piece at the end of the dish. Spoon a little tomato sauce over the meat and serve the rest in a sauce bowl. Sprinkle with 2 tablespoons of finely chopped parsley. Serves 6 to 8.

VEAL AND HAM PIE

2 pounds raw veal or 4 cups
cubed cooked veal
1 pound ham steak or 2 cups
cubed cooked ham
2 to 4 tablespoons ham fat or
butter

3 tablespoons flour
salt, cayenne
4 hard-boiled eggs, sliced
1 tablespoon chopped parsley
½ teaspoon grated lemon rind
pastry for crust

Trim the veal and ham of surplus fat and cut into 1-inch cubes.
Heat 2 tablespoons of butter or ham fat in a heavy deep saucepan
and quickly brown the cubed meat; put only as many pieces in
the pan at one time as will fit without touching, adding more fat
if necessary. When they are all browned, put them back into the
pan in layers, sprinkling each layer lightly with flour, using 3
tablespoons in all. Add enough water to come to within an inch
of the top of the meat and season with salt and cayenne pepper.
Bring to a boil, lower the heat to simmering and cook for 1½ hours
unless the meats were cooked previously and then ½ hour is sufficient.

While the meat is simmering, prepare the pastry recipe on page
44.

When the meat is tender, take the pan off the fire and let the
meat cool a little. Add 4 thinly sliced hard-boiled eggs, 1 tablespoon of chopped parsley and ½ teaspoon of grated lemon rind.
Put the meat and gravy into a deep pie dish and cover with the
pastry. Place on a cookie sheet and bake in a hot oven at 400°
for about 30 minutes, until the top is nicely browned.

Serve in the baking dish. Serves 6 to 8.

COLD VEAL AND TUNA FISH

1 cup rice
½ cup diced cooked green beans
½ cup diced cooked carrots
½ cup French dressing

8 thin slices cold roast veal
4 ounces tuna fish
¼ pound butter
salt, pepper

watercress

Prepare the following rice salad. Cook 1 cup of rice in plenty of boiling salted water for 13 to 14 minutes, until just tender. Drain and wash well in cold water. Let stand until cold. Mix with ½ cup cold diced cooked green beans, ½ cup cold diced carrots and ½ cup of French dressing.

Cut the veal into neat symmetrical slices. Pound 4 ounces of tuna fish in a mortar with a pestle until smooth. Cream ¼ pound of butter, blend with the tuna fish and season with salt and pepper. Or the tuna and butter can be beaten in an electric mixer. Fill a pastry bag with a large plain tube. Pipe a layer on 4 slices of veal and top, sandwich fashion, with the remaining 4 slices.

To Serve: Make a bed of the rice salad on a cold serving dish. Arrange the veal on top and garnish with watercress. Serves 4.

CÔTES DE VEAU À LA CRÈME
(Veal Chops with Cream)

4 veal chops	*3 tablespoons flour*
4 tablespoons butter	*1 cup veal stock or water*
2 tablespoons brandy	*1 cup heavy cream*
1 small clove garlic, crushed	*salt, pepper*
¼ pound mushrooms, sliced	*1 bay leaf*
½ teaspoon meat glaze	*¼ teaspoon dried thyme*
2 tablespoons grated Parmesan cheese	

Brown the chops quickly on both sides in 2 tablespoons of hot butter. Heat 2 tablespoons of brandy in a small pan, ignite and pour over the chops. Remove the chops from the pan. Add 1 tablespoon of butter to the pan, then 1 small clove of crushed garlic and cook ½ minute. Add ¼ pound of mushrooms, sliced, and cook another 2 to 3 minutes. Blend in, off the fire, ½ teaspoon meat glaze and 3 tablespoons of flour. Pour on 1 cup of veal stock or water and stir over the fire until the mixture comes to a boil. Still stirring constantly, slowly add 1 cup of heavy cream. Return the meat to the sauce with salt, pepper, a bay leaf and ¼ teaspoon of dried thyme. Cover and simmer for 40 to 50 minutes, or until the meat is tender.

To Serve: Arrange the chops on a hot serving dish and cover with the sauce. Sprinkle with 2 tablespoons of grated Parmesan cheese, dot with the remaining 1 tablespoon of butter and brown under the broiler. Serves 4.

CÔTES DE VEAU À LA BONNE FEMME
(Veal Chops and Vegetables in Casserole)

4 lean veal chops	*2 tablespoons dry white wine*
1 small clove garlic, crushed	*½ teaspoon meat glaze*
4 tablespoons butter	*½ cup veal or chicken stock*
12 very small white onions	*salt, freshly ground pepper*
8 to 10 very small new potatoes	*½ teaspoon lemon juice*
¼ pound salt pork, diced	*1 tablespoon chopped parsley*

Rub chops with crushed garlic. Heat 1 tablespoon of butter in a thick shallow pan and when the butter is very hot, brown the chops quickly on both sides. Remove chops from the pan. Melt another 3 tablespoons of butter in the pan and add 12 small white onions, 8 to 10 very small new potatoes and ¼ pound diced salt pork. Brown very slowly for 10 to 15 minutes. Add 2 tablespoons of dry white wine and mix well to lift the glaze.

Blend in, off the fire, ½ teaspoon of meat glaze, ½ cup of veal or chicken stock, salt, pepper and ½ teaspoon of lemon juice. Bring slowly to a boil. Put the chops back in the pan, cover and bake in a moderate oven at 350° for 30 to 40 minutes. Place chops in a hot casserole, arrange vegetables around them and pour sauce over all. Sprinkle with a tablespoon of finely chopped parsley just before serving. Serves 4.

Note: A casserole may be used for cooking this whole dish — and then it can be served right in the casserole — as long as it is the kind that can be used on the top of the stove as well as in it.

CÔTES DE VEAU AUX FINES HERBES
(Veal Chops with Fresh Herbs)

4 veal chops
1 to 2 tablespoons flour
4 tablespoons butter
½ teaspoon meat glaze
¼ cup dry white wine
½ teaspoon lemon juice

¼ teaspoon tomato paste
2 tablespoons water
salt
freshly cracked black pepper
1 tablespoon finely chopped mixed fresh herbs

few sprigs watercress

Dust the chops lightly with flour, using 1 to 2 tablespoons. Brown them well on both sides in 3 tablespoons of hot butter. Cover and cook very slowly for 15 to 20 minutes. Remove the chops and keep them warm. Add to the pan ½ teaspoon of meat glaze, ¼ cup dry white wine, ½ teaspoon lemon juice, ¼ teaspoon tomato paste, 2 tablespoons water, salt and freshly cracked black pepper. Simmer for 3 to 4 minutes. Arrange chops on a hot serving dish. Add 1 tablespoon finely chopped fresh herbs to the sauce with the remaining tablespoon of butter. Pour over the veal. Garnish with a few sprigs of fresh watercress and serve immediately. Serves 4.

CÔTES DE VEAU AUX OLIVES
(Veal Chops with Black Olives)

4 veal chops
5 tablespoons butter
1 cup dry white wine

salt, pepper
6 to 8 large ripe olives
1 tablespoon chopped parsley or chives

Heat 3 tablespoons of butter in a large skillet. When the butter is on the point of turning color, put in the chops and brown them on both sides. When they are browned, put another 2 tablespoons of butter in the pan and ½ cup of dry white wine. Season with salt and pepper. Cover and cook over a low heat for 40 to 50 minutes, until the chops are tender. Add the other ½ cup of wine a little at a time as the chops are cooking. Chop 6 to 8 large ripe olives very finely. Put them into the pan with the chops when they are almost done.

To Serve: Arrange the chops on a hot serving dish and spoon all the sauce over them; there won't be too much since most of the butter and wine will be absorbed during the cooking. If you wish more sauce, heat a little additional butter and wine in the pan. Sprinkle with 1 tablespoon of finely chopped parsley or chives. Pile small buttered potato balls at each end of the dish. Serves 4.

CÔTES DE VEAU AU MARSALA
(Veal Chops with Marsala)

4 veal chops	3 teaspoons potato flour or 3
3 tablespoons butter	tablespoons flour
3 tablespoons sherry	1 cup veal stock or water
1 small clove garlic, crushed	¼ cup Marsala
½ teaspoon tomato paste	¼ cup dry white wine
½ teaspoon meat glaze	salt, pepper

4 tomatoes, skinned and sliced

Heat 2 tablespoons of butter in a large skillet. When the butter is on the point of turning color, put in the chops and brown them quickly on both sides. Heat 3 tablespoons of sherry in a small pan, ignite and pour over the meat. Remove chops from the pan. Put 1 small clove of garlic, crushed, and another tablespoon of butter in the pan and cook for ½ minute. Blend in, off the fire, ½ teaspoon of tomato paste, ½ teaspoon of meat glaze and 3 teaspoons of potato flour (or 3 tablespoons of flour). Add 1 cup of veal stock or water, ¼ cup of Marsala and ¼ cup of dry white wine. Stir over the fire until the mixture comes to a boil. Season with salt and pepper. Put back the chops, cover the pan and cook slowly until the chops are tender, about 40 to 50 minutes. Add 4 skinned and sliced tomatoes and cook another 5 minutes.

To Serve: Arrange the chops on a hot serving dish and pour the sauce over them. Serves 4.

CÔTES DE VEAU EN PAPILLOTES
(Veal Chops in Parchment Paper)

4 veal chops	1 teaspoon chopped parsley
salt, pepper	1 teaspoon chopped chives or
4 tablespoons butter	marjoram
1 large yellow onion, chopped	1 tablespoon sour cream
¼ pound mushrooms, chopped	4 thin slices cooked ham
1 teaspoon lemon juice	1 bunch watercress

Put the chops between 2 pieces of waxed paper and beat lightly with a wooden mallet. Season with salt and pepper. Brown rather slowly on both sides in 2 tablespoons of hot butter. Remove from the pan.

Peel and finely chop 1 large yellow onion. Put another tablespoon of butter in the same pan and cook the onion slowly until golden brown. Finely chop ¼ pound of mushrooms and cook briskly for about 5 minutes with 1 tablespoon of butter, 1 teaspoon of lemon juice, salt and pepper. Mix together the cooked onion, mushrooms, 1 teaspoon of finely chopped parsley, 1 teaspoon of finely chopped chives or marjoram, 1 tablespoon of sour cream and a little salt and pepper. Spread this mixture evenly over one side of each chop. Top with a slice of cooked ham, neatly trimmed to fit the chops. Wrap each chop securely in parchment paper. Bake in a moderate oven at 350° for 45 minutes; the paper will turn dark brown.

Serve in the paper on a hot serving dish, preferably silver, and garnish with watercress. Serves 4.

VEAL CUTLET

1 veal cutlet, 1½ to 2 pounds	1 medium-size can Italian toma-
about 2 tablespoons flour	toes
1 egg	salt and pepper
about ½ cup dry bread crumbs	¼ teaspoon oregano
4 tablespoons butter	¼ cup sherry
1 medium-size onion, finely	1 small Mozzarella cheese
chopped	½ cup grated Parmesan cheese

Dust the veal cutlet lightly with flour, brush with an egg which has been slightly beaten with 1 tablespoon of water, then roll in bread crumbs. Heat 3 tablespoons of butter in a heavy skillet. Brown the veal cutlet slowly on both sides, taking 10 to 15 minutes for each side. While the veal is browning, sauté a medium-size finely chopped onion in 1 tablespoon of butter until soft but not brown. Add a medium-size can of tomatoes, season with salt, pepper and ¼ teaspoon oregano, and let simmer for 15 to 20 minutes.

When the meat is browned, pour ¼ cup sherry over it. Remove the skillet from the fire. Cut a small Mozzarella cheese into small dice and put half of it on top of the meat. Sprinkle with ¼ cup grated Parmesan cheese and cover with half the tomatoes. Repeat these layers once again. Cook in a moderate oven at 325° uncovered for about 30 minutes; longer will not matter.

If a skillet such as a good-looking enamel-glazed cast-iron skillet is used, it can be used for serving. Otherwise serve the cutlet on a hot serving platter. Serves 5 or 6.

WIENER SCHNITZEL

1½ pounds leg of veal	*fine dry bread crumbs*
flour for breading	*4 tablespoons butter*
salt, pepper	*4 slices lemon*
1 egg	*4 anchovy filets, optional*
4 capers, optional	

Remove any fat and sinew from the veal and cut it into 4 neat serving pieces. Pound with a wooden mallet to break down the tissues a little. Dust very lightly with seasoned flour, patting off any excess. Beat 1 egg thoroughly with 1 tablespoon of water and brush the veal with it. Then coat with fine bread crumbs. If time allows, let the veal stand on a cake rack for ½ hour to dry the coating.

Melt 3 tablespoons of butter in a skillet. Cook the veal slowly until golden brown on both sides. It should take 50 to 60 minutes to brown and cook the cutlets. Remove from the pan and arrange on a hot serving dish. Melt another tablespoon of butter in the pan and pour the pan juices over the veal. Garnish with slices of lemon. If you wish, a rolled-up anchovy filet topped with a caper can be placed on each slice of lemon. Serves 4.

BLANQUETTE DE VEAU
(Veal in Cream Sauce)

2½ *pounds shoulder or leg of veal*	5 *tablespoons butter*
salt, cayenne	3 *tablespoons flour*
1 *carrot, sliced*	2 *cups stock*
4 *whole cloves*	24 *small white onions*
1 *leek, sliced*	8 *to* 10 *small white mushrooms*
1 *small stalk celery, sliced*	2 *egg yolks*
6 *peppercorns*	½ *cup light cream*
bouquet of herbs: 1 *bay leaf,* 2 *sprigs parsley,* 1 *sprig thyme*	1 *teaspoon lemon juice*
	6 *croutons of bread*

Trim off all the tissue and most of the fat from the veal and cut into pieces 2 inches long, 1 inch wide and ½ inch thick. Place in a heavy saucepan and just cover with cold water. Season with a little salt and bring slowly to a boil; skim. Add a sliced carrot (1 slice stuck with 4 cloves), a sliced leek, a sliced stalk of celery, 6 peppercorns and a bouquet of herbs consisting of 1 bay leaf, 2 sprigs of parsley and a sprig of thyme. Cover and simmer for about 1 hour, until the meat is tender. Remove from the fire and let the meat stand in the stock.

Melt 3 tablespoons of butter. Blend in, off the fire, 3 tablespoons of flour. Add salt, cayenne and 2 cups of strained stock the meat was cooked in. Stir over the fire until the sauce comes to a boil. Let simmer for 10 to 15 minutes, stirring occasionally.

In the meantime cover 24 small white onions with cold water, bring slowly to a boil and drain. Sauté until golden brown in 1 tablespoon of butter. Remove onions, add another tablespoon of butter and sauté 8 to 10 small white mushrooms until lightly browned. Remove the veal from the stock and add it to the sauce. Also add the onions and mushrooms and a little salt.

Beat 2 egg yolks with ½ cup of light cream and stir slowly into the sauce. Add 1 teaspoon of lemon juice.

Serve on a hot serving dish with croutons of fried bread arranged around the sides of the dish. This will serve 6 people.

HUNGARIAN GOULASH

1½ pounds veal from leg or shoulder	1 green pepper, shredded
3 tablespoons butter	1 tablespoon paprika
1 large yellow onion, sliced	½ teaspoon tomato paste
2 carrots, sliced	3 tablespoons flour
1 stalk celery, sliced	1½ cups stock
1 clove garlic, crushed	salt and pepper
	1 bay leaf
1 cup sour cream	

Cut the veal into 1-inch cubes, or have the butcher do it. Heat 2 tablespoons of butter in a deep heavy saucepan and when the butter is on the point of turning color, quickly brown the veal all over. Remove the veal with a slotted spoon. Put another tablespoon of butter in the pan. Add a large sliced onion, 2 sliced carrots, 1 sliced stalk of celery, a crushed clove of garlic and half the shredded pepper. Cook slowly for 5 to 6 minutes. Stir in 1 tablespoon of paprika (preferably Spanish) and cook another minute or so.

Blend in, off the fire, ½ teaspoon of tomato paste and 3 table-spoons of flour. Pour on 1½ cups of stock and stir over the fire until the mixture comes to a boil. Season with salt and pepper, and put back the veal with a bay leaf. Cover the pan and let the meat simmer for 30 to 40 minutes, until tender.

Remove the veal and put it in a shallow casserole. Strain the sauce and return to the fire. Slowly blend in ¾ cup of sour cream with a small wire whisk. Pour the sauce over the veal. Spoon 3 to 4 tablespoons of sour cream over the center and garnish with strips of green pepper and a little paprika. In Hungary this is served with egg dumplings, browned rice or boiled potatoes. Serves 4.

Note: Beef may be used instead of veal.

VEAL CASSEROLE WITH SOUR CREAM

2 pounds veal from leg	1 teaspoon tomato paste
3 tablespoons butter	3 tablespoons flour
2 tablespoons Marsala	1 cup stock
1 small clove garlic, crushed	1 cup sour cream
	4 tomatoes, skinned and chopped
3 mushrooms, sliced	salt and pepper
1 teaspoon meat glaze	1 bay leaf

1 tablespoon finely chopped chives

Trim meat, cut into large 1-inch squares and brown quickly all over in 2 tablespoons of hot butter. Heat 2 tablespoons of Marsala in a small pan, ignite and pour over the veal. Remove veal from the pan. Add remaining 1 tablespoon of butter to the pan with a small clove of garlic, crushed, and cook for 1 minute. Add 3 sliced mushrooms and cook another 2 minutes. Blend in, off the fire, 1 teaspoon of meat glaze, 1 teaspoon of tomato paste and 3 tablespoons of flour. Pour on 1 cup of stock and stir over the fire until the mixture comes to a boil. Still stirring constantly, slowly add 1 cup of sour cream. Return the veal to the pan with 4 skinned chopped tomatoes. Season with salt, pepper and a bay leaf. Cover and simmer until the meat is tender, about 45 minutes, stirring occasionally.

Serve in a heated casserole and sprinkle with 1 tablespoon of finely chopped chives. Serves 4 to 6.

Note: This dish can be cooked right in a casserole if it is the kind that can be used on top of the stove.

PAUPIETTES DE VEAU À LA GRECQUE
(Stuffed Veal Birds)

6 thin slices veal from leg	1 teaspoon tomato paste
1 large yellow onion, finely chopped	½ teaspoon meat glaze
6 tablespoons butter	2 teaspoons potato flour
2 hard-boiled eggs, finely chopped	1 cup stock
2 tablespoons chopped chives	¼ cup dry white wine
salt and pepper	1 bay leaf
3 tablespoons brandy	1½ cups rice, cooked

Put the slices of veal between 2 pieces of waxed paper and beat with a wooden mallet until very thin. Cook the finely chopped yellow onion in 1 tablespoon of butter until soft but not browned, using a slow fire. Mix with 2 finely chopped hard-boiled eggs, 2 tablespoons of chopped chives, salt and pepper. Spread a generous spoonful of this mixture on each slice of veal. Roll up tightly and fasten each end with string. These veal birds are called paupiettes. Add 2 tablespoons of butter to the pan the onion was cooked in and when very hot, quickly brown the veal birds all over. Heat 3 tablespoons of brandy in a small pan, ignite and pour over the meat. Remove meat from the pan. Blend in, off the fire, 1 teaspoon of tomato paste, ½ teaspoon of meat glaze and 2 teaspoons of potato flour. Pour on 1 cup of stock and ¼ cup of dry white wine and stir over the fire until the sauce comes to a boil. Put back the veal birds with a bay leaf, cover and simmer for 25 to 30 minutes.

To Serve: Season hot cooked rice with salt and pepper, and mix in 3 tablespoons of melted butter with a fork. Put into a shallow, round, greased cake tin, press down gently with a fork and turn out on a hot serving dish. (The pan may be placed in a 350° oven for 10 minutes or so if necessary to heat the rice.) Remove the veal birds from the sauce and cut off the threads. Arrange on top of the rice. Strain the sauce over all. Serves 6.

PAUPIETTES DE VEAU FONTANGES
(Veal Birds with Pea Purée)

6 thin slices leg of veal	3 tablespoons brandy
4 chicken livers	½ teaspoon tomato paste
4 tablespoons butter	1 teaspoon meat glaze
¼ pound mushrooms	2 teaspoons potato flour
8 thin slices cooked tongue	1 cup veal or beef stock
salt, pepper	¼ cup dry white wine

1 bay leaf

PEA PURÉE

3 pounds peas or 2 packages frozen peas	2 tablespoons butter
	2 tablespoons flour
salt, pepper	3 tablespoons sour cream

Put the slices of veal between 2 pieces of waxed paper and beat until very thin with a wooden mallet. Brown 4 chicken livers quickly in 1 tablespoon of very hot butter. Remove the livers, put another tablespoon of butter in the pan and sauté ¼ pound sliced mushrooms until golden brown. Shred the chicken livers and 8 slices of tongue and combine with the sautéed mushrooms. Season with salt and pepper. Spread a generous spoonful of this mixture on each veal slice. Roll up each slice and fasten each end with thread; these veal birds are called paupiettes. Heat 2 tablespoons of butter in the pan the chicken livers and mushrooms were cooked in and quickly brown the paupiettes all over. Heat 3 tablespoons of brandy in a small pan, ignite and pour over the veal birds. Remove them from the pan.

Blend into the pan juices ½ teaspoon tomato paste, 1 teaspoon of meat glaze and 2 teaspoons of potato flour, off the fire. Pour on 1 cup of stock and ¼ cup of dry white wine and stir over the fire until the mixture comes to a boil. Taste for seasoning and put in the veal birds with a bay leaf. Cover with waxed paper and a lid and simmer for 45 minutes. Meanwhile prepare a pea purée.

Pea Purée: Cook 3 pounds of peas, shelled (or 2 packages of frozen peas) in boiling salted water until soft. Drain well and put through a strainer. Melt 2 tablespoons of butter in a small pan, stir in 2 tablespoons of flour and brown slowly until a dark amber color. Add the strained peas, salt and pepper and 3 tablespoons of sour cream; heat thoroughly.

To Serve: Make a bed of the pea purée on a hot serving dish. Remove the strings from the veal birds and arrange on top of the pea purée. Strain the gravy over the veal birds and serve immediately. Serves 6.

ESCALOPES DE VEAU VALENTINO
(Veal Scallops with Asparagus)

12 thin slices of veal from the leg	*1 teaspoon meat glaze*
4 tablespoons butter	*3 teaspoons potato flour or 3 tablespoons flour*
3 tablespoons brandy	*1 cup stock*
½ pound mushrooms	*½ cup dry white wine*
½ teaspoon tomato paste	*1 pound fresh asparagus or 1 package frozen asparagus*

Use 12 thin slices of veal cut from the best part of the leg. Heat 1 tablespoon of butter in a heavy skillet and when it is on the point of turning color, put in the veal and brown it on both sides. Brown only as many slices at one time as will fit into the pan without overlapping, adding another tablespoon of butter as needed. When all the meat is browned, put it back into the pan. Heat 3 tablespoons of brandy in a small pan, ignite and pour over the veal. Remove the veal from the pan.

Leave 6 whole mushrooms for the garnish and slice the rest. Melt 2 tablespoons of butter in the same pan and lightly brown all the mushrooms. Remove the whole caps, leaving the sliced mushrooms in the pan. Blend in, off the fire, ½ teaspoon of tomato paste, 1 teaspoon of meat glaze and 3 teaspoons of potato flour (or 3 tablespoons of flour). Pour on 1 cup of stock and ½ cup of dry white wine and stir over the fire until the sauce comes to a boil. Put back the veal with any pan juices, cover and simmer about 25 minutes, until the veal is tender.

Meanwhile cook 1 pound of fresh asparagus or 1 package of frozen asparagus spears in boiling salted water until just tender. Trim off the ends neatly, leaving the tips about 2 inches long. Put the tips into the sauce with the veal when it is about done.

To Serve: Arrange the slices of veal slightly overlapping on a hot serving dish. Spoon the sauce over the veal. Top with the sautéed mushroom caps. Serves 6.

SCALLOPINI WITH MARSALA

12 *thin slices leg of veal*	¼ *cup finely chopped onion*
1 *to 2 tablespoons flour*	½ *cup Marsala or sherry*
4 *tablespoons butter*	*salt, pepper*
¼ *cup finely chopped mushrooms*	1 *lemon*

Put the slices of veal between 2 pieces of waxed paper and beat with a wooden mallet until very thin. Dust lightly with flour. Heat 2 tablespoons of butter in a large skillet and when the butter is just turning color, put in the veal and brown quickly on both sides. Remove the veal from the pan. Lower the heat, add another 2 tablespoons of butter to the pan and slowly cook ¼ cup each of finely chopped mushrooms and onion for 5 minutes. Return the veal to the pan, pour on ½ cup of Marsala or sherry, season with salt and pepper, and simmer covered until the veal is tender, which will be in about 10 to 15 minutes.

To Serve: Arrange the slices of veal slightly overlapping on a hot serving dish. Boil down the sauce for a minute or so and pour it over the veal. Serve with slices of lemon. Serves 6.

SCALLOPINI WITH SORREL PURÉE

6 *large thin slices leg of veal*	¼ *cup dry white wine*
6 *tablespoons butter*	*salt, pepper*
3 *tablespoons Marsala*	1 *bay leaf*
1 *small clove garlic, crushed*	3 *pounds sorrel*
1 *cup stock*	2 *tablespoons flour*
¼ *cup cream*	

Brown the slices of veal quickly in 1 tablespoon of hot butter. Heat 3 tablespoons of Marsala in a small pan, ignite and pour over the veal. Remove veal. Melt another 2 tablespoons of butter in the pan, put in a small clove of crushed garlic and cook for 1 minute. Pour on 1 cup of stock and ¼ cup of dry white wine. Return the veal to the pan. Season with salt, pepper and a bay leaf. Cover and simmer for 10 to 15 minutes, or until the veal is tender.

Meanwhile prepare a purée of sorrel. Wash 3 pounds of sorrel in several changes of lukewarm water. Put into a saucepan with a tablespoon of butter, salt and pepper. Cook briskly for 5 to 6 minutes, stirring occasionally. Drain, chop coarsely and put through a strainer. Melt 2 tablespoons of butter. Blend in 2 tablespoons of flour and cook slowly until golden brown. Mix with the sorrel, seasoning and ¼ cup of heavy cream. Cook over a slow fire until thoroughly heated.

To Serve: Make a smooth bed of sorrel purée on a hot serving dish. Arrange the scallopini on top, slightly overlapping. Strain over the sauce. Garnish with any cooked vegetable such as carrots, peas, beans, asparagus or baby onions. Serves 6.

ESCALOPES DE VEAU MAINTENON
(Scallops of Veal with Ham)

6 *thin slices leg of veal*	1 *cup milk*
6 *tablespoons butter*	4 *tablespoons grated Parmesan*
4 *chicken livers*	*cheese*
¼ *pound firm white mushrooms*	½ *teaspoon dry mustard*
salt, pepper, cayenne	½ *teaspoon tomato paste*
¼ *pound cooked ham, shredded*	2 *tablespoons sherry*
3 *tablespoons flour*	½ *teaspoon meat glaze*

¼ *cup stock or water*

Place slices of veal between 2 pieces of waxed paper and beat until thin with a heavy wooden mallet. Brown on one side only in 1 tablespoon of hot butter.

In another pan quickly brown 4 chicken livers in 1 tablespoon of hot butter. Remove the livers and coarsely chop them. Put another tablespoon of butter in the pan, then the mushrooms, sliced, salt and pepper. Cook briskly for 3 to 4 minutes. Add the chopped chicken livers and the shredded ham and cook for 1 minute. Spread a generous spoonful of this mixture on each slice of veal, on the uncooked side. Place on a cookie sheet.

Melt 2 tablespoons of butter. Blend in, off the fire, 3 tablespoons of flour, salt and cayenne pepper. Add 1 cup of milk and stir over the fire until the mixture comes to a boil. Add 2 tablespoons of grated Parmesan cheese and ½ teaspoon of dry mustard. Let simmer for 2 to 3 minutes. Cover each slice of veal with a spoonful of this sauce. Sprinkle with 2 tablespoons of grated cheese and dot with 1 tablespoon of butter. Brown under the broiler. Arrange on a hot serving dish.

In the pan the veal was cooked in put ½ teaspoon of tomato paste, 2 tablespoons of sherry, ½ teaspoon of meat glaze and ¼ cup of stock or water. Bring to a boil, taste for seasoning and strain around the veal. Pile noisette potatoes (see page 122) at each end of the dish and serve immediately. Serves 6.

VEAU PROVENÇALE
(Veal with Rice and Tomatoes)

1½ pounds leg of veal	*2 zucchini*
4 tablespoons butter	*1 teaspoon meat glaze*
2 tablespoons sherry	*1 teaspoon tomato paste*
1 small clove garlic, crushed	*2 cups stock*
1 medium-size yellow onion, chopped	*2 tomatoes, skinned and sliced*
2 or 3 mushrooms, sliced	*¼ cup grated Parmesan cheese*
1 cup rice	*1 to 2 tablespoons chopped parsley*

Cut the veal in small ½-inch cubes and brown quickly all over in 2 tablespoons of hot butter. Heat 2 tablespoons of sherry in a small pan, ignite and pour over the veal. Remove veal from the pan. Add remaining 2 tablespoons of butter, 1 small clove of crushed garlic and a medium-size yellow onion, finely chopped; cook slowly until lightly browned. Add 2 or 3 sliced mushrooms and cook another minute or so. Add a cup of rice and cook slowly for 3 minutes, stirring constantly.

Meanwhile cover 2 zucchini with cold water, bring slowly to a boil and drain. Stir into the rice mixture 1 teaspoon of meat glaze, 1 teaspoon of tomato paste and the zucchini, sliced. Return the veal to the pan, add 1 cup of stock and cook covered until all the stock is absorbed. Add remaining cup of stock and cook covered over a very slow fire until the veal and rice are tender, about 20 to 30 minutes. Add 2 skinned and sliced tomatoes and cook for 1 or 2 minutes.

To Serve: Place in a casserole and sprinkle the top with grated cheese and 1 to 2 tablespoons of finely chopped parsley. Serves 4 or 5.

VEAU MAJORCA
(Veal with Peppers and Tomatoes)

2 pounds veal from leg	1 tablespoon shredded orange
4 tablespoons butter	rind
2 tablespoons brandy	½ teaspoon meat glaze
1 green pepper	3 teaspoons potato flour or 3
1 red pepper	tablespoons flour
1 large yellow onion	¼ cup red wine
2 tomatoes	1½ cups stock
1 large clove garlic, crushed	1 bay leaf
2 mushrooms, sliced	salt and pepper

Cut the veal into 1-inch cubes. Brown quickly all over in 2 table-spoons of hot butter. Heat 2 tablespoons of brandy in a small pan, ignite and pour over the veal. Remove the veal from the pan.

Meanwhile core, seed and dice 1 green pepper and 1 red pepper. Finely chop 1 large yellow onion. Skin 2 tomatoes, remove the seedy pulp and cut into shreds. Heat another 2 tablespoons of butter in the pan the veal was cooked in, add the peppers, onion, tomatoes and 1 large clove of garlic, crushed; cook briskly for about 5 minutes. Add 2 sliced mushrooms and 1 tablespoon of shredded orange rind and cook another minute or two.

Stir in, off the fire, ½ teaspoon of meat glaze and 3 teaspoons of potato flour (or 3 tablespoons of flour). Pour on ¼ cup of red wine and 1½ cups of stock and stir over the fire until the mixture comes to a boil. Put back the veal with a bay leaf. Season with salt and pepper. Cover the pan and let simmer for 30 to 40 minutes, or until the veal is tender. Remove the bay leaf.

Serve on a hot platter and garnish with straw potatoes. Serves 4 to 6.

VEAU VIENNOISE
(Veal Cooked in Beer)

12 thin slices leg of veal
3 tablespoons butter
1 green pepper, finely chopped
2 tablespoons finely chopped onion
¼ cup finely chopped mushrooms
1 small clove garlic, crushed
1 teaspoon tomato paste
1 teaspoon meat glaze
3 teaspoons potato flour or 3 tablespoons flour
1 bottle light lager beer (12 oz.)
salt
black pepper
½ teaspoon dry mustard
1 bay leaf
2 tomatoes, skinned and shredded
2 tablespoons grated Parmesan cheese
1 teaspoon finely chopped chives

Put the slices of veal between 2 pieces of waxed paper and beat them as thin as possible with a wooden mallet. Heat 1 tablespoon of butter in a heavy skillet. When it is just turning color, put in the veal and brown each slice quickly on both sides. Do just a few at a time so that the meat does not overlap, adding more butter if necessary. Remove veal from pan. Add remaining 1 to 2 tablespoons of butter, then a finely chopped green pepper, 2 tablespoons of finely chopped onion, ¼ cup finely chopped mushrooms and a small clove of garlic, crushed. Cook very slowly for 4 to 5 minutes. Remove pan from fire and blend in 1 teaspoon of tomato paste, 1 teaspoon of meat glaze and 3 teaspoons of potato flour (or 3 tablespoons of flour). Slowly pour on 1 bottle of light lager beer. Season with salt, pepper and ½ teaspoon of dry mustard. Return to the fire and stir until the mixture comes to a boil. Replace the veal in the sauce, add a bay leaf and cover pan with waxed paper and a lid. Simmer gently for 25 to 30 minutes, stirring once or twice.

To Serve: Arrange veal slices overlapping on a hot ovenproof serving dish. Add 2 skinned and shredded tomatoes to the sauce and boil 1 minute. Pour the sauce over the veal. Sprinkle with 2 tablespoons of grated Parmesan cheese and brown under the broiler. Top with 1 teaspoon of finely chopped chives. Serves 6.

ESCALOPES DE VEAU ITALIENNE
(Veal with Tomatoes and Spinach)

12 thin slices leg of veal	3 pounds spinach
4 tablespoons butter	2 tablespoons sour cream
3 tablespoons sherry	2 large cloves garlic, crushed
1 cup stock	1 small onion, finely chopped
bay leaf	6 tomatoes, skinned and sliced
salt, pepper	6 slices Cheddar cheese

Put the slices of veal between 2 pieces of waxed paper and beat with a wooden mallet until about ¼ inch thick. Brown on both sides in 2 tablespoons of hot butter. Heat 3 tablespoons of sherry in a small pan, ignite and pour over the veal. Pour on 1 cup of stock. Add a bay leaf, salt and pepper. Cover and simmer for 15 to 20 minutes, until the veal is tender.

In the meantime wash 3 pounds of spinach well. Place in a saucepan with 1 tablespoon of butter, salt and pepper. Cook rapidly for 5 to 6 minutes, stirring occasionally. Drain well and chop coarsely. Mix with 2 tablespoons of sour cream.

In another pan melt 2 tablespoons of butter. Add 2 large cloves of crushed garlic and a small finely chopped onion and cook briskly for 2 to 3 minutes. Add 6 skinned and sliced tomatoes and cook another 5 minutes or so.

To Serve: Make a smooth bed of the spinach on an ovenproof serving dish. Remove the veal from the sauce and arrange the slices slightly overlapping on top of the spinach. Spoon the tomato mixture over the veal and cover with 6 thin slices of Cheddar cheese. Brown under the broiler. Strain the gravy around the edge of the dish and serve immediately. Serves 6.

VEAL PARMIGIANA

8 slices veal from the leg
3 cloves garlic, crushed
about 3 tablespoons flour
6 to 7 tablespoons butter
½ cup white wine
salt, pepper
1 large eggplant
½ cup olive oil
4 large tomatoes, skinned and
    sliced

2 small onions, peeled and finely
    chopped
8 slices Cheddar cheese
1 teaspoon tomato paste
1 teaspoon meat glaze
3 teaspoons potato flour or 3
    tablespoons flour
½ cup red wine
1 cup stock
½ cup grated Parmesan cheese

Put each slice of veal between 2 pieces of waxed paper and beat
with a wooden mallet. Rub each slice with a little garlic and dust
lightly with flour. Heat 2 tablespoons of butter in a heavy skillet
and cook the veal over a quick fire until golden brown on each
side. Brown only as many slices at one time as will fit into the
pan without overlapping. Add another tablespoon of butter if
necessary to keep the meat from sticking to the pan. When all
the meat is browned, put it in the pan, pour over ½ cup of white
wine, season with salt and pepper, cover and cook slowly for
10 to 15 minutes.

Meanwhile cut 1 large eggplant into ½-inch slices. Sprinkle with
salt and let stand for ½ hour. Drain and dry, spread with a little
garlic, dust lightly with flour and fry in ½ cup of olive oil until
brown on each side. Remove and in the same pan cook 4 large
sliced tomatoes and 2 small finely chopped onions for about 5
minutes, until lightly browned. Arrange the eggplant slices overlapping on a hot serving dish. Cover with the cooked tomatoes
and onions, then the veal slices, also slightly overlapping. Place
8 slices of cheddar cheese on top and pour over the following
sauce.

Melt 2 tablespoons of butter in the pan the veal was cooked in.
Stir in, off the fire, 1 teaspoon of tomato paste, 1 teaspoon of meat
glaze and 3 teaspoons of potato flour (or 3 tablespoons of flour).
Pour on ½ cup of red wine and 1 cup of stock and stir over the
fire until the sauce comes to a boil. Taste for seasoning and sim-

mer for a few minutes. Spoon the sauce over the veal, sprinkle with ½ cup of grated Parmesan cheese, dot with 2 tablespoons of butter and brown under the broiler. Serves 4 to 6.

SCALLOPINI WITH EGGPLANT

1 small eggplant	*1 3-ounce package cream*
salt, pepper	*cheese*
¼ to ½ cup olive oil	*¼ pound cottage cheese*
12 thin slices leg of veal	*2 tablespoons sour cream*
3 tablespoons butter	*1 tablespoon chopped chives*
1 cup stock	*1 large clove garlic, crushed*

freshly cracked black pepper

Cut the eggplant in half lengthwise and then into thin slices. Sprinkle with salt and let stand ½ hour. Drain and dry. Fry until golden brown in ¼ to ½ cup of olive oil. Keep warm in a very slow oven.

Meanwhile put 12 thin slices of leg of veal between 2 pieces of waxed paper and beat with a wooden mallet. Brown slowly on both sides in 3 tablespoons of hot butter. Pour on 1 cup of stock and simmer for 10 to 15 minutes. Remove the veal from the pan and spread each piece with a spoonful of the following mixture. Blend together 1 small 3-ounce package of cream cheese, ¼ pound of cottage cheese, 2 tablespoons of sour cream, 1 tablespoon of chopped chives, 1 large clove of crushed garlic, salt and freshly cracked black pepper.

To Serve: Arrange overlapping slices of eggplant on a hot serving dish. Place the veal on top and strain the sauce over all. Serves 6.

BROCHETTES DE VEAU
(Broiled Pieces of Veal on Skewers)

1½-pound filet of veal or	*¾ pound smoked bacon, in 1 piece*
veal cutlet	*salt*
1 clove garlic, crushed	*freshly ground black pepper*
6 tablespoons melted butter	*about 1 cup dry bread crumbs*

½ bunch watercress

Trim all bone and sinew from the veal and cut into 1-inch cubes. Rub with a little crushed garlic and roll the pieces in melted butter. Cut the bacon into ½-inch cubes and drop into boiling water for ½ minute. Remove and drain on absorbent paper. Thread the veal and bacon alternately on 4 long steel skewers. Season with salt and freshly cracked black pepper and roll in bread crumbs, coating the meat well. Sprinkle with the remaining butter. Place under the broiler at least 3 inches away from the flame. Broil for 7 to 8 minutes on each side, basting a few times with the pan juices. Serve on the skewers on a long hot platter and garnish with sprigs of watercress. Serves 4.

BREAST OF VEAL WITH RAISINS AND SOUR CREAM

3 pounds breast of veal	*3 tablespoons flour*
4 tablespoons butter	*1½ cups veal stock*
2 tablespoons sherry	*1 tablespoon currant jelly*
¾ cup white sultana raisins	*salt, cayenne*
¼ pound mushrooms, sliced	*1 bay leaf*
	1 cup light sour cream

Bone the meat or have the butcher do it. Cut into 1-inch cubes and brown quickly in 2 tablespoons of hot butter. Heat 2 tablespoons of sherry in a small pan, ignite and pour over the veal. Remove veal from the pan. Melt another 2 tablespoons of butter in the pan, add ¾ cup white sultana raisins and cook briskly for 2 to 3 minutes. Add ¼ pound sliced mushrooms and cook another 2 minutes.

Blend in, off the fire, 3 tablespoons of flour. Pour on 1½ cups of veal stock and stir over the fire until the mixture comes to a boil. Add 1 tablespoon currant jelly, salt, cayenne and a bay leaf. Return the veal to the pan and simmer covered until tender, about 30 to 40 minutes. Slowly blend in 1 cup of light sour cream.

To Serve: Serve in a casserole with a bowl of boiled rice. It can be cooked and served in the same casserole if you use one that can be used for top-of-the-stove cooking and is suitable for serving. This is a good party dish since it can wait almost indefinitely at a simmering heat. Serves 5 or 6.

BONED STUFFED BREAST OF VEAL

3 pounds breast of veal
½ pound chicken livers or
  calves' liver
1 tablespoon butter
½ pound sausage
½ cup fried bread crumbs
½ cup chopped cooked onion

1 small clove garlic, crushed
1 tablespoon chopped herbs
1 tablespoon chopped mushroom
salt, pepper
1 to 2 tablespoons water
½ cup dry white wine

Bone the veal or have the butcher do it. Sauté ½ pound of chicken livers or calves' liver quickly in 1 tablespoon of very hot butter. Remove and chop coarsely. Mix together the liver, ½ pound of sausage meat, ½ cup of fried bread crumbs, ½ cup chopped cooked onion, 1 small clove of crushed garlic, 1 tablespoon of chopped fresh herbs such as parsley and chives, and 1 tablespoon of chopped mushroom. Season with salt and pepper and bind with 1 to 2 tablespoons of water. Spread evenly on the veal, leaving a margin of an inch around the outside edge. Roll and tie with string at 1½-inch intervals. Place in a shallow roasting pan and cook in a moderate oven at 350° until browned. Then pour ½ cup of dry white wine into the pan, cover and continue cooking for 1 to 1½ hours.

To Serve: Remove the meat from the oven and cut off enough slices for one meal. Arrange them slightly overlapping on a hot serving dish with the uncut piece at one end. Strain the pan gravy over the meat. Surround with little mounds of cooked vegetables such as peas, green beans, mushrooms, zucchini, lima beans, broiled tomatoes and sautéed potato balls. Serves 5 or 6.

VEAU ROULADE
(Roast Rolled Breast of Veal)

1 piece breast of veal, 3½ to	*2 tablespoons olive oil*
4 pounds	*1 small onion, sliced*
salt, pepper	*1 carrot, sliced*
1 small clove garlic, crushed	*½ cup rosé or white wine*
¼ pound sliced prosciutto	*½ cup water*
(Italian ham)	*½ pound mushrooms, sliced*
1 small Mozzarella cheese	*2 tablespoons butter*
1 to 2 teaspoons chopped parsley	*2 tablespoons flour*

Bone the breast of veal or have the butcher do it. Spread it out flat and trim off any excess fat. Season with salt, pepper and a clove of crushed garlic. Cover with the sliced prosciutto (regular boiled ham may be used if prosciutto is not available). Cut the Mozzarella into thin slices and place on top of the ham. Sprinkle with 1 to 2 teaspoons of chopped parsley. Roll lengthwise and tie with string at 1½-inch intervals. Place in a shallow baking dish and brush with 2 tablespoons of olive oil. Put into the pan a small sliced onion, a sliced carrot, ½ cup of rosé or white wine, ½ cup of water and the veal bones. Roast for 1¼ to 1½ hours in a moderate oven at 375° basting occasionally with the pan juices. Remove the veal and keep warm while you prepare the following sauce.

Sauce: Sauté ½ pound of sliced mushrooms in 2 tablespoons of butter until lightly browned. Blend in 2 tablespoons of flour, off the fire. Strain the pan juices and if there are not 2 cups of stock, add enough water to make that amount. Pour into the pan with the mushrooms and stir over the fire until the sauce comes to a boil. Taste for seasoning.

To Serve: Cut the strings off the veal and carve as many slices as are needed for one meal. Arrange them slightly overlapping on a hot serving dish with the uncut piece at one end. Spoon a little of the sauce over the veal and serve the rest in a sauce bowl. Serves 5 or 6.

VEAL MOUSSE

2 pounds lean veal   1½ cups light cream
3 egg whites, unbeaten   salt, pepper

HOLLANDAISE SAUCE

2 egg yolks   salt, cayenne
1 tablespoon tarragon vinegar   1 tablespoon cream
                   ¼ pound butter

3 cucumbers   2 tablespoons finely chopped
¼ cup melted butter   parsley
            freshly cracked black pepper

4 tomatoes   1 teaspoon Dijon mustard
1 clove garlic, crushed   4 tablespoons bread crumbs
2 tablespoons softened butter 4 tablespoons grated Parmesan
                                 cheese

Veal Mousse: Put the veal through a meat grinder twice. Beat in 3 egg whites, then slowly beat in 1½ cups of light cream. Season with salt and a little pepper. Grease a ring mold well with vegetable shortening and fill with the mousse to within ½ inch of the top. Cover with greased waxed paper and place the mold in a pan with an inch of boiling water in the bottom. Bake in a moderate oven at 350° for 25 to 30 minutes or until firm to the touch. Meanwhile prepare the sauce and garnishes.

Hollandaise Sauce: Put 2 egg yolks, 1 tablespoon of vinegar, salt and a little cayenne pepper into a small bowl and beat until smooth with a wire whisk. Beat in 1 tablespoon of cream. Place the bowl in a skillet with simmering water in the bottom and beat until the mixture begins to thicken. Then beat in ¼ pound of butter, bit by bit.

Cucumbers: Peel cucumbers and cut into small olive-shaped pieces. Cook for 5 minutes in boiling salted water, then drain. Mix with ¼ cup of melted butter, 2 tablespoons of finely chopped parsley, salt and plenty of freshly cracked black pepper.

Broiled Tomatoes: Skin 4 tomatoes and cut in half. Blend together 1 clove of crushed garlic, 2 tablespoons of softened butter and 1 teaspoon of Dijon mustard and spread on the tomatoes. Sprinkle with 4 tablespoons of bread crumbs and 4 tablespoons of grated Parmesan cheese and broil until lightly browned.

To Serve: Remove the mousse from the oven and let stand for 5 minutes, then run a sharp knife around the edge and unmold on a round hot serving platter. Spoon Hollandaise sauce over the mousse, fill the center with cooked cucumbers and surround with broiled tomatoes. Serves 7 or 8.

VEAL LOAF

2 pounds ground lean veal	*1 egg, slightly beaten*
¼ pound salt pork, ground	*1 cup light cream*
1 cup soft bread crumbs	*2 tablespoons chopped parsley*
1 tablespoon finely chopped onion	*salt, pepper*
	dash of nutmeg
1 tablespoon lemon juice	*2 tablespoons melted butter*

Blend together all of the ingredients except the melted butter, preferably with one hand which has been dipped in cold water. Place in a greased 9 × 5-inch loaf pan. Brush the top well with 2 tablespoons of melted butter. Bake in a moderate oven at 350° for 1½ hours. Remove, let stand for 5 minutes, then turn out on a hot serving dish. Garnish with small mounds of cooked, fresh, seasonal vegetables. Serves 7 or 8.

JELLIED VEAL LOAF

4 to 6 pounds knuckle of veal	*salt, pepper*
1 medium-size onion, sliced	*1 bay leaf*
1 large carrot, sliced	*2 hard-boiled eggs, sliced*
2 stalks celery, sliced	*stuffed olives, sliced*

Ask the butcher to crack the knuckle bone. Put it into a large, deep, heavy saucepan and cover with cold water, using about 2 quarts. Bring slowly to a boil and skim. Cover and simmer for 1 hour. Add a medium-size sliced onion, 1 large sliced carrot, 2 stalks of sliced celery, 3 to 4 teaspoons of salt, pepper and a bay leaf. Simmer for another 1 to 2 hours. Strain, reserving the stock. Remove all meat from the bone and chop it very finely. Put it into a saucepan with 4 cups of the strained stock and simmer for ½ hour.

Slice 2 hard-boiled eggs and arrange them on the bottom of a 9 × 5-inch loaf pan. Place small rounds of stuffed olives between the slices of egg. Place the veal mixture in the pan carefully so as not to disturb the eggs and olives. Chill for several hours or overnight in the refrigerator.

To Serve: Run a sharp knife around the edge of the pan and unmold the veal loaf. Cut into slices and arrange them slightly overlapping on a cold serving dish, preferably silver. Serves 8 to 10.

VEAL STOCK

3 pounds knuckle veal bone, cracked
1 piece veal, about 1 pound
4 quarts water
2 cups mixed sliced onion, carrot and celery
1 tablespoon salt
bouquet of fresh herbs, including 1 whole nutmeg
1 cup dry white wine
6 peppercorns

Veal stock has so many uses that it is worth making, especially since it can be frozen to provide veal stock at all times.

Put the cracked knuckle of veal in a large saucepan, preferably an earthenware cocotte. Cut the piece of veal into small cubes; any cut will do since it is used just for flavor. Put it into the pan with 4 quarts of cold water. Bring slowly to a boil. Skim carefully. Add 2 cups of mixed sliced onion, carrot and celery. Also add the bouquet of fresh herbs with a whole nutmeg, 1 cup of dry white wine, 6 peppercorns and 1 tablespoon of salt. Simmer for 3 to 4 hours. Strain, cool and remove any fat that rises to the top.

Veal stock will keep about 1 week in the refrigerator. In the summer it should be boiled up once or twice. When freezing it, use small containers rather than one large one, just enough for individual dishes.

FOIE DE VEAU SAUTÉ AUX FINES HERBES
(Sautéed Calves' Liver with Mixed Herbs)

4 tablespoons butter	1 to 2 teaspoons lemon juice
8 small slices calves' liver	½ cup dry white wine
8 slices grilled smoked bacon	¼ cup chopped mixed herbs
1 tablespoon very finely chopped onion	salt
	freshly cracked black pepper

Heat 2 tablespoons of butter in a heavy skillet. When the butter is foaming and on the point of turning color, brown the slices of liver quickly on each side. Remove them and arrange slightly overlapping on a hot serving dish alternately with the slices of grilled bacon. Keep warm in a very slow oven. Melt the remaining 2 tablespoons of butter in the pan the liver was cooked in. Add 1 tablespoon of very finely chopped onion and sauté briskly for 2 to 3 minutes. Then add 1 to 2 teaspoons of lemon juice, ½ cup of dry white wine and ¼ cup of finely chopped mixed fresh herbs. This mixture should use 2 or 3 of the following herbs: parsley, tarragon, chives, chervil or thyme. Season with salt and freshly cracked black pepper, boil up quickly and pour over the liver. Serve immediately. Serves 4.

LIVER WITH ORANGE

4 large slices calves' liver	2 teaspoons potato flour
3 tablespoons butter	1 cup stock
¼ cup finely chopped onion	¼ cup sherry
½ teaspoon tomato paste	2 tablespoons shredded orange rind
1 teaspoon meat glaze	salt, pepper

GLAZED ORANGES

2 large seedless oranges	1 tablespoon sugar
2 tablespoons butter	

Heat 2 tablespoons of butter in a large skillet and quickly brown the liver on both sides. Remove the liver from the pan and keep warm. Add another tablespoon of butter to the pan and ¼ cup of finely chopped onion and cook slowly for about 5 minutes, until the onion is soft but not brown. Blend in, off the fire, ½ teaspoon of tomato paste, 1 teaspoon of meat glaze and 2 teaspoons of potato flour. Pour on 1 cup of stock and ¼ cup of sherry and stir over the fire until the sauce comes to a boil. Add 2 tablespoons of shredded orange rind, season with salt and pepper, and simmer for a few minutes. Meanwhile prepare the orange garnish.

Glazed Oranges: Cut 2 oranges into thick slices leaving the skin on. Sprinkle lightly with about 1 tablespoon of sugar. Brown quickly until a good dark color in 2 tablespoons of hot butter.

To Serve: Arrange the slices of liver slightly overlapping on a hot serving dish. Spoon the sauce over it and top with glazed oranges. Serve with rice pilaff (see page 125). Serves 4.

LARDED BRAISED CALVES' LIVER

1 whole calves' liver, about 1½ pounds	*¼ pound salt pork*
	3 slices bacon
	1 tablespoon butter

BROWN SAUCE

2 tablespoons butter	*3 teaspoons potato flour*
½ teaspoon tomato paste	*1½ cups stock*
½ teaspoon meat glaze	*¼ cup dry white wine*
salt, pepper	

STUFFED CABBAGE LEAVES

8 cabbage leaves	*2 chopped hard-boiled eggs*
1 cup cooked rice	*¾ cup chopped sautéed mush-rooms*
½ cup chopped sautéed onion	
1 tablespoon chopped parsley	

BROILED TOMATOES

4 tomatoes	*2 tablespoons butter*
½ cup grated Parmesan cheese	

Lard the calves' liver several times with long thin strips of salt pork. Trim off the ends leaving about ¼ inch of the fat at each end. (See page 17 for larding instructions.) Heat 1 tablespoon of butter in a deep heavy saucepan. When it is just turning color, quickly brown the calves' liver on each side. Remove the liver from the pan, wrap 3 slices of bacon around it and secure the bacon with string. Prepare the following brown sauce in the pan the liver was cooked in.

Brown Sauce: Melt another 2 tablespoons of butter in the pan. Blend in, off the fire, ½ teaspoon of tomato paste, ½ teaspoon of meat glaze and 3 teaspoons of potato flour. Pour on 1½ cups of stock and ¼ cup of dry white wine and stir over the fire until the sauce comes to a boil. Season with salt and pepper. Put the liver into the sauce, cover and simmer for 45 minutes.

Stuffed Cabbage Leaves: Put a medium-size green cabbage into a saucepan, cover with cold water, bring slowly to a boil and simmer for 5 minutes. Remove, cut off the core and use 8 of the large outside leaves. Mix together 1 cup of cooked rice, ½ cup chopped sautéed onion, 2 chopped hard-boiled eggs, ¾ cup chopped sautéed mushrooms, 1 tablespoon of finely chopped parsley and a little seasoning. Put a heaping spoonful on each leaf and fold the leaf over the filling making a neat triangle. Place the stuffed cabbages in the pan with the liver to cook for 15 to 20 minutes.

Broiled Tomatoes: Cut the tomatoes in half. Sprinkle with ½ cup of grated Parmesan cheese, salt and pepper, and dot with 2 tablespoons of butter. Brown under the broiler just before serving.

To Serve: Remove the liver, cut off the strings and carve into slices. Arrange them slightly overlapping on a hot serving dish. Spoon over the sauce. Place the stuffed cabbage leaves and broiled tomatoes alternately around the edge of the dish. Serves 4.

CALVES' LIVER RISOTTO

½ pound calves' liver	1½ cups rice
5 tablespoons butter	¼ pound mushrooms, sliced
¼ cup olive oil	1 teaspoon meat glaze
1 large yellow onion, chopped	1 teaspoon tomato paste
2 small cloves garlic, crushed	3 cups chicken or veal stock
½ teaspoon Spanish saffron	1 cup grated Parmesan cheese

2 tablespoons finely chopped parsley

Cut the liver into small thick strips. Heat 2 tablespoons of butter in a large, heavy, deep saucepan and when the butter is very hot, quickly brown the liver all over. Remove the liver from the pan. Add ¼ cup of olive oil to the same pan and when it is hot, add a finely chopped large yellow onion. Cook over a slow fire for 5 minutes. Add 2 small cloves of crushed garlic and cook another minute. Crush ½ teaspoon of saffron in a mortar with a pestle, adding a little water, and put into the pan with 1½ cups of rice. Cook over a very slow fire for 5 to 6 minutes, stirring occasionally.

In the meantime sauté ¼ pound of sliced mushrooms in 1 table-spoon of butter. Blend in 1 teaspoon of meat glaze and 1 teaspoon of tomato paste. Pour on 1 cup of stock and add this mixture to the rice. Stir well, then add the other 2 cups of stock. Taste for seasoning; it may not need any if the stock was well seasoned. Cover with waxed paper and a lid and place in a moderate oven at 350° for 40 to 45 minutes. Remove and stir in lightly with a fork the strips of liver and ¼ cup of grated Parmesan cheese. Dot the top with 2 tablespoons of butter, cover and leave over the lowest possible fire for 10 minutes.

To Serve: Pile up in a casserole or hot deep dish. Sprinkle with a little cheese and 2 tablespoons of finely chopped parsley. Serve the rest of the grated cheese separately. Serves 4 to 6.

PETITES CRÈMES DE FOIE
(Little Liver Creams)

½ *pound ground calves' liver*   ½ *cup cream*
2 *eggs, beaten*   *salt, pepper*
pinch ground nutmeg

NOISETTE POTATOES
2 *pounds old potatoes*   4 *tablespoons butter*
salt, pepper

HOLLANDAISE SAUCE
2 *egg yolks*   3 *tablespoons cream*
1 *tablespoon tarragon vinegar*   ¼ *pound butter*
salt, cayenne pepper

Mix together the ground liver, 2 beaten eggs, ½ cup of cream, salt, pepper and a pinch of ground nutmeg. Rub through a fine strainer. Grease 8 small upright molds well with vegetable shortening and fill with the liver mixture. Place the molds in a pan and pour in boiling water to come halfway up the molds. Cover them with greased waxed paper. Bake for about 20 minutes in a moderate oven at 375° or until set.

Noisette Potatoes: Pare 2 pounds of old potatoes and cut them into small balls with a round potato cutter. Sauté in 4 tablespoons of butter over a moderate fire for 15 to 20 minutes, until the potatoes are soft and well browned. Shake the pan often so that the potatoes will brown evenly. Just before serving season with salt and pepper.

Hollandaise Sauce: Place 2 egg yolks in a small bowl. Beat in 1 tablespoon of tarragon vinegar with a wire whisk. Add salt, a pinch of cayenne pepper and 1 tablespoon of cream. Place the bowl in a skillet of gently boiling water and beat until the mixture begins to thicken. Then beat in ¼ pound of butter, bit by bit, and another 2 tablespoons of cream.

To Serve: Remove the molds from the oven, let stand for 5 minutes, then turn them out. Arrange the liver creams in a circle on a hot serving dish. Spoon Hollandaise sauce over them and fill the center with noisette potatoes. Serves 4.

FOIE DE VEAU À LA CRÈME
(Calves' Liver with Sour Cream)

4 large slices calves' liver	*1 cup stock*
4 tablespoons butter	*3 tablespoons sherry*
½ teaspoon tomato paste	*¾ cup sour cream*
½ teaspoon meat glaze	*4 tablespoons grated Parmesan*
3 tablespoons flour	*cheese*
1 small clove garlic, crushed	salt
freshly cracked black pepper	

Dry the liver well. Heat a heavy skillet and when hot add 1 tablespoon of butter. When it is just on the point of turning color, quickly brown the liver on both sides. Remove the liver from the pan. Melt another 3 tablespoons of butter in the pan. Blend in, off the fire, ½ teaspoon of tomato paste, ½ teaspoon of meat glaze, 3 tablespoons of flour and a small clove of crushed garlic. Pour on 1 cup of stock and 3 tablespoons of sherry and stir over the fire until the mixture comes to a boil. Add ¾ cup of sour cream slowly, stirring well all the time. Add 2 tablespoons of grated Parmesan cheese, salt and freshly cracked black pepper. Place the liver in a shallow casserole and cover it with the sauce. Sprinkle the remaining 2 tablespoons of cheese over the top. Bake in a moderate oven at 350° for 10 to 15 minutes. Remove and serve in the casserole. Serves 4.

PÂTÉ MAISON
(Cold Meat Pâté)

2 pounds ground calves' liver
2 pounds sausage meat
salt and pepper
6 slices of bacon
6 chicken livers

2 hard-boiled eggs
6 ounces cooked ham, in one piece
6 ounces cooked tongue, in one piece
6 ounces liverwurst, sliced

Mix the ground liver and sausage meat together and season with plenty of salt and pepper. Grease a loaf pan very well. Line with 6 slices of bacon and half fill with the liver and sausage mixture. Cut 2 hard-boiled eggs in half lengthwise and place down the center of the pan. Cut the ham and tongue into finger-size strips and place them with the liverwurst and chicken livers on top of the eggs. Fill with the rest of the liver and sausage mixture. Cover with waxed paper. Put the loaf pan into another pan and pour in enough water to come halfway up the sides. Bake in a moderate oven at 350° for 1½ hours. Remove and place a brick on top of the pan to press down the pâté. Chill for several hours in the refrigerator. Turn out of the pan, cut in slices and serve as a pâté. This makes an attractive buffet dish if the pâté is covered with a thin layer of aspic and is garnished with chopped set aspic. See index for aspic recipes.

RIZ DE VEAU AU BEURRE NOIR
(Sweetbreads with Black Butter)

2 pairs large sweetbreads	about 2 tablespoons flour
1 tablespoon lemon juice or vinegar	salt, cayenne pepper
2 tablespoons butter	

BEURRE NOIR

butter in pan and 3 more tablespoons	½ cup dry white wine
1 small clove garlic, crushed	1 teaspoon lemon juice
2 tablespoons capers	

Soak the sweetbreads for about an hour in cold water. Drain, put into a saucepan with cold water to cover and 1 tablespoon of lemon juice or vinegar and bring slowly to a boil. Simmer for 5 minutes, drain and put into a bowl of iced water for a few minutes. Remove from the water and take off the skin and any sinew. Dust lightly with flour which has been seasoned with salt and cayenne pepper. Brown quickly on both sides in 2 tablespoons of hot butter, then cook slowly about 5 minutes on each side. Arrange on a hot serving dish and place in a very slow oven to keep warm while you prepare the following sauce.

Beurre Noir: Melt another 3 tablespoons of butter in the pan the sweetbreads were cooked in and brown it very slowly, which may take up to 10 minutes. Add a small clove of crushed garlic and cook another 1 or 2 minutes. Add ½ cup of dry white wine, 1 teaspoon of lemon juice and 2 tablespoons of capers and cook for 1 minute.

Pour the sauce over the sweetbreads and serve immediately. Serves 4.

SWEETBREADS EN BROCHETTE

2 pairs large sweetbreads	2 green peppers
1 tablespoon lemon juice or vinegar	½ pound mushrooms
½ pound sliced bacon	1 clove garlic, crushed
1 large yellow onion	¼ cup melted butter
salt, pepper	

RICE PILAFF

1 cup rice	3 tablespoons melted butter
¼ to ½ teaspoon saffron	½ cup raisins
3 tablespoons warm water	½ cup sliced sautéed mushrooms
1 teaspoon meat glaze	½ cup blanched browned almonds

Soak 2 pairs of large sweetbreads in cold water for 1 hour. Drain. Place in a saucepan with cold water to cover and 1 tablespoon of lemon juice or vinegar and bring slowly to a boil. Drain again and put into iced water for at least 5 minutes. Remove any membrane and sinew. Cut into 1-inch cubes. Cut ½ pound of bacon in half crosswise and wrap each piece of sweetbread with half a slice of bacon. Peel a large yellow onion, quarter it and separate into sections. Core and seed 2 green peppers and cut into 1-inch squares. Thread 4 skewers with pieces of sweetbread alternating them with whole mushroom caps, sections of onion and pieces of pepper. Place the skewers on a cookie sheet. Spread with a large clove of crushed garlic and brush with ¼ cup of melted butter. Season with salt and pepper. Place under the broiler at least 3 inches away from the flame and cook for about 10 minutes or until golden brown, turning once.

Rice Pilaff: Boil 1 cup of rice in plenty of salted water (or chicken stock) for 13 to 14 minutes, or until just tender. Drain and place in a large strainer over simmering water for 10 to 15 minutes to steam. Dissolve ¼ to ½ teaspoon saffron in 3 tablespoons of warm water with 1 teaspoon of meat glaze. Blend into the rice with 3 tablespoons of melted butter, ½ cup of raisins, ½ cup sliced sautéed mushrooms and ½ cup blanched browned almonds.

To Serve: Make a smooth bed of rice pilaff on a hot serving platter. Place the skewers on top of the rice. Add ¼ cup of water to the pan juices, bring to a boil and pour over the sweetbreads. Serves 4.

SWEETBREADS TALLEYRAND

2 pairs large sweetbreads	½ teaspoon tomato paste
lemon juice	2 teaspoons potato flour
2 tablespoons flour	1 cup stock
5 tablespoons butter	½ cup dry white wine
3 tablespoons brandy	2 truffles, finely chopped
salt, pepper	1 small clove garlic, crushed
8 large mushroom caps	8 rounds white bread
1 teaspoon meat glaze	8 thin slices cooked ham

1 tablespoon finely chopped parsley

Soak the sweetbreads for 1 hour in cold water. Drain. Put into a saucepan with cold water to cover and 1 tablespoon of lemon juice and bring slowly to a boil. Simmer for 5 minutes, drain again and put into a bowl of iced water for at least 10 to 15 minutes, or until ready to use. Remove skin and sinews and dry on a cloth. Cut in half lengthwise and dust lightly with flour. Brown rather slowly on both sides in 2 tablespoons of hot butter. Heat 3 tablespoons of brandy in a small pan, ignite and pour over the sweetbreads. Remove breads from the pan and keep warm. Add another tablespoon of butter to the pan with 1 teaspoon of lemon juice, salt and pepper. Sauté 8 large mushroom caps until golden brown. Remove them and keep warm with the sweetbreads.

Blend into the pan juices, off the fire, 1 teaspoon of meat glaze, ½ teaspoon of tomato paste and 2 teaspoons of potato flour. Pour on 1 cup of stock and ½ cup of dry white wine and stir over the fire until the sauce comes to a boil. Add 2 finely chopped truffles and a small clove of crushed garlic and simmer a few minutes. Cut 8 rounds of bread a little larger than the sweetbreads and about ½ inch thick and fry until golden brown in 2 tablespoons of butter.

To Serve: Arrange the rounds of bread on a hot serving dish. Place a slice of ham on each round topped with a sweetbread and a mushroom cap. Spoon the sauce over all and sprinkle with 1 tablespoon of finely chopped parsley. Serves 8.

LARDED SWEETBREADS WITH SUPRÊME SAUCE

2 pairs large sweetbreads	3 tablespoons butter
lemon juice	½ pound small white mushrooms
½ pound salt pork	salt, pepper
	1 small truffle

SUPRÊME SAUCE

3 tablespoons butter	¾ cup light cream
2 tablespoons flour	salt, white pepper
¾ cup chicken or veal stock	1 to 2 tablespoons brandy
	pan juices

Soak the sweetbreads for an hour in cold water. Drain. Put in a saucepan with cold water to cover and 1 tablespoon of lemon juice. Bring slowly to a boil, simmer for 5 minutes and drain again. Put immediately into a bowl of iced water and let stand for 10 to 15 minutes. Remove the skin and sinews. Cut ½ pound of salt pork into long thin strips and lard each piece of sweetbread about 4 times with a larding needle (see page 17 for larding instructions). Trim off the ends. Brown the sweetbreads on both sides in 2 tablespoons of butter over a moderate fire. Remove the sweetbreads and keep them warm.

Put another tablespoon of butter in the same pan. Sauté ½ pound small white mushrooms with 1 teaspoon of lemon juice, salt and pepper, until light brown. Meanwhile make the sauce.

Suprême Sauce: Melt 2 tablespoons of butter. Blend in, off the fire, 2 tablespoons of flour. Pour on ¾ cup of chicken or veal stock and stir over the fire until the mixture comes to a boil. Slowly add ¾ cup of light cream. Season with salt and white pepper. Beat in 1 tablespoon of butter, bit by bit. Lastly add 1 to 2 tablespoons of brandy and the strained pan juices.

To Serve: Arrange the sweetbreads in a circle on a hot serving dish with the sautéed mushrooms in the center. Spoon the sauce over the sweetbreads and top each one with a slice of truffle. Serves 4.

LARDED BRAISED SWEETBREADS

3 pairs large sweetbreads
1 tablespoon lemon juice or vine-
gar
¼ pound salt pork
5 tablespoons butter
1 large yellow onion, sliced
1 large carrot, sliced

4 slices bacon
salt
freshly cracked black pepper
½ cup dry white wine
4 tablespoons chicken stock
2 large heads chicory
⅓ cup heavy cream

1 tablespoon chopped parsley

Soak the sweetbreads in cold water for 1 hour. Drain, put into a saucepan with cold water to cover and 1 tablespoon of lemon juice or vinegar. Bring slowly to a boil and simmer for 5 minutes. Remove and put into a bowl of iced water for a few minutes. Drain and dry on a cloth. Remove the skin and any tissue and lard with a larding needle, using long thin strips of salt pork (see page 17 for larding method). Spread the bottom of a heavy pan with 3 tablespoons of softened butter. Cover with a large sliced onion and carrot and slices of bacon. Season with salt and freshly cracked black pepper. Place the sweetbreads on top and season them. Bake covered in a moderate oven at 350° for 30 minutes.

Remove cover, place the pan high in the oven and turn up the heat to 425°. When the sweetbreads are brown, in about 15 minutes, pour over ½ cup of dry white wine and 4 tablespoons of chicken stock. Baste the sweetbreads well, then drain off the juice into a small saucepan. Bring it to a boil and add 2 tablespoons of butter, bit by bit, over a high flame.

In the meantime wash 2 large heads of chicory and cook it in boiling salted water for 6 to 8 minutes, or until tender. Drain well and chop rather fine. Season with salt and freshly cracked black pepper and mix in ⅓ cup heavy cream.

To Serve: Make a bed of the chicory down the center of a hot serving dish. Place the sweetbreads on top. Pour over the sauce and sprinkle with 1 tablespoon of finely chopped parsley. Serves 6.

BRAISED SWEETBREADS

3 pairs large sweetbreads
1 tablespoon lemon juice or vinegar
5 tablespoons butter
2 tablespoons Marsala
1 small clove garlic, crushed
¼ pound mushrooms, sliced
½ teaspoon meat glaze
3 teaspoons potato flour
1 cup stock, veal or beef
¾ cup sour cream
salt and pepper
¼ teaspoon dried thyme
1 cucumber
¾ cup grated Parmesan cheese

Soak the sweetbreads in cold water for 1 hour. Drain. Place in a saucepan with cold water to cover, add 1 tablespoon of lemon juice or vinegar and bring slowly to a boil. Simmer for 5 minutes and drain again. Put into a bowl of iced water for a few minutes. Remove, trim off skin, membranes and tubes and cut in half lengthwise. Brown quickly on both sides in 2 tablespoons of hot butter. Heat 2 tablespoons of Marsala in a small pan, ignite and pour over the sweetbreads. Remove the sweetbreads from the pan. Add another 2 tablespoons of butter to the pan with 1 small clove of crushed garlic and ¼ pound of sliced mushrooms and cook briskly for 2 minutes. Blend in, off the fire, ½ teaspoon of meat glaze and 3 teaspoons of potato flour. Pour on 1 cup of veal or beef stock and stir over the fire until the mixture comes to a boil. Still stirring constantly, add ¾ cup of sour cream a little at a time. Season with salt, pepper and ¼ teaspoon of dried thyme. Return the sweetbreads to the pan, cover and simmer for 15 to 20 minutes.

Peel 1 cucumber and cut into thin slices. Add cold salted water to cover, bring slowly to a boil, simmer a minute or so, then drain thoroughly. Put into the pan with the sweetbreads.

To Serve: Place sweetbreads and sauce on a hot ovenproof serving dish, sprinkle with ¾ cup of grated Parmesan cheese, dot with 1 tablespoon of butter and brown under the broiler. Serves 6.

BRAISED SWEETBREADS WITH PEA PURÉE

2 pairs large sweetbreads
1 tablespoon lemon juice or vinegar
3 tablespoons butter
3 tablespoons sherry
¼ pound mushrooms, thinly sliced

salt and pepper
½ teaspoon tomato paste
3 teaspoons potato flour
1½ cups stock
1 bay leaf

PEA PURÉE

3 pounds peas or 2 packages frozen peas
2 tablespoons butter

2 tablespoons flour
salt, pepper
3 or 4 tablespoons sour cream

Soak the sweetbreads in cold water for ½ to 1 hour. Drain, put them into a saucepan with cold water to cover, salt and 1 tablespoon lemon juice or vinegar. Bring slowly to a boil and simmer about 5 minutes. Drain again and put into a bowl of iced water for a few minutes. Remove the skin and any sinew. Brown quickly on both sides in 2 tablespoons of hot butter. Heat 3 tablespoons of sherry in a small pan, ignite and pour over the sweetbreads. Remove the sweetbreads from the pan. Melt another tablespoon of butter in the same pan and cook ¼ pound sliced mushrooms quickly for 3 or 4 minutes. Season with salt and pepper. Blend in, off the fire, ½ teaspoon of tomato paste and 3 teaspoons of potato flour. Add 1½ cups of stock and stir over the fire until the mixture comes to a boil. Put back the sweetbreads with a bay leaf and simmer covered for about 15 minutes. In the meantime prepare the pea purée.

Pea Purée: Cook 3 pounds of fresh peas or 2 packages of frozen peas until soft. Drain well and put through a strainer. Melt 2 tablespoons of butter. Stir in 2 tablespoons of flour, salt and pepper, and brown slowly. Add the strained peas and cook until thoroughly heated. Stir in 3 or 4 tablespoons of sour cream.

To Serve: Make a bed of the pea purée on a hot serving dish. Arrange the sweetbreads on top and strain the sauce over all. Serves 4.

ROGNONS DE VEAU FLAMBÉS
(Veal Kidneys with Brandy)

3 veal kidneys	¼ teaspoon dry mustard
3 tablespoons butter	1 cup heavy cream, whipped
¼ cup brandy	salt, pepper
¼ pound mushrooms, sliced	1 tablespoon finely chopped parsley

Remove the fat and membrane from the kidneys and cut them into small 1-inch cubes. Heat 1 tablespoon of butter in a heavy skillet. When it is on the point of turning color, put in the kidneys and brown them quickly all over, shaking the pan often to brown them evenly. Heat ¼ cup of brandy in a small pan, ignite and pour over the kidneys. Remove the kidneys with a slotted spoon.

Melt another 2 tablespoons of butter in the same pan and cook the sliced mushrooms over a moderate fire for about 5 minutes until lightly browned. Stir in ¼ teaspoon of dry mustard, then 1 cup of heavy cream, whipped. Put back the kidneys and season with salt and pepper. Cook just until the kidneys are heated through, since overcooking will make them tough.

Serve in a shallow casserole, sprinkle with a tablespoon of finely chopped parsley. Serves 4 or 5.

ROGNONS DE VEAU GRILLÉS, SAUCE MOUTARDE
(Grilled Veal Kidneys with Mustard Sauce)

4 veal kidneys	1 small clove garlic, crushed
salt	8 slices bacon
freshly cracked black pepper	4 slices thin white bread
1 bunch watercress	

MUSTARD SAUCE

2 egg yolks	salt
½ teaspoon dry mustard	cayenne pepper
½ teaspoon tomato paste	4 tablespoons light cream
1 tablespoon tarragon vinegar	¼ pound butter

Wash kidneys and remove outer membrane. Cut in half length-wise and remove white centers, fat and tubes. Season centers with salt, freshly cracked black pepper and garlic. Reshape, wrap each one with 2 slices of bacon and fasten with toothpicks. Place on a baking sheet and bake in a moderate oven at 350° for 15 minutes. Brown under the broiler for 3 minutes more on each side.

Toast 4 slices of thin white bread, trim off the crusts and ar-range kidneys on toast on a hot serving dish. Garnish with sprigs of fresh watercress and serve the following sauce in a separate bowl.

Mustard Sauce: Put into a small earthenware bowl 2 egg yolks, ½ teaspoon dry mustard, ½ teaspoon tomato paste, 1 tablespoon of tarragon vinegar, salt and a pinch of cayenne pepper. Beat until smooth with a wire whisk. Then beat in 1 tablespoon of light cream. Place the bowl in a skillet of hot water over low heat and beat until the sauce begins to thicken. Beat in ¼ pound butter, bit by bit. Thin slightly with 3 tablespoons of light cream. Serves 4.

VEAL KIDNEY STEW

4 veal kidneys	*3 tablespoons flour*
3 tablespoons butter	*1 cup dry white wine*
2 shallots	*1 cup stock or water*
12 baby white onions	*salt and pepper*
½ pound mushrooms, sliced	*1 tablespoon chopped parsley*

Remove the membrane from the kidneys and cut into small dice. Heat 1 tablespoon of butter in a heavy skillet and when it is just turning color, put in the kidneys and brown them quickly all over. Remove the kidneys. Lower the fire a little and put another 2 tablespoons of butter in the pan. Finely chop 2 shallots and put them into the pan with 12 baby white onions. Cook over a moder-ate fire until the onions are lightly browned, shaking the pan oc-casionally. Add ½ pound of sliced mushrooms and cook another 2 to 3 minutes. Blend in 3 tablespoons of flour, off the fire. Add 1 cup of dry white wine and 1 cup of stock or water and stir over the fire until the mixture comes to a boil. Season with salt and pepper and put back the kidneys. Simmer covered for about 30 minutes.

Serve in a casserole and sprinkle with a tablespoon of finely chopped parsley. Serves 5 or 6.

STUFFED VEAL HEARTS

2 veal hearts	salt, pepper
milk or buttermilk	1 tablespoon chopped parsley
½ pound sausage meat	about 2 tablespoons flour
½ cup finely chopped onion	2 tablespoons butter
½ cup chopped mushroom	1 cup red wine
1 cup soft bread crumbs	1 cup water

Hearts have had a lot of exercise, so they require rather long, moist cooking — in other words, braising — to make them tender. Veal hearts weigh ¾ to 1 pound each and are better than the larger beef hearts because they are not as tough. Wash them well in several changes of water to remove all the blood. Soaking them for an hour in cold milk or buttermilk helps tenderize them. Cut out the veins and arteries, making a pocket for the stuffing.

For the stuffing cook ½ pound of sausage meat until brown and crisp. Remove the meat with a slotted spoon. Sauté ½ cup of finely chopped onion and ½ cup of chopped mushroom slowly in the sausage fat until lightly browned. Blend with 1 cup of soft bread crumbs, the sausage meat, salt, pepper and 1 tablespoon of chopped parsley.

Dry the hearts well and stuff them. Secure the stuffing with skewers and string. Dust the hearts lightly with about 1 tablespoon of flour. Brown quickly on both sides in 1 tablespoon of hot butter. Pour on 1 cup of red wine and 1 cup of water. Cover and simmer until the hearts are tender, about 2 hours.

To Serve: Remove the hearts and cut them into slices crosswise. Arrange them slightly overlapping on a hot serving dish. Thicken the gravy with 1 tablespoon of flour to a smooth paste with 1 tablespoon of butter. Spoon over the heart slices. Serves 4.

TÊTE DE VEAU
(Calf's Head)

1 calf's head	2 cloves
1 large carrot, sliced	2 sprigs dill
1 medium-size onion, sliced	2 cloves garlic
1 slice lemon	1 tablespoon salt
2 bay leaves	12 peppercorns

SAUCE

3 tablespoons butter	2 teaspoons brandy
3 tablespoons flour	2 egg yolks
1½ cups stock, strained	½ cup cream
salt, cayenne	2 tablespoons chopped parsley

triangles of fried bread

Get a skinned calf's head from the butcher and have it split in half, taking care not to split the tongue. Soak in plenty of cold water for several hours, changing the water occasionally. Remove the brains and tongue. Skin the brains and soak in iced water for ½ hour. Put the following ingredients into a large kettle: 4 quarts of water, 1 large sliced carrot, 1 medium-size sliced onion, 1 slice of lemon, 2 bay leaves, 2 cloves, 2 sprigs of dill, 2 cloves of garlic, 1 tablespoon of salt and 12 peppercorns. Bring slowly to a boil and simmer for 10 minutes. Add the calf's head and tongue and simmer for 1½ to 2 hours, until the meat is tender. Remove the head and let the brains simmer for 15 minutes. Meanwhile take all the meat off the head and dice it. Skin the tongue, remove the roots and slice the rest. Dice the brains. Prepare the following sauce.

Melt 3 tablespoons of butter. Blend in, off the fire, 3 tablespoons of flour. Add 1½ cups of the strained stock the head was cooked in and stir over the fire until the mixture comes to a boil. Season with salt and a pinch of cayenne and add 2 teaspoons of brandy. Beat 2 egg yolks lightly with a fork and blend in ½ cup of cream. Add to the sauce and cook until well heated but do not let it boil. Put all the meat into the sauce and 2 tablespoons of chopped parsley and heat well.

Serve in a casserole surrounded with triangles of fried bread. The top may be covered with a few very thin slices of Gruyère cheese. Serves 5 or 6.

Note: Tête de veau is often served with vinaigrette sauce (see page 82). Place the diced meat on a plate and sprinkle well with parsley. Serve the sauce in a separate bowl.

LAMB

In many European countries lamb is the staple meat. Lambs obviously need far less grazing space than beef steers, and they are slaughtered so young that they are an inexpensive meat to raise. But aside from the practical aspects there are other reasons why lamb is so favored. All of the meat on a lamb is good. Because lambs are killed before they are a year old (lambs over a year are called mutton), they do not have time to develop strong, tough muscles. Some cuts may have more bone and cartilage than others, but none of them has tough connective tissues and muscles.

Lamb is marketed at three ages. Baby lamb is the rarest — lamb which has not yet been weaned, very small, very expensive and also rather flavorless. Young lamb which has just started to graze is a great delicacy with a more pronounced and delicious flavor than baby lamb. Young lamb hasn't had time to develop much fat, so care must be taken to add some when cooking it. It should also be well cooked rather than rare or pinkish. It only reaches the markets for a limited time in the spring and because of the price is a treat rather than a regular item on our menus. As is the case with many of the scarce meats, hotels and restaurants buy a large share and not much is left for the general public.

Lamb 3 to 12 months old is what we usually find in the markets. Although technically spring lamb is only 3 to 5 months old, lamb is often called spring lamb regardless of its age or the time of year. Older lambs are naturally larger than young ones and have a stronger flavor.

There is a wide choice of cuts, prices and uses. The most expensive cuts are the loin and rib section, and the leg. In the loin and rib section we get loin lamb chops, which correspond to a T-bone steak in beef, and rib chops. Rib chops are sometimes Frenched — the fat and meat at the end of the bone are trimmed off — giving them a neater appearance although it does take away some good eating. Loin lamb chops have an end piece of meat and fat which is usually rolled around the center part and tied or skewered to keep it in place; a kidney can be enclosed. The famous English mutton chops are a double loin chop with the backbone removed and the kidney left in. Lamb chops are usually broiled and should be cooked so that the outside is brown and crisp, with the inside still a little pink and juicy. Overcooking dries them out and they are not nearly as good. Both the loin and the rib are also roasted whole. The loin is called the saddle and the ribs are prepared as a rack of lamb. They are relatively more expensive to roast than the leg because there is less meat in proportion to bone, but because the meat is so delicious, they are worth the extra cost for special occasions.

The leg lends itself to many uses. The most frequent one is roasting. Legs are sometimes butchered with some of the loin left at the end, which can be cut off and used separately as chops if you wish. The leg can either be roasted whole or part can be roasted and the rest cut up for any of the recipes in the following section using cubed meat — ragout, shashlik, pilaff and so on. The leg is actually the best cut for cubed meat because it is solid meat; the shoulder and breast have more fat and cartilage. But it is also more expensive. The center part of the leg can also be cut into steaks, which are broiled the same as beef steaks and are excellent. So a leg can be a good buy even for a small family, since part of it can be roasted, the center broiled as steaks and the shank end cubed for curry, stew and a number of other uses. Roast leg of lamb is also fine cold, and some recipes using it follow in this lamb section. In America leg of lamb is often roasted until well done, with the meat cooked until it is dark — and often dry and even tough. In France a leg of lamb is served when the inside is still pink or even rare. You may not like it rare, but try it pink and see how much more juicy it will be. Baby and young lamb should be well done, but older or spring lamb is best medium rare.

The moderate-cost cuts are the shoulder, breast, neck and shank. The shoulder has a bone in the middle which makes it awkward to carve if left whole. But the shoulder can be boned and roasted stuffed (using the same recipe as rump of veal on page 89). The whole shoulder includes 5 or 6 chops which can be cut off and broiled the same as rib and loin chops, while the remainder of the shoulder can be cubed for curry, pilaff and so on. The breast has all the breast bones covered with a rather thin layer of tender meat and usually a little fat. It is easy to bone the breast and roast it stuffed, and it can also be cubed. The neck is the cheapest cut of all. Although it has vertebrae running the entire length, the meat is nice and tender and makes a good stew.

In judging lamb the fat should be creamy white, the flesh firm and medium to light red. The whole lamb is covered with a papery sheath called the fell. This is cut off chops but can be left on the leg or removed, as you wish. Some people seem to think it has a disagreeable flavor, but that is a debatable point.

Lambs' liver is mild-flavored and tender, costs less than calves' liver and can replace it in any of the recipes on pages 118–122. The brains and heart are also fine but small and are not often found in retail markets. Therefore the only part of the inside of the lamb that we have recipes for is the kidneys, which are delicious. The outer membrane should be removed; the butcher usually does this, but it is an easy matter to do it yourself. Then cut the kidneys in half lengthwise. There is a white center core which should be removed. Hold the core with your left hand and use a small sharp knife and a sawing motion; the core will come out in a few seconds. Wash the kidneys if you like — it isn't at all necessary. But don't soak them or you will dissipate some of the flavor. To keep them tender and juicy use a high heat, a preheated pan and very little fat. When browning them cook the cut side first to seal in juices, and the whole browning only takes about 2 to 3 minutes. Overcooking makes them tough unless they are cooked for a long time in plenty of liquid as in a steak and kidney pie.

ROAST LEG OF LAMB

1 leg of lamb, 6 to 8 pounds	1 bunch small carrots
2 cloves garlic	1 bunch small white turnips
7 tablespoons butter	salt, pepper
1 cup red wine	2 pounds old potatoes

Loosen the skin from around the bone end of the lamb and push in 2 cloves of garlic. Rub the top with a tablespoon of softened butter. Place in a roasting pan and pour ½ cup of red wine into the pan. Roast in a moderately slow oven at 325° for about 20 minutes to the pound. A meat thermometer will register 170° when the meat is done and it should be slightly pink. Baste every 15 minutes or so, adding an additional tablespoon of wine each time. Meanwhile prepare the following vegetable garnish.

Cut a bunch of small carrots and a bunch of small white turnips into small even shapes. Cook until just tender in boiling salted water, drain and mix in 2 tablespoons of melted butter, salt and pepper. Cut 2 pounds of old potatoes into large olive shapes and sauté until golden brown in 3 tablespoons of hot butter. Or, either whole peeled onions or medium-size potatoes — or both — can be cooked right in the pan with the lamb. You will then need an extra half cup of wine.

To Serve: Remove the lamb from the pan. Rub another tablespoon of butter over the top. Cut as many slices, preferably across the grain, as are needed for one meal and arrange them slightly overlapping on a hot serving dish. Place the uncut piece at one end. Surround the meat with little piles of the cooked vegetables. Pour ½ to 1 cup of water into the roasting pan and bring to a boil to dissolve the glaze. Strain a little of this gravy over the lamb and serve the rest in a gravy bowl. A 6-pound leg of lamb will serve 6 to 8.

CROWN ROAST OF LAMB

1 crown roast of lamb, 12 to 16 ribs	fresh mint
¼ pound salt pork	½ pound mushrooms
salt, pepper	5 to 6 tablespoons butter
3 pounds old potatoes	1 teaspoon lemon juice
2 to 3 pounds peas	½ cup heavy cream

A crown roast of lamb is made of the rack or ribs of lamb. Since a double rib is figured for each serving, 2 racks are joined together for a crown large enough to serve 6 to 8 people. It isn't a cheap cut but is very good and makes an attractive party dish.

Have the butcher prepare the crown. He will remove the chine bones to facilitate carving and trim the meat and fat from the ends of the bones — in other words, French them. The 2 racks are then joined together to form the crown, with the bones on the outside. The center is sometimes filled with a meat or bread crumbs stuffing, but it adds nothing to this excellent meat and so is not recommended. Tie a piece of salt pork on the tip of each rib to prevent the bone from charring. Season the meat with salt and pepper. Place in a roasting pan and roast in a moderate oven at 325° for 1¼ to 1½ hours. Meanwhile prepare the following vegetable garnish.

Potatoes and Peas: Peel 3 pounds of old potatoes and cut them into small balls with a potato baller. Cook until just tender in boiling salted water. Drain and dry over a slow fire for a minute or so. Cook 2 to 3 pounds of peas in boiling unsalted water with 2 or 3 sprigs of fresh mint. Drain. Sauté ½ pound of sliced mushrooms in 2 tablespoons of butter with salt, pepper and 1 teaspoon of lemon juice; use a gentle fire and cook only until lightly browned. Combine the potatoes, peas, mushrooms and 3 to 4 tablespoons of melted butter. Season, add ½ cup of heavy cream and cook over a slow fire until thoroughly heated.

To Serve: Place the lamb on a hot serving dish. Remove the salt pork and cover each rib with a paper frill. Fill the center of the crown with the vegetables. Allow a double rib for each serving. Serves 6 to 8.

SADDLE OF LAMB

1 saddle of lamb, about 8 pounds	2 small onions
salt, pepper	1 clove garlic
1 cup water or ½ cup water and ½ cup rosé wine	sprig parsley and thyme
1 pound dried marrow beans	¼ pound butter
	2 to 3 tablespoons chopped parsley

Have the butcher prepare a saddle of lamb. The saddle consists of the loin and sometimes part of the leg. To facilitate carving, it is best to have it boned. Also any excess fat should be trimmed off and the whole saddle tied neatly with string. A saddle weighs about 8 pounds before it is trimmed. Find out what the trimmed weight is in order to gauge the cooking time. Place on a rack in a roasting pan and roast in a moderate oven at 350° for about 15 to 18 minutes to the pound, or until a meat thermometer registers 170°. Season with salt and pepper after it has cooked ½ hour.

Marrow Beans: Soak 1 pound of dried white marrow beans in plenty of cold water for 8 hours or overnight. Drain. Put into a large saucepan with 3 quarts of cold water and bring slowly to a boil. Add 2 small white onions, 1 clove of garlic, salt and a sprig of parsley and thyme. Simmer until the beans are tender, about 2 to 2½ hours. Drain and blend with ¼ pound of melted butter and 2 to 3 tablespoons of chopped parsley.

To Serve: Place the lamb on a hot serving dish. Add 1 cup of water or ½ cup of water and ½ cup of rosé wine to the juices in the pan and bring to a boil. Serve the gravy in a separate gravy bowl and also serve the beans separately. Serves 6 to 8.

RACK OF LAMB BOULANGÈRE
(Rack of Lamb with Vegetable Garnish)

1 small rack of lamb, with	*1½ cups stock*
6 to 8 chops	*salt, pepper*
6 tablespoons butter	*12 small white onions*
3 teaspoons potato flour	*¼ pound mushrooms, quartered*
1 teaspoon tomato paste	*1 cup each cooked peas, baby lima*
1 teaspoon meat glaze	*beans and Frenched green beans*

Trim the ends of the rib bones, leaving about 2 inches of the bone free from meat and fat. Place the lamb in a baking pan and dot the top with 2 tablespoons of butter. Broil until the lamb is very well browned and the bones charred, turning once to brown both sides. This will take about 30 minutes in all; the outside should be well cooked and the inside still pink and juicy.

Meanwhile make a brown sauce. Melt 2 tablespoons of butter in a small saucepan. Blend in, off the fire, 3 teaspoons of potato flour, 1 teaspoon of tomato paste and 1 teaspoon of meat glaze. Pour on 1½ cups of stock and stir over the fire until the mixture comes to a boil. Season with salt and pepper and simmer for a few minutes. Brown 12 small white onions slowly in 2 tablespoons of butter. Add ¼ pound of quartered mushrooms and cook another 2 to 3 minutes. Pour the brown sauce over the onions and mushrooms and let simmer until ready to use.

To Serve: Place the lamb on a hot serving dish. Spoon some of the sauce over the meat and pour the rest around it. Put cutlet frills on the ends of the bones. Surround the lamb with small mounds of cooked peas, baby lima beans and Frenched green beans. Allow 1 to 2 ribs for each serving.

STUFFED LEG OF LAMB

1 leg of lamb, 6 to 7 pounds
2 thin slices white bread
½ cup light cream
½ pound mushrooms, chopped
1 small onion, finely chopped
4 tablespoons butter
½ pound smoked ham, ground
¼ pound lean veal, ground
1 egg
½ teaspoon grated lemon rind
about ¼ teaspoon grated nutmeg
salt, pepper
1 tablespoon tomato paste
1 cup dry white wine
watercress or parsley

Have the butcher bone the lamb neatly, leaving the last 2 inches or so of the shank bone in. Soak 2 thin slices of white bread in ½ cup of light cream in a large mixing bowl. Sauté ½ pound of chopped mushrooms and 1 small finely chopped onion in 2 tablespoons of butter until lightly browned. Add to the soaked bread the ground ham and veal, 1 egg, ½ teaspoon of grated lemon rind, about ¼ teaspoon of grated nutmeg, salt and pepper, and the sautéed mushrooms and onion. Blend until thoroughly mixed. Fill the lamb and secure the opening with skewers and string.

Place the lamb on a rack in a roasting pan. Spread the top with 2 tablespoons of softened butter. Mix 1 tablespoon of tomato paste with 1 cup of dry white wine and pour into the pan. Roast uncovered in a moderate oven at 350° for about 45 minutes to the pound, or until a meat thermometer registers 185°. (Boned meat takes longer to cook than meat with the bone in.) Baste occasionally with the pan juices.

To Serve: Place the lamb on a hot serving dish and garnish with parsley or watercress. Add 1 cup of water to the pan juices, bring to a boil and serve in a separate gravy bowl. Serves 6 to 8.

BROILED LEG OF LAMB

1 leg of lamb, 6 to 8 pounds
1 medium-size onion, sliced
1 carrot, sliced
about ¼ teaspoon dried oregano

½ cup olive oil
1 cup red wine vinegar
few peppercorns
1 small clove garlic, optional

Broiled leg of lamb is delicious with a good browned crust on the outside and the meat slightly pink and very juicy inside.

The whole leg can be broiled, or the lower part of the leg can be cut into cubes for shashlik (see following recipe), and the rest broiled. The lamb must be boned, which either you or the butcher can do. Then place it in a large mixing bowl and add the following marinade. Sprinkle 1 medium-size sliced onion, a sliced carrot and ¼ teaspoon of dried oregano over the lamb. Blend together ½ cup of olive oil and 1 cup of red wine vinegar and pour over the meat. Add a few peppercorns and a clove of garlic if you wish. Let the meat stand in the marinade in a cool place for several hours or overnight, turning it occasionally.

Preheat the broiling unit and pan. Remove the meat from the marinade but do not dry it. Spread it out flat and put it in the hot broiler pan about 2½ to 3 inches away from the fire. Broil for just 20 minutes on each side. When you turn the meat after the first 20 minutes, brush a little of the marinade over the cooked part and season it with salt.

Serve on a hot platter. Garnish with scooped-out tomato halves filled with peas which have been cooked with a little mint. A whole leg of lamb will serve 7 or 8 people. If part is used for shashlik, the rest will serve 4 people.

Note: The remaining marinade may be used for shashlik.

SHASHLIK

1½ pounds leg or shoulder of
  lamb
about ½ pound lean bacon
4 lamb kidneys
8 chicken livers
1 large yellow onion
1 green pepper

2 tomatoes
12 small mushroom caps
salt
freshly cracked black pepper
1 small clove garlic, crushed
1 to 2 tablespoons butter
3 tablespoons brandy

PILAFF

½ cup white raisins
¼ cup white wine
2 tablespoons butter
¾ cup pine nuts

1½ cups rice
3 cups stock
salt, pepper

Cut the lamb into cubes about 1 inch square. Shoulder lamb
should be marinated for several hours, since marinating helps
tenderize meat (see preceding recipe for marinade). Although
leg of lamb does not need marinating, it will give it a delicious
flavor.

Cut the bacon in half crosswise — you will need about ½
pound. Cut the kidneys in half and remove the center white
core. Wrap each half kidney, 8 chicken livers and each piece of
lamb in half a slice of bacon. Peel and quarter a large yellow
onion and separate into sections. Core and seed a green pepper
and cut into eighths. Peel and quarter 2 tomatoes. Lightly sauté
12 small mushroom caps. Thread all these ingredients on shashlik
sticks alternating a piece of meat with a vegetable. Season with
salt and freshly cracked black pepper and rub with a small clove
of crushed garlic and 1 to 2 tablespoons of softened butter.
Place on a cookie sheet and broil until well browned, turning
once to brown both sides. The total cooking time will be about
8 to 10 minutes.

Pilaff: Soak ½ cup of white raisins in ¼ cup of white wine
about 10 minutes. Heat 2 tablespoons of butter in a medium-size
skillet. Add 1½ cups of rice and stir over a slow fire for 2 to 3
minutes. Add 3 cups of stock, the raisins and wine, salt and pepper.

Bring to a boil. Cover and cook without stirring for 20 minutes. Add ¾ cup of pine nuts and cook another 5 minutes or so. Just before serving blend in all the pan juices from the shashlik.

To Serve: Make a bed of rice pilaff on a hot serving dish. Slide the shashlik gently off the skewers on top of the rice. Heat 3 tablespoons of brandy in a small pan, ignite, pour over all and serve flaming. Serves 4.

LAMB STEW

2 *pounds boned shoulder of lamb*	3 *tablespoons flour*
or 3 pounds breast or neck	6 *cups of water*
3 *to 4 tablespoons butter*	*salt, pepper*
18 *baby white onions*	2 *tomatoes*
12 *small pieces carrot*	18 *small potatoes*
12 *small pieces turnip*	1 *pound peas*
1 *to 2 teaspoons chopped parsley*	

Cut the lamb into neat 1-inch squares. The breast and neck have a rather high proportion of bone, which is why you need more of these cuts; the bone adds flavor so is no disadvantage. Heat 1 tablespoon of butter in a deep heavy saucepan. When it is on the point of turning color, quickly brown the lamb all over, adding more butter if necessary. When it is all browned remove it from the pan. Put another 2 tablespoons of butter in the same pan and slowly brown 18 baby white onions, 12 small pieces of carrot and 12 small pieces of turnip. Remove them from the pan. Put back the lamb and sprinkle it with 3 tablespoons of flour. Add 6 cups of water, salt and pepper, and 2 skinned diced tomatoes. Bring slowly to a boil. Cover and simmer for 1½ hours. Add the browned onions, carrots and turnips, and 18 small peeled potatoes. Cook uncovered until the potatoes are tender, another 30 minutes or so. When the potatoes have cooked for 20 minutes add 1 pound of peas. The stew is done when the meat is easily pierced with a fork.

To Serve: Put the stew into a large, shallow, ovenproof serving dish and brown it under the broiler. (This isn't essential but does give it an appetizing flavor and appearance.) Sprinkle with 1 to 2 teaspoons of chopped parsley. Serves 4 to 6.

LAMB WITH ROQUEFORT TOPPING

2½ pounds breast of lamb, boned and rolled
6 slices bacon
5 tablespoons butter
3 tablespoons sherry
1 small clove garlic, crushed
1 teaspoon tomato paste
1 teaspoon meat glaze
2 teaspoons potato flour

1½ cups stock
salt, pepper
1 bay leaf
6 tomatoes
1 tablespoon finely chopped chives
½ pound Roquefort cheese
¼ teaspoon dry mustard
6 sautéed mushroom caps

Wrap 6 slices of bacon around the rolled breast of lamb and tie each piece with string. Cut into slices between the slices of bacon. Heat 1 tablespoon of butter in a heavy skillet and quickly brown the lamb on both sides. Heat 3 tablespoons of sherry in a small pan, ignite and pour over the meat. Remove the meat from the pan. If there are more than 2 tablespoons of fat in the pan, remove the extra amount. Blend into the pan juices 1 small clove of crushed garlic, 1 teaspoon of tomato paste, 1 teaspoon of meat glaze and 2 teaspoons of potato flour. Pour on 1½ cups of stock and stir over the fire until the mixture comes to a boil. Season with salt, pepper and a bay leaf. Put back the lamb, cover with waxed paper and a lid, and simmer for 45 to 50 minutes, until the lamb is tender.

Broiled Tomatoes: Sprinkle 6 halved tomatoes with 1 tablespoon of finely chopped chives, dot with 2 tablespoons of butter and broil until nicely browned.

Roquefort Topping: Blend thoroughly together, preferably in an electric mixer, ½ pound of Roquefort cheese, 2 tablespoons of softened butter, ¼ teaspoon of dry mustard and a little salt.

To Serve: Place the lamb in the center of a hot serving dish and spoon the sauce around it. Pipe a mound of the Roquefort topping on each piece and top with a sautéed mushroom cap. Garnish with broiled tomatoes. Serves 6.

LAMB CURRY

2 *pounds boned and rolled shoulder of lamb*	4 *tablespoons flour*
6 *tablespoons butter*	1 *tablespoon tomato paste*
2 *cloves garlic, crushed*	1 *teaspoon meat glaze*
salt	2 *cups stock*
freshly cracked black pepper	*juice of 1 orange*
1 *cup water*	*juice of ½ lemon*
2 *tablespoons salad oil*	¼ *cup coconut milk*
1 *cup finely sliced mixed onion, carrot, celery*	1 *tablespoon red currant jelly*
1 *apple, sliced with skin on*	3 *tablespoons shredded coconut*
4 *to 5 tablespoons curry powder*	2 *cardamon seeds, crushed*
	salt, pepper
2 *cups rice, boiled*	

Remove most of the fat from the lamb and cut it into ¾-inch squares. Heat 2 tablespoons of butter in a heavy skillet. Add 2 cloves of crushed garlic and cook for 1 minute. Then quickly brown the meat all over. Season with salt and freshly cracked black pepper. Add 1 cup of water and simmer covered until the lamb is tender, about 1 to 1¼ hours.

Meanwhile prepare the sauce. Heat 4 tablespoons of butter and 2 tablespoons of salad oil in a deep heavy saucepan. Add 1 cup of sliced mixed onion, carrot and celery, and an apple sliced with the skin on. Cook slowly for 5 minutes. Add 4 to 5 tablespoons of a good curry powder and cook another 10 minutes. Blend in, off the fire, 4 tablespoons of flour, 1 tablespoon of tomato paste and 1 teaspoon of meat glaze. Pour on 2 cups of stock and stir over a slow fire until the mixture comes to a boil. Add the juice of 1 orange, juice of ½ lemon, ¼ cup of coconut milk, 1 tablespoon of red currant jelly, 3 tablespoons of shredded coconut and 2 crushed cardamon seeds. Season with salt and pepper. Simmer for 35 to 40 minutes, then put through a strainer. Reheat in a double boiler until ready to use.

When the lamb is cooked add it to the sauce with any pan juices.

To Serve: Fill a lightly greased ring mold with boiled rice, press down gently with a fork and turn out on a hot serving dish. Fill the center with the curry. Serve condiments separately in little individual bowls on a tray. Use several or all of the following condiments: 1 finely diced green pepper, 3 finely chopped hard-boiled egg whites, 3 finely chopped hard-boiled egg yolks, 1 cup of chutney, 1 ripe avocado pear diced and mixed with ½ cup diced sautéed bacon, 1 finely chopped yellow onion mixed with bacon fat and cayenne, ½ cup chopped parsley, ½ cup black raisins, ½ cup white raisins, 1 cup shredded coconut, ½ cup ground peanuts. Serves 4 to 6.

LAMB PILAFF

1½ pounds shoulder or leg of lamb, cubed	*3 cups water*
	salt, pepper
3 tablespoons butter	*¼ teaspoon dried oregano*
1 large yellow onion	*2 tablespoons chopped parsley*
1½ cups raw rice	*1 lemon*

Cut the lamb into small ¾-inch cubes. Heat 1 tablespoon of butter in a heavy casserole. When it is just turning color, quickly brown the lamb all over. Have only a single layer of meat in the pan at one time, and you will need an additional tablespoon of butter to brown it all. Remove the meat from the pan. Put the remaining tablespoon of butter into the pan. Thinly slice a large yellow onion and cook it over a moderate fire until golden brown. Add 1½ cups of raw rice (it need not be washed) and stir over the fire for about 2 minutes. Pour on 3 cups of water; there will be enough glaze in the pan to flavor and color the water so that stock is not needed. Season with salt, pepper and

¼ teaspoon of dried oregano. Put the meat back into the pan. Cover and cook in a moderate oven at 350° for 1 hour.

Serve in the casserole and sprinkle 2 tablespoons of finely chopped parsley over the top. Serve lemon wedges separately. Serves 4 to 6.

LAMB RAGOUT

2 *pounds boned and rolled shoulder of lamb*	½ *pound green beans*
5 *tablespoons butter*	1 *teaspoon tomato paste*
2 *tablespoons brandy*	1 *teaspoon meat glaze*
1 *bunch of carrots*	3 *tablespoons flour*
1 *pound white turnips*	½ *cup red wine or sherry*
1 *pound baby white onions*	1 *cup stock*
½ *pound mushrooms, quartered*	*salt, pepper*
1 *pound peas*	2 *tomatoes*
	2 *tablespoons chopped chives*

Cut the meat into 1-inch squares. Heat 2 tablespoons of butter in a heavy deep saucepan and brown the meat quickly on all sides. Heat 2 tablespoons of brandy in a small pan, ignite and pour over the meat. Remove the meat from the pan. Cut the carrots and turnips into small olive shapes. Put another 2 tablespoons of butter in the pan, then the carrots, turnips and baby onions. Brown them quickly. Add ½ pound of quartered mushrooms, 1 pound of peas and ½ pound of Frenched green beans and cook 2 to 3 minutes. Melt the remaining tablespoon of butter in the pan. Blend in, off the fire, 1 teaspoon of tomato paste, 1 teaspoon of meat glaze and 3 tablespoons of flour. Pour on ½ cup of red wine or sherry and 1 cup of stock and stir over the fire until the mixture comes to a boil. Put back the lamb and season with salt and pepper. Cover and simmer for about an hour, or until the lamb is tender. At the end of the cooking period add 2 peeled and sliced tomatoes.

Serve in a casserole and sprinkle with 2 tablespoons of finely chopped chives. Serves 4 to 6.

Note: This dish can be cooked and served in the same casserole if it is the type — such as a copper or enamel-glazed cast-iron casserole — that is suitable for both top-of-the-stove cooking and for serving.

CASSOULET
(Ragout of Beans with Pork and Lamb)

2 pounds dried white beans	salt
1 small onion, stuck with 1 clove	¾ pound fresh pork rind
	½ pound lean salt pork
3 cloves garlic	1 pound link sausage
bouquet garni (parsley, thyme, bay leaf)	2 pounds boned shoulder of lamb

Cassoulet is an economical dish, combining beans with a variety of meats. Various meats may be used and goose may be one of them if you have some cooked goose on hand.

Soak 2 pounds of dried white beans in cold water to cover for several hours or overnight. Drain. Put into a large saucepan with 4 quarts of cold water and bring slowly to a boil. Add a small white onion which has been stuck with 1 clove, 3 cloves of garlic, a bouquet garni consisting of a sprig of parsley and thyme and a bay leaf, salt, ¾ pound of fresh pork rind and ½ pound of lean salt pork. Simmer for 1½ hours.

Meanwhile cook 1 pound of link sausage until brown and crisp. Remove the sausage from the pan. Cut 2 pounds of boned shoulder of lamb into 1-inch cubes and brown them in the sausage fat. Pour on 2 cups of the bean liquid and simmer until the lamb is tender, about 1 hour.

Drain the beans, reserving the liquid. Cut the pork rind and salt pork into small ½-inch cubes. Slice the sausage. Put one third of the beans into a large earthenware casserole. Cover with half the meat — sausage, lamb, pork rind and salt pork. Repeat these layers once and top with the remaining beans. Pour on the lamb juice and enough bean stock to cover the beans. Bake covered in a slow oven at 300° for 1 to 2 hours, adding more bean stock if necessary to keep the beans covered.

Serve in the casserole. Serves 10 to 12.

SWEDISH LAMB WITH DILL SAUCE

2 to 2½ pounds breast or shoulder of lamb	*few peppercorns*
1 tablespoon salt	*1 bay leaf*
	fresh dill

DILL SAUCE

3 tablespoons butter	*1 to 2 teaspoons sugar*
4 tablespoons flour	*2 tablespoons finely chopped dill*
2 cups stock	
1½ tablespoons vinegar	*1 egg yolk*

If breast of lamb is used, have it boned and then cut into 1½ to 2-inch squares. Shoulder of lamb should be cubed. Place the meat in a deep heavy saucepan and add about 1 quart of cold water, just enough to barely cover the meat. Bring slowly to a boil and skim. Season with 1 tablespoon of salt, a few peppercorns, 1 bay leaf and 2 or 3 sprigs of dill. Cover and simmer for 1¼ to 1½ hours, until the lamb is tender. Strain off 2 cups of the stock and keep the lamb warm in the remaining stock while the sauce is prepared.

Dill Sauce: Melt 3 tablespoons of butter. Blend in 4 tablespoons of flour, off the fire. Pour on 2 cups of lamb stock and stir over the fire until the mixture comes to a boil. Add 1½ tablespoons of vinegar, 1 to 2 teaspoons of sugar and 2 tablespoons of finely chopped dill; simmer for 5 minutes or so. Slightly beat 1 egg yolk. Blend it with a little of the sauce, then add to the sauce and stir well; do not let the sauce boil after the egg yolk has been added.

To Serve: Drain the lamb thoroughly and place on a hot serving dish. Cover with the sauce and garnish with a few sprigs of fresh dill. Serve with plainly boiled potatoes. Serves 4 to 6.

ROAST STUFFED BREAST OF LAMB

1 piece breast of lamb, about 2 pounds	2 tablespoons bread crumbs
salt, pepper	½ large yellow onion, chopped
1 clove garlic, crushed	6 to 8 slices bacon
1 slice calves' liver	½ cup red wine
3 tablespoons butter	3 teaspoons potato flour
½ pound sausage meat	½ teaspoon tomato paste
	1 teaspoon meat glaze
1½ cups stock	

Have the butcher bone the lamb or do it yourself with a sharp knife. To enlarge the surface for stuffing, cut the lamb in half horizontally but do not cut right through one end and be careful not to break the skin. Season with salt, pepper and a clove of crushed garlic. Prepare the following stuffing. Sauté a slice of calves' liver quickly on both sides in 1 tablespoon of very hot butter. Remove and chop. Blend together the chopped liver, ½ pound of sausage meat, 2 tablespoons of bread crumbs and half a finely chopped large yellow onion. Spread the stuffing evenly on the lamb, leaving a 1-inch margin around the edge. Roll up the meat lengthwise. Cover with 6 to 8 strips of bacon and tie with string at 2-inch intervals. Place in a baking pan with ½ cup of red wine. Bake for 1 to 1¼ hours in a moderate oven at 350° and baste every 15 minutes.

When the meat has cooked about ½ hour, make a brown sauce. Melt 2 tablespoons of butter. Blend in, off the fire, 3 teaspoons of potato flour, ½ teaspoon of tomato paste and 1 teaspoon of meat glaze. Pour on 1½ cups of stock and stir over the fire until the sauce comes to a boil. Season and simmer until ready to use.

To Serve: Remove lamb, cut off strings and cut as many slices as will be needed for one meal. Arrange slices overlapping on a hot flat serving dish, with the uncut piece at one end. Strain pan juices into the brown sauce and spoon this over the meat. Garnish with cooked vegetables such as peas, green beans, zucchini, carrots, broiled tomatoes and sautéed potato balls. Serves 4.

LAMB CHOPS WITH WHITE WINE

4 shoulder lamb chops
3 tablespoons butter
2 medium-size yellow onions,
   thinly sliced
¼ pound mushrooms, sliced

2 tablespoons flour
1 teaspoon tomato paste
½ cup dry white wine
¾ cup water
salt
freshly cracked black pepper

Heat a heavy skillet. Put in 1 tablespoon of butter and when it just starts turning color, brown the chops quickly on both sides. Peel and thinly slice 2 medium-size yellow onions and cut ½ pound of mushrooms into rather thick slices. Melt 2 tablespoons of butter in a heavy casserole and sauté the onions and mushrooms over a medium fire until lightly browned. Blend in 2 tablespoons of flour and 1 teaspoon of tomato paste, off the fire. Add ½ cup of dry white wine and ¾ cup of water and stir over the fire until the mixture comes to a boil. Season with salt and freshly cracked black pepper. Put the browned chops into this sauce. (Ordinarily the sauce would be made in the pan the chops were browned in, but as the chops brown, some of the lamb fat is tried out, and this would add a rather unpleasant taste to the sauce.) Cover and simmer for about 40 minutes, until the chops are tender.

Serve in the casserole. This is a good dish for informal entertaining since it can wait almost indefinitely over a simmering heat. Serves 4.

STUFFED LAMB CHOPS

6 thick loin lamb chops
½ cup ground raw bacon
1 egg white, unbeaten
¾ cup light cream
salt, pepper
2 cloves garlic
6 tablespoons butter
1 teaspoon meat glaze

½ teaspoon tomato paste
3 teaspoons potato flour
1½ cups stock
¼ cup dry white wine
6 slices bread
3 large tomatoes
1 large yellow onion
½ cup grated Parmesan cheese

Bone the chops and make an incision in the center of each one where the bone was forming a pocket. Fill the pockets with the following stuffing. Put ½ cup of raw ground bacon into a bowl and beat in 1 egg white. Slowly beat in ¾ cup of light cream, preferably in an electric mixer. Season with salt and pepper. Secure the filling with a toothpick or small skewer. Make 2 or 3 small incisions in the tops and insert slices of garlic.

Heat a large skillet. Put in 1 tablespoon of butter and when it is just turning color, quickly brown the chops on both sides. Remove the chops from the pan. Add another tablespoon of butter to the pan. Blend in, off the fire, 1 teaspoon of meat glaze, ½ teaspoon of tomato paste and 3 teaspoons of potato flour. Add 1½ cups of stock and ¼ cup of dry white wine and stir over the fire until the sauce comes to a boil. Taste for seasoning. Put back the chops, cover and simmer for 20 to 30 minutes, until the chops are tender.

Cut 6 rounds of white bread and fry them in 2 tablespoons of hot butter until golden brown on each side.

Broiled Tomatoes: Cut 3 tomatoes in half. Top each half with a thin slice of onion, a tablespoon of grated Parmesan cheese, 1 teaspoon of butter, salt and pepper. Broil until nicely browned.

To Serve: Arrange the rounds of bread on a hot serving dish. Place the lamb chops on top and strain the sauce over the meat. Surround the chops with broiled tomatoes. Serves 6.

BROILED LOIN LAMB CHOPS

4 large loin lamb chops with kidney	about 1 cup bread crumbs
	salt, pepper
4 large firm tomatoes	3 tablespoons butter
½ pound sausage meat	8 large mushrooms
1 small onion, finely chopped	¼ pound cooked ham, ground
6 chicken livers	fresh watercress or parsley

Have 4 loin lamb chops cut about 1¼ inches thick and rolled around a lamb kidney. Broil for 6 minutes on one side. Turn over. Place the following stuffed tomatoes and stuffed mushrooms on a shallow baking dish and put them under the broiler while the chops cook another 6 minutes. Watch the tomatoes and mush-rooms since they may brown before the chops are done.

Stuffed Tomatoes: Cut the tops off 4 large firm tomatoes and scoop out the inside pulp with a spoon. Put ½ pound of sausage meat into a skillet, break it apart with a fork and cook until well browned. Remove the sausage meat with a slotted spoon and sauté a small finely chopped onion in the sausage fat. Remove the onion, turn up the heat and quickly brown 6 chicken livers. Take them out of the pan and chop them. Blend together the cooked sausage, onion, half the chicken livers and ½ cup of bread crumbs. Season lightly and fill the tomatoes. Sprinkle the tops with about ¼ cup of bread crumbs and dot with 1 tablespoon of butter.

Stuffed Mushrooms: Remove the stems from 8 large mushrooms and finely chop these stems. Sauté the caps and stems. Blend to-gether ¼ pound of ground ham, the rest of the chicken livers and the sautéed stems. Fill the caps, sprinkle with bread crumbs and dot with 1 tablespoon of butter.

To Serve: Arrange the chops on a hot serving dish. Brush them with melted butter and season with salt and pepper. Place the stuffed tomatoes and mushrooms alternately around them and garnish with watercress or parsley. Serves 4.

LAMB CHOPS IN WINE

4 *thick loin chops*	½ *cup water*
3 *tablespoons butter*	½ *pound mushrooms, sliced*
8 *baby white onions*	½ *cup white wine*
8 *small pieces of carrot*	*salt, pepper*
	few drops lemon juice

Heat 1 tablespoon of butter in a large skillet and when it is on the point of turning color, brown the chops on both sides. Remove the chops. Melt another 2 tablespoons of butter in the pan and brown 8 baby white onions and 8 small olive-shaped pieces of carrot over a moderate fire, shaking the pan often to brown them evenly. Lift the glaze with ½ cup of water. Put back the chops with ½ pound of sliced mushrooms, ½ cup of white wine, salt and pepper. Cover and simmer for 30 minutes. Just before serving sprinkle with a few drops of lemon juice.

To Serve: Make a bed of the vegetables and sauce on a hot serving dish. Arrange the chops down the center of the dish. Serves 4.

LOIN LAMB CHOPS WITH SHERRY SAUCE

4 loin lamb chops, about 1 inch thick	salt, pepper
7 tablespoons butter	2 tablespoons white wine
3 tablespoons sherry	1 small cauliflower
½ teaspoon tomato paste	½ cup bread crumbs
1 teaspoon meat glaze	¾ cup grated Parmesan cheese
3 teaspoons potato flour	8 large mushroom caps
1½ cups stock	8 small mushroom caps
1 bay leaf	3 ounces cream cheese
	1 teaspoon finely chopped chives

Brown the chops quickly on each side in 2 tablespoons of hot butter. Heat 3 tablespoons of sherry in a small pan, ignite and pour over the meat. Remove the lamb from the pan. Put another tablespoon of butter in the pan. Blend in, off the fire, ½ teaspoon of tomato paste, 1 teaspoon of meat glaze and 3 teaspoons of potato flour. Add 1½ cups of stock and stir over the fire until the mixture comes to a boil. Return the lamb to the pan with a bay leaf, salt and pepper, and 2 tablespoons of white wine. Cover and simmer for 20 to 25 minutes, until the meat is tender.

Meanwhile prepare the following vegetable garnish.

Cauliflower: Separate a small cauliflower into flowerets and cook in a small amount of boiling salted water until tender. Drain and dry on a cloth. Sprinkle with ½ cup of bread crumbs and ¾ cup of grated Parmesan cheese, dot with 1 tablespoon of butter and brown under the broiler.

Stuffed Mushrooms: Sauté 8 large and 8 small mushroom caps. Mix together thoroughly 3 ounces of cream cheese and 3 tablespoons of softened butter, preferably with an electric mixer.

Season with a little pepper and blend in 1 teaspoon of finely chopped chives. Put into a pastry bag with a small plain tube and fill the stem end of the large mushroom caps. Top with the small mushroom caps.

To Serve: Arrange chops on a hot serving dish and pour over the sauce. Garnish with mushrooms placed alternately with the cauliflower flowerets around the platter. Serves 4.

CÔTELETTES D'AGNEAU NELSON
(Lamb Chops with Onion Purée)

6 large rib lamb chops	6 small mushrooms
4 large yellow onions	12 large mushroom caps
1 cup milk	1 teaspoon meat glaze
salt, pepper	½ teaspoon tomato paste
5 tablespoons butter	3 teaspoons potato flour
1 egg white	1 cup stock
½ cup dry bread crumbs	½ cup red wine
½ cup grated Parmesan cheese	2 tablespoons brandy

Brown the chops quickly on both sides under the broiler. Place them on a baking dish. Cover the tops with the following soubise (onion purée). Peel and slice 4 large yellow onions and cook until very soft in 1 cup of seasoned milk. Drain and put through a fine strainer. Melt 1 tablespoon of butter in a small saucepan, add the onion purée and cook slowly until it is reduced and thick. Blend in 1 unbeaten egg white, then ½ cup of bread crumbs. Season. Place on top of the chops and dome with a spoon. Sprinkle with ½ cup of grated Parmesan cheese and dot with 1 tablespoon of butter. Bake in a moderate oven at 350° for 25 minutes or until nicely browned.

Meanwhile prepare the mushrooms and the sauce. Chop 6 small mushrooms finely and sauté in 1 tablespoon of hot butter. Remove them with a slotted spoon. Put another tablespoon of butter in the pan and sauté 12 large mushroom caps. Fill the center of the caps with the cooked chopped mushrooms and keep warm.

Sauce: Melt another tablespoon of butter in the pan the mushrooms were cooked in. Blend in, off the fire, 1 teaspoon of meat glaze, ½ teaspoon of tomato paste and 3 teaspoons of potato flour. Pour on 1 cup of stock and ½ cup of red wine and stir over the fire until the mixture comes to a boil. Let simmer a few minutes. Just before serving add 2 tablespoons of brandy.

To Serve: Cover the bottom of a hot serving dish, preferably a round one, with the sauce. Arrange the chops in the form of a crown on top of the sauce. Surround them with the stuffed mushrooms. If the chops have been Frenched (trimmed), cover the end bones with cutlet frills, which are usually obtainable from your butcher. Serves 6.

CÔTELETTES D'AGNEAU EN PAPILLOTES
(Lamb Cutlets in Parchment Paper)

4 thick loin lamb chops	*1 teaspoon meat glaze*
½ pound mushrooms, sliced	*1 cup stock*
4 tablespoons butter	*½ cup Madeira*
4 or 8 thin slices cooked ham	*salt, pepper*
2 teaspoons potato flour	*1 teaspoon red currant jelly*
1 teaspoon tomato paste	*1 tablespoon chopped truffle*

Cut 4 pieces of parchment paper about 10 inches square. Bone 4 thick loin lamb chops and put a skewer in each one to hold in place. Broil about 5 minutes on each side, until well browned and almost done. Sauté ½ pound of sliced mushrooms in 2 tablespoons of butter. Brush the center of each piece of paper with a little softened butter. Spread a thin layer of mushrooms about the size of the chops over the butter. Cover the mushrooms with a thin piece of ham — if it is regular boiled ham, cut each slice in half; if you are using a ham you have on hand, cut the slices approximately the same size as the chops. Place the chops on the ham and cover them with a few mushrooms and another piece of ham. Fold the parchment around the chops. Place on a cookie sheet and bake in a hot oven at 425° about 10 minutes, until the paper is dark brown. Meanwhile make the sauce.

Melt another tablespoon of butter in the pan the mushrooms were cooked in. Blend in, off the fire, 2 teaspoons of potato flour, 1 teaspoon of tomato paste and 1 teaspoon of meat glaze. Pour on

1 cup of stock and ½ cup of Madeira and stir over the fire until the sauce comes to a boil. Season with salt and pepper and add 1 teaspoon of red currant jelly and 1 tablespoon of finely chopped truffle. Simmer until ready to use.

Serve the chops in the parchment paper on a hot serving dish on a starched napkin, with the sauce in a separate bowl. Serves 4.

ENGLISH MIXED GRILL

4 thick loin lamb chops, with kidney	4 tomatoes
salt, pepper	8 thick slices onion
8 sausages	2 to 3 tablespoons butter
	8 large mushroom caps
8 slices bacon	

Place the chops on a preheated broiler rack. Have the rack 3 inches or so from the broiler flame and broil them about 10 minutes on one side. Turn them, season with salt and pepper, and broil for another ten minutes on the second side. When they start cooking prepare the rest of the ingredients.

Put 8 sausages in a shallow skillet with an inch of water, bring to a boil, simmer for 5 minutes and drain. Core and halve 4 tomatoes and top each half with a thick slice of onion, salt and pepper, and dot with 1 to 2 tablespoons of butter. Brush 8 large mushroom caps with 1 tablespoon of melted butter. Put the sausages, tomatoes, mushrooms and 8 slices of bacon in a shallow baking pan. Put into the broiler with the chops when you turn them. Broil until nicely browned, turning the bacon and sausages once.

Serve on a hot platter or on hot plates. If you add some shoe-string potatoes, you have a whole quickly prepared meal. Serves 4.

BRAISED LAMB SHANKS

4 lamb shanks, about 1 pound each	2 tablespoons olive oil
3 tablespoons flour	1 large onion, thinly sliced
salt, pepper	¾ cup red wine
paprika	1¼ cups water
2 tablespoons butter	¼ teaspoon chopped fresh rosemary

Lamb shanks are an economical cut; they are the upper part of a lamb's foreleg with solid pieces of excellent meat around long slender bones.

Season 1 tablespoon of flour with salt and a little paprika and lightly dust the shanks. Heat 2 tablespoons of butter and 2 tablespoons of olive oil in a deep heavy saucepan and brown the shanks all over. Remove them from the pan and lightly brown 1 large thinly sliced onion. Put back the meat with ¾ cup of red wine, ¾ cup of water and ¼ teaspoon chopped fresh rosemary. Season with salt and pepper. Cover and cook in a moderate oven at 375° for about 2 hours, or until the meat is easily pierced with a fork.

Take the lamb shanks out of the gravy. Blend 2 tablespoons of flour with ½ cup of cold water, add it to the pan liquid and stir over the fire until the gravy thickens and comes to a boil. Simmer for 2 to 3 minutes, then strain.

To Serve: The shanks can be served as they are on a hot platter, with the gravy in a separate gravy bowl. Or the meat can be cut off the bones and arranged on a hot serving dish; spoon a little of the gravy over the meat and serve the rest separately. Serves 4.

LAMB CASSEROLE

1 large yellow onion, thinly sliced	2 tablespoons flour
	½ teaspoon tomato paste
5 to 6 tablespoons butter	1 cup stock
1 green pepper	½ cup red or rosé wine
4 cups diced cooked lamb	salt
1 small clove garlic, crushed	freshly cracked black pepper
2 tomatoes	½ cup bread crumbs

Peel and thinly slice a large yellow onion. Heat 2 tablespoons of butter in a deep heavy saucepan and cook the onion over a slow fire until it is a good dark brown. Remove the onion from the pan with a slotted spoon. Core, seed and dice a green pepper. Raise the heat under the pan, add 1 tablespoon of butter and quickly brown the green pepper and 4 cups of diced cooked lamb. Remove them from the pan. Add another tablespoon of butter, 1 small clove of crushed garlic and 2 peeled diced tomatoes and cook for 1 minute. Blend in 2 tablespoons of flour and ½ teaspoon of tomato paste, off the fire. Pour on 1 cup of stock and ½ cup of red or rosé wine and stir over the fire until the mixture comes to a boil. Put back the onion, lamb and green pepper. Season with salt and freshly cracked black pepper. Cover and simmer for 10 minutes.

Put into a casserole. Lightly brown ½ cup of bread crumbs with 1 to 2 tablespoons of butter and sprinkle over the top. Bake uncovered in a moderate oven at 375° for 20 minutes; or until the top is nicely browned. Serve in the casserole. Serves 4 to 6.

COLD LAMB WITH MINT SAUCE

Slice cold roast lamb and serve with mint sauce. Put the following ingredients in a small screw-top jar: ¾ cup finely chopped fresh mint, ½ teaspoon of salt, ¼ cup of cider vinegar, 1 tablespoon of sugar, a little freshly cracked black pepper and ½ teaspoon of lemon juice. Chill thoroughly before serving.

AUBERGINES FARCIES ITALIENNE
(Stuffed Eggplant with Lamb)

2 *medium-size eggplants*	*1 cup finely chopped mushrooms*
salt, pepper	*1 teaspoon tomato paste*
4 tablespoons salad oil	*2 cups ground cooked lamb*
6 tablespoons butter	*3 tablespoons bread crumbs*
1 large yellow onion, finely chopped	*3 tomatoes, skinned and shredded*
1 carrot, finely diced	*½ cup grated Parmesan cheese*
¼ pound green beans, diced	*2 tablespoons chopped parsley or chives*

Cut the eggplants in half lengthwise. Make crisscross incisions on the cut side with a sharp knife, sprinkle well with salt and let stand for ½ hour. Drain off any liquid that accumulates and dry the eggplants. Place on a cookie sheet and brush the tops with 4 tablespoons of salad oil. Bake for 40 minutes in a moderate oven at 350°. Remove, scoop out all the meat, leaving a ½-inch shell, and chop the meat finely.

Meanwhile melt 3 tablespoons of butter. Add 1 large finely chopped onion, a diced carrot and ¼ pound diced green beans. Season with salt and pepper, cover and cook very slowly until soft, about 15 minutes. Add 1 cup of finely chopped mushrooms and cook for 2 minutes. Stir in 1 teaspoon of tomato paste, 2 cups of ground cooked lamb, 3 tablespoons of bread crumbs and a little more seasoning. Cover and cook for 5 minutes. Remove and combine with 3 skinned and shredded tomatoes and the eggplant meat. Put the mixture into the shells, rounding it well. Sprinkle with ½ cup of grated Parmesan cheese and 3 tablespoons of melted butter and brown under the broiler.

To Serve: Arrange the eggplant on a hot serving dish, sprinkle with 2 tablespoons of finely chopped parsley or chives and serve immediately. Serves 4.

LAMB WITH OLIVES

12 slices cooked roast lamb	*2 tablespoons flour*
3 tablespoons butter	*1½ cups stock*
½ cup finely chopped onion	*salt, pepper*
15 to 18 stuffed olives, sliced	

Arrange the slices of lamb slightly overlapping on an ovenproof baking dish. Melt 3 tablespoons of butter in a skillet. Add ½ cup of finely chopped onion and sauté until the onion is lightly browned. Blend in 2 tablespoons of flour, off the fire. Pour on 1½ cups of stock and stir over the fire until the mixture comes to a boil. Season with salt and pepper and simmer for 2 to 3 minutes. A pinch of ground cloves may be added, if you wish. Cover the lamb with the sauce and 15 to 18 sliced stuffed olives. Bake uncovered in a moderate oven at 350° until thoroughly heated, about 15 to 20 minutes.

Serve in the baking dish. Serves 4 to 6.

ROGNONS SAUTÉS HENRI VI
(Sautéed Kidneys with Béarnaise Sauce)

1 loaf unsliced white bread	*8 large mushroom caps*
6 to 8 tablespoons butter	*8 small mushroom caps*
8 lamb kidneys	*shoestring potatoes*
	watercress

BÉARNAISE SAUCE

2 egg yolks	*1 tablespoon cream*
.1 tablespoon tarragon vinegar	*¼ pound butter*
salt, cayenne	*2 truffles, finely chopped*

Cut 8 rounds of bread about 2 inches in diameter and ½ inch thick. Fry until golden brown on both sides in 3 to 4 tablespoons of hot butter. Remove and keep warm. Cut the kidneys in half lengthwise and remove the white center cores. Heat another 1 to 2 tablespoons of butter in the pan the bread was fried in and sauté the kidneys over a brisk fire, starting with the cut side down and browning both sides. Remove and keep warm. Heat another 2 tablespoons of butter in the pan and lightly brown 8 large and 8 small mushroom caps.

Béarnaise Sauce: Put 2 egg yolks, 1 tablespoon of tarragon vinegar, salt and a pinch of cayenne pepper into a small mixing bowl. Beat until blended with a small wire whisk. Beat in 1 tablespoon of cream. Put the bowl into a skillet with an inch of hot water in the bottom and beat over a slow fire until the mixture begins to thicken. Then beat in ¼ pound of butter, bit by bit. Just before serving add 2 finely chopped truffles.

To Serve: Arrange the rounds of bread on a hot serving dish. Place a large mushroom cap on each round, stem side up. Put a heaping spoonful of Béarnaise sauce in each mushroom cap, then a whole kidney topped with a small mushroom cap. Allow 1 to 2 kidneys for each serving.

ROGNONS TURBIGOS
(Kidneys Sautéed with Onions and Red Wine)

8 lamb kidneys	½ teaspoon tomato paste
4 tablespoons butter	2 teaspoons potato flour
12 cocktail sausages	1 cup light stock
12 small white onions	¼ cup red wine
6 white mushrooms, quartered	2 tablespoons sherry
1 teaspoon meat glaze	salt, pepper
1 to 2 tablespoons chopped parsley or chives	

Skin the kidneys, cut in half lengthwise and remove the white
center cores. Heat 2 tablespoons of butter in a heavy skillet. When
very hot put in the kidneys, cut side down to seal in the juices,
and brown quickly on both sides. Remove kidneys from the pan.
Put another tablespoon of butter in the pan, brown 12 cocktail
sausages and remove them. Add the remaining tablespoon of butter to the pan and slowly brown 12 small white onions for 10 to
15 minutes. Add 6 quartered mushrooms and cook 1 minute. Blend
in, off the fire, 1 teaspoon of meat glaze, ½ teaspoon of tomato
paste and 2 teaspoons of potato flour. Stir until smooth and add 1
cup of stock, ¼ cup of red wine and 2 tablespoons of sherry.
Season with salt and pepper and stir over the fire until the mixture
comes to a boil. Put the kidneys and sausages back into the sauce
and cook until thoroughly heated.

Serve in a casserole and sprinkle with 1 to 2 tablespoons of
finely chopped parsley or chives. Serves 4 to 6.

KIDNEYS IN MUSTARD SAUCE

8 lamb kidneys	3 tablespoons flour
4 tablespoons butter	salt, pepper
1 clove garlic, crushed	1½ cups stock
¼ pound mushrooms, finely sliced	¼ cup red wine
1 teaspoon dry mustard	2 tablespoons sour cream
½ teaspoon meat glaze	1 to 2 tablespoons chopped parsley

Remove the outer membrane of the kidneys, if the butcher hasn't already done it. Cut in half lengthwise and remove the white center core. Cut into thick slices and brown very quickly on both sides in 2 tablespoons of hot butter. Remove the kidneys from the pan. Add to the pan another 2 tablespoons of butter, a clove of crushed garlic and ¼ pound of finely sliced mushrooms. Cook over a moderate fire for about 3 minutes, or until the mushrooms are lightly browned. Blend in, off the fire, 1 teaspoon of dry mustard, ½ teaspoon of meat glaze, 3 tablespoons of flour, salt and pepper. Pour on 1½ cups of stock and ¼ cup of red wine and stir over the fire until the mixture comes to a boil. Simmer for 5 to 10 minutes. Beat in 2 tablespoons of sour cream with a small wire whisk, a little at a time. Replace the kidneys and cook just until the kidneys are heated through. Serve in a casserole and sprinkle with 1 to 2 tablespoons of finely chopped parsley. Boiled, buttered rice goes well with this dish. Serves 4 to 6.

LAMB KIDNEYS EN BROCHETTE

8 lamb kidneys	*4 tablespoons butter*
8 slices bacon	*2 green peppers*
½ pound boiled ham, in 1 piece	*1 clove garlic, crushed*
8 mushroom caps	*salt, pepper*
8 baby white onions	*1 bunch watercress*

SAFFRON RICE

1½ cups rice	*½ cup melted butter*
¼ teaspoon saffron	*salt, pepper*
2 tablespoons hot water	*1 tablespoon chopped parsley*

Cut the kidneys in half and remove the center white cores. Cut 8 slices of bacon in half crosswise and wrap each piece of kidney in half a slice of bacon. Cut the ham in ½-inch cubes. Sauté 8 mushroom caps. Slowly brown 8 baby white onions in 1 tablespoon of butter. Core and seed 2 green peppers and cut into pieces the same size as the ham. Thread all these ingredients on skewers, alternating a piece of meat with a vegetable. Melt 3 tablespoons of butter in the pan the onions were cooked in. Add a clove of crushed garlic and cook 1 minute. Place the skewers on a cookie sheet. Pour the butter over them and season with salt and pepper. Broil for 5 minutes on each side in a preheated broiler.

Saffron Rice: Cook 1½ cups of rice in 2 quarts of boiling salted water for 13 minutes, or until the grains are just tender. Drain and put in a colander on top of a pan with a little boiling water in it. Steam for 10 to 15 minutes, or until ready to use. Crush ¼ teaspoon saffron in 2 tablespoons of hot water in a mortar with a pestle. Add ½ cup of melted butter. Mix into the rice with a fork, add salt, pepper and 1 tablespoon of finely chopped parsley.

To Serve: Make a bed of saffron rice on a hot serving dish. Place the skewers on the top of the rice and garnish with watercress. Serves 4.

HAM AND PORK

Pork is popular all over the world. Each country has its own cuts and methods of preparation, since no other animal offers such variety. Pigs are easy to raise, needing no elaborate acreage for pasturing and not being fussy about their diet. The result is that pig meat is plentiful and not too expensive, is fine meat nutritionally and adaptable to many uses. There are hams, both smoked and fresh, roast pork, pork chops, pork shoulders, spareribs, tenderloins as well as bacon, sausage and salt pork.

Pigs are generally slaughtered when they are 7 to 12 months old, so the meat is tender and has plenty of fat. However, pork is always well cooked, usually at a low temperature, to tenderize the connective tissue. Bacon and sausage are broiled or pan-fried, but all the other cuts are best cooked by slow methods.

Hams, or the legs of a pig, are one of the leading pork cuts. The majority of hams are smoked, and in this country they are also tenderized. Tenderizing means that most of the cooking is already done when you purchase the ham, and all the ham needs is a short baking period. (For some reason, when you cook a ham in the oven, it is called baking it rather than roasting as with other meats.) Hams that have not been tenderized are quite salty so are usually soaked for several hours, then boiled and finally baked in the oven for a nice crust. But none of this is necessary with a tenderized ham. There are considerable differences between tenderized hams of various brands, and some are rather lacking in flavor compared with European hams, so it is worth shopping around to find a brand you like. Whole hams weigh 10 to 20 pounds. You can also buy half a ham, either the shank or butt end, and have a steak cut off the center parts. Hams are an economical buy because there is a lot of meat in proportion to bone; it is as good cold as it is hot; and there are numerous ways of using cooked ham.

The more expensive pork cuts include the loin, ribs and tenderloin. The loin can be roasted, and so can the ribs as a crown roast. The ribs are also used as chops, which should be baked or braised rather than broiled for the best flavor and for tenderness. Broiling hardens the fibers and tends to dry out the meat. Less expensive cuts are the spareribs, shoulder and feet.

Pork is a rich, rather heavy meat, with plenty of fat. Therefore it is often served with something sharp to complement it. Applesauce and sweet potatoes seem to be traditional with pork in this country, probably because it is the one meat that goes with anything sweet. In France, however, sweet potatoes — especially with marshmallows on top — would be considered more suitable for dessert. But flavored with something tangy they are good. And mustard, which is a standard accompaniment to ham, is fine.

BAKED HAM

1 whole ham, 10 to 12 pounds	1 to 1½ cups brown sugar
whole cloves	1 teaspoon dry mustard
½ cup brandy	

PEACH GARNISH

3 peaches	¼ cup water
1 cup apricot jam	6 blanched almonds

STUFFED PEPPERS

6 green peppers	1½ cups cooked rice
¾ cup sautéed chopped onion	salt, pepper
1 cup sautéed sliced mushrooms	½ cup grated Parmesan cheese
2 tablespoons butter	

SAUCE

1 cup juice from ham	½ cup red wine
2 teaspoons potato flour	½ cup stock
½ teaspoon tomato paste	

With a sharp knife carefully loosen the rind as far as the shank.

Bone all of the ham except the shank, or have the butcher do it. Boning isn't essential but it makes carving easier and cuts any possible waste if it is done skillfully. Score the top fat in a ¼ inch deep diamond pattern. Put 1 whole clove in each diamond. Blend 1 to 1½ cups of brown sugar with 1 teaspoon of dry mustard and spread on top of the ham. Replace the rind. Bake in a moderate oven at 325° 15 to 20 minutes to the pound (a meat thermometer will register 150°). Boned hams take a little longer than hams with the bone in. When it has cooked an hour remove the rind, pour ½ cup of brandy into the pan and start basting every 15 minutes with the pan juices.

Peach Garnish: Peel and halve 3 peaches, removing the pit. Thin 1 cup of apricot jam with ¼ cup of water. Simmer the peaches in the jam until they are tender but still hold their shape.

Stuffed Peppers: Put 6 green peppers in a pan with cold water to cover. Bring slowly to a boil and drain. Cut off the tops and scoop out the seeds. Blend together ¾ cup sautéed chopped onion, 1 cup sautéed sliced mushrooms, 1½ cups of cooked rice, salt and pepper. Fill the peppers. Sprinkle the tops with ½ cup of grated Parmesan cheese and dot with 2 tablespoons of butter. Bake for 15 to 20 minutes in a moderate oven at 325°; they can bake while the ham is being carved.

To Serve: Remove the ham and let stand for 15 minutes before carving. Put 1 cup of the pan juices into a saucepan. Blend 2 teaspoons of potato flour with a little cold water and add to the juices with ½ cup of red wine, ½ cup of stock and ½ teaspoon of tomato paste. Stir over the fire until the sauce comes to a boil. Let simmer until ready to serve. Carve as many slices of ham as needed for one meal. Do not separate them from the ham but serve it whole. Spoon a little of the sauce over the ham and serve the rest in a sauce bowl. Garnish the ham with stuffed peppers and the peaches with a blanched almond placed in each one. A whole ham will serve at least 15 to 18 people. This is enough garnish for 6 people and should be increased if you are serving more.

JAMBON EN CROÛTE
(Ham in Crust)

1 whole ham, 10 to 12 pounds   *½ cup Madeira*

CRUST

6 cups flour	*4 teaspoons baking powder*
1 cup butter	*2 to 3 teaspoons salt*
½ cup lard	*3 egg yolks*

about 1 cup ice water

BRAISED CELERY

2 bunches celery	*2 small onions, sliced*
2 tablespoons butter	*salt, pepper*
8 slices bacon	*1½ cups strong stock*
2 carrots, sliced	*1 tablespoon chopped parsley*

SAUCE

4 tablespoons butter	*1 cup celery stock*
3 tablespoons flour	*1 cup heavy cream*

salt, white pepper

This is a delicious and handsome dish for parties. Have a whole ham weighing about 10 to 12 pounds boned by removing the leg bone from the shank end. This isn't essential but does make carving easier. Bake it until tender. Remove the rind and the thick end of the loin and let the ham cool. If the layer of fat covering the ham is more than ½ inch thick, trim off the excess. Make the following crust.

Crust: Put 6 cups of flour on a pastry board or marble slab. Make a well in the center and in it put 1 cup of butter, ½ cup of lard, 4 teaspoons of baking powder, 2 to 3 teaspoons of salt, 3 egg yolks and about 1 cup of ice water. Work center ingredients to a smooth paste. Then work in the flour with the heel of your hand. Roll out about ½ inch thick.

Wrap the pastry around the ham and seal it on the bottom. Decorate with motifs of pastry and brush with milk or slightly beaten egg. Make a few slits in the top for steam to escape. Place on a cookie sheet and bake in a moderate oven at 375° for 1 to 1¼ hours, or until golden brown. Meanwhile prepare the braised celery and the sauce.

Braised Celery: Remove the leafy tops from 2 bunches of celery and cut the stalks in half lengthwise. Cook in boiling salted water for 15 minutes. Drain, reserving the stock, and dry on a cloth. Grease a deep oblong baking dish with 1 tablespoon of butter and place 4 strips of bacon on the bottom. Scatter half the carrot and onion slices over the bacon and season. Place the celery in the pan, cover with the rest of the carrot and onion, then the remaining 4 slices of bacon. Pour over 1½ cups of stock and cover with waxed paper. Bake in a moderate oven at 375° for 50 minutes, or until the celery is clear and tender. Remove the celery and place it on a hot serving dish. Strain the liquid and boil until it thickens a little. Add the remaining 1 tablespoon of butter, bit by bit. Pour the sauce over the celery and sprinkle with 1 tablespoon of chopped parsley.

Sauce: Boil the celery cooking water down to 1 cup. Melt 3 tablespoons of butter. Blend in 3 tablespoons of flour, off the fire. Add the 1 cup of celery cooking water and stir over the fire until the mixture comes to a boil. Slowly add 1 cup of heavy cream. Season with salt and white pepper. Beat in 1 tablespoon of butter, bit by bit.

To Serve: Place the ham on a large silver platter. Pour ½ cup of Madeira in the slits in the crust. Let stand for 15 minutes. Serve the celery and sauce separately. A whole ham will serve at least 15 to 18 people. The celery and sauce is sufficient for 6 people and both recipes can easily be increased.

ROAST FRESH HAM

6 to 8 pounds fresh ham	*1 cup red wine*
salt, pepper	*¼ cup vinegar*
1 medium-size red cabbage	*½ cup brown sugar*
2 apples, peeled and diced	

The ham will have a skin which should be left on because it gets brown and crisp and is delicious to eat. The ham can be boned and stuffed, if you wish, but the bone helps flavor the meat so is best left in. Score the skin in diamonds with a sharp knife and season with salt and pepper. Put skin side up in a roasting pan. Roast for 35 to 40 minutes to the pound — 45 to 50 minutes if it has been boned — or until a meat thermometer registers 185°. Serve with the following red cabbage.

Red Cabbage: Core a red cabbage and cut it into thin slices. Put it into a saucepan with 1 cup of red wine, ¼ cup of vinegar, ½ cup of brown sugar, 2 peeled and diced apples and some salt. Cook gently for about 30 minutes or until the cabbage is tender, adding a little more wine or water if the mixture looks dry.

To Serve: Place the ham on a hot serving dish and serve the cabbage separately. A whole ham will serve at least 8 to 10 people. One cabbage will serve 5 or 6.

MADEIRA SAUCE FOR HAM

⅓ cup brown sugar
½ cup white raisins
1 tablespoon red currant jelly
1 cup ham liquor
pinch of cloves
juice of ½ lemon

¼ teaspoon dry mustard
salt
2 teaspoons potato flour
½ cup Madeira
¼ cup almonds, blanched and chopped

Put ⅓ cup brown sugar, ½ cup white raisins, 1 tablespoon of red currant jelly, 1 cup of ham liquor, pinch of cloves, the juice of ½ lemon and ¼ teaspoon dry mustard into a saucepan. Bring slowly to a boil and taste for seasoning. Salt will be needed unless the ham liquor is very salty. Blend 2 teaspoons of potato flour with 1 tablespoon of cold water. Add to the sauce and stir until it thickens. Just before serving add ½ cup of Madeira and ¼ cup of blanched chopped almonds. Do not let the sauce boil after the wine has been added or some of its flavor will be dissipated.

JAMBON AUX ÉPINARDS
(Ham with Spinach)

8 slices cooked ham	salt, pepper
2 packages frozen chopped spinach	½ pound mushrooms, sliced
	2 teaspoons potato flour
5 tablespoons butter	1 teaspoon meat glaze
2 tablespoons flour	½ teaspoon tomato paste
3 to 4 tablespoons sour cream	½ cup sherry
1 cup stock	

Cut 8 slices of baked or boiled ham about ¼ inch thick. Cook 2 packages of frozen chopped spinach until tender in boiling salted water; or use 3 pounds of fresh spinach and chop it finely after it is cooked. Drain thoroughly. Melt 2 tablespoons of butter. Blend in 2 tablespoons of flour and cook until lightly browned. Add the drained spinach and 3 to 4 tablespoons of sour cream. Season with salt and pepper. Cook until well heated, or until ready to use.

Heat the slices of ham in 1 tablespoon of butter in a large skillet. Make a smooth bed of spinach purée on a hot serving dish. Arrange the slices of ham slightly overlapping on top. Keep warm while the sauce is being prepared.

Melt another 2 tablespoons of butter in the skillet the ham was cooked in. Sauté ½ pound of sliced mushrooms until lightly browned. Blend in, off the fire, 2 teaspoons of potato flour, 1 teaspoon of meat glaze and ½ teaspoon of tomato paste. Add ½ cup of sherry and 1 cup of stock and stir over the fire until the sauce comes to a boil. Taste for seasoning. Simmer for 2 to 3 minutes, then spoon over the ham. Serves 4.

CORNETS DE JAMBON LUCULLUS
(Cornets of Ham with Aspic)

8 thin slices cooked ham	3 tablespoons butter
¾ pound pâté or liverwurst	salt, cayenne
2 truffles or black olives	

ASPIC

3 cups strong stock	2 tablespoons tomato paste
4 tablespoons gelatine	¼ cup white wine or sherry
3 egg whites, stiffly beaten	

RICE SALAD

| 1½ cups rice, cooked | 2 cups mixed diced cooked green beans and carrots |
| ½ to ¾ cup French dressing | |

Line 8 cornet molds with thin slices of cooked ham. Strain ¾ pound pâté or liverwurst and mix with 3 tablespoons of softened butter. Cream well and season with salt and cayenne. Put into a pastry bag with a small round tube and pipe into the cornets. Put a slice of truffle or ripe olive on top of each and place in the refrigerator to set for at least 1 hour. Remove the cornets from the molds, place on a cake rack, coat each one with aspic on the point of setting and return to the refrigerator for the aspic to set, or until ready to use.

Aspic: Put 3 cups of stock, 4 tablespoons of gelatine, 2 tablespoons of tomato paste, ¼ cup white wine or sherry and 3 stiffly beaten egg whites into a large saucepan. The stock should be cold and free from fat and can be made with cold water and 2 to 3 teaspoons of meat glaze. Beat with a large wire whisk over a slow fire until the mixture comes to a boil. Remove and let stand at least 10 minutes. Strain through a cloth which has been wrung out in cold water and is placed over a large strainer. Put about half the aspic into a shallow cake or pie tin and into the refrigerator to set for the garnish. Place the rest over a bowl of ice and stir until on the point of setting; use this to coat the cornets.

Rice Salad: Blend 1½ cups of rice, cooked, with 2 cups of mixed diced cooked green beans and carrots. Chill. Mix with ½ to ¾ cup of French dressing.

To Serve: Put the rice salad into a round cake tin, press down gently. Unmold on a serving platter, preferably silver. Arrange the cornets in a crown on top of the rice. Garnish with chopped set aspic. Serves 8.

HAM SOUFFLÉ

2 cups ground cooked ham	cayenne
5 tablespoons butter	¾ cup milk
3 tablespoons flour	4 egg yolks, unbeaten
½ teaspoon dry mustard	1 pound mushrooms
6 egg whites, stiffly beaten	

Put enough ham through the fine cutter of a meat grinder to make 2 cups. Melt 3 tablespoons of butter in a medium-size saucepan. Blend in, off the fire, 3 tablespoons of flour, ½ teaspoon of dry mustard and a pinch of cayenne. Pour on ¾ cup of milk and stir over the fire until the mixture comes to a boil. Remove from the fire. Add the ground ham. Then add 4 egg yolks, one at a time, stirring well after each addition. Let cool a little — in fact at this stage the mixture can stand for several hours.

Remove the stems from a pound of mushrooms and slice the caps. Sauté in 2 tablespoons of butter until lightly browned. Grease a soufflé dish with butter and tie a band of buttered waxed paper around the outside.

Stiffly beat 6 egg whites and fold them gently into the ham mixture. Place a third of the soufflé mixture in the dish and cover with half the sautéed mushrooms. Then another third of the soufflé mixture, the rest of the mushrooms and the remaining soufflé. Bake in a moderate oven at 375° for 30 to 40 minutes, until nicely browned. Remove, carefully take off the waxed paper and serve immediately. Serves 4 to 6.

Note: The mushrooms may be omitted and the soufflé sprinkled with grated Parmesan cheese before it is baked.

HOT HAM MOUSSE

2 pounds lean boiled ham	salt, cayenne
8 tablespoons butter	¼ teaspoon nutmeg
8 tablespoons flour	½ cup sour cream
1½ cups milk	¼ cup heavy cream
3 eggs	1 tablespoon tomato paste

SAUCE

5 tablespoons butter	½ cup light cream
3 tablespoons flour	4 tablespoons dry sherry
1½ cups veal stock	1 tablespoon chopped truffle
2 egg yolks	or black olives

Put the ham through the fine blade of a meat chopper 3 times. Melt 8 tablespoons of butter. Blend in 8 tablespoons of flour, off the fire. Pour on 1½ cups of milk and stir over the fire until the mixture comes to a boil. Put on a plate and let it get cold. Mix with the ground ham and put through a strainer. Beat 3 eggs until well blended but not frothy and add to the ham mixture. Season with salt, cayenne and ¼ teaspoon of nutmeg. Blend in ½ cup of sour cream, ¼ cup of heavy cream and 1 tablespoon of tomato paste. Put into a well-greased ring mold and cover with a piece of greased waxed paper. Set in a pan and pour in enough boiling water to come within 1½ inches of the top of the mold. Bake in a moderate oven at 350° for 1 to 1½ hours, until set. Meanwhile prepare the following sauce.

Sauce: Melt 3 tablespoons of butter. Blend in 3 tablespoons of flour, off the fire. Pour on 1½ cups of veal stock and stir over the fire until the mixture comes to a boil. Season with salt and cayenne. Beat in the remaining 2 tablespoons of butter, bit by bit. Just before serving beat 2 egg yolks lightly with a fork, add ½ cup of light cream and 4 tablespoons of dry sherry. Stir into the sauce and continue stirring until the sauce is very hot but not boiling. Add 1 tablespoon of chopped truffle or black olives.

To Serve: Remove the mold from the water bath and let stand for 5 minutes. Slide a small sharp knife around the edge of the mold, give it a little knock and turn out on a serving platter. Spoon the sauce over the mousse. Serves 6 to 8.

COLD HAM MOUSSE

2 pounds lean boiled ham	1 cup milk
5 tablespoons butter	1 cup heavy cream, whipped
6 tablespoons water	2 egg whites, stiffly beaten
6 tablespoons flour	salt, cayenne
2 tablespoons gelatine	2 truffles

ASPIC

3 cups cold clear stock	1 tablespoon tomato paste
2 tablespoons sherry	3 tablespoons gelatine
4 tablespoons red wine	2 egg whites, stiffly beaten

Put 2 pounds of ham through the meat chopper twice. Make the following sauce. Melt 1 tablespoon of butter in 6 tablespoons of water. Stir in, off the fire, 6 tablespoons of flour which have been mixed with 2 tablespoons of dry gelatine. Pour on 1 cup of milk. Stir over the fire until the sauce comes to a boil. Pour on a plate and let it get cold. Blend thoroughly with the ground ham and rub through a fine strainer. Mix in 4 tablespoons of well-creamed butter, 1 cup of heavy cream, whipped, 2 stiffly beaten egg whites, salt and cayenne. Put into a soufflé dish. Cover with ½-inch layer of aspic on the point of setting and place in the refrigerator until set. Decorate suitably with truffles and pour over another thin layer of aspic on the point of setting. Leave in the refrigerator until set or until ready to use. Serve garnished with chopped set aspic. Serves 6 to 8.

Aspic: Put 3 cups of cold clear stock (cold water and meat glaze may be used), 2 tablespoons of sherry, 4 tablespoons of red wine, 1 tablespoon of tomato paste and 3 tablespoons of dry gelatine into a deep saucepan. Blend together and add 2 stiffly beaten egg whites. Beat with a large wire whisk over a slow fire until it comes to a real boil. Remove from the fire and let stand for 15 minutes. Strain through a damp cloth placed over a large strainer. Put half the aspic into a shallow cake pan and into the refrigerator to set for the garnish. Stir the rest over ice until on the point of setting.

CROQUE MONSIEUR
(French Ham and Cheese Sandwiches)

8 thin slices white bread	½ pound mushrooms, sliced
8 slices Swiss or Gruyère cheese	and sautéed
	1 egg
4 slices cooked ham	¼ cup milk
2 to 3 tablespoons butter	

HOLLANDAISE SAUCE

2 egg yolks	salt, cayenne
1 tablespoon tarragon	1 tablespoon cream
vinegar	¼ pound butter

Remove the crusts from 8 thin slices of white bread and make into sandwiches, putting into each one a slice of cheese, a slice of ham, a spoonful of sautéed mushrooms and another slice of cheese. Beat 1 egg with ¼ cup of milk and dip both sides of each sandwich in this mixture. Fry the sandwiches in 2 to 3 tablespoons of butter until golden brown on each side. Place them on an ovenproof serving dish and keep warm while you make the following Hollandaise sauce.

Hollandaise Sauce: Put 2 egg yolks in a small bowl. Beat in 1 tablespoon of tarragon vinegar, salt and a little cayenne with a small wire whisk. Then beat in 1 tablespoon of cream. Place the bowl in a pan with an inch of simmering water in the bottom and beat until the mixture begins to thicken. Then beat in ¼ pound of butter, bit by bit.

To Serve: Spoon the Hollandaise sauce over each sandwich and brown lightly under the broiler. Serves 4.

HAM WITH SWEET AND SOUR SAUCE I

6 large slices cooked ham
3 tablespoons butter
¼ cup diced pimento or red pepper
¼ cup diced green pepper
¼ cup finely chopped onion
¼ cup seeded raisins
¼ cup chopped mushrooms
½ teaspoon tomato paste
2 teaspoons potato flour
¾ cup stock

¼ cup sherry
¼ cup claret
¼ cup Marsala
salt, pepper
3 pounds fresh spinach or 2 packages frozen chopped spinach
3 tablespoons sour cream
1 small clove garlic, crushed
½ cup shredded browned almonds

Lightly brown 6 slices of ham in 1 tablespoon of hot butter in a deep heavy saucepan. Remove the ham. Melt another 2 tablespoons of butter in the pan. Add ¼ cup each of diced pimento or red pepper, diced green pepper, finely chopped onion, seeded raisins and chopped mushrooms. Cook briskly for 2 to 3 minutes. Blend in, off the fire, ½ teaspoon of tomato paste and 2 table-spoons of potato flour. Pour on ¾ cup of stock and stir until smooth. Then add ¼ cup of sherry, ¼ cup of claret and ¼ cup of Marsala. Stir over the fire until the sauce comes to a boil. Taste for seasoning. Put back the ham and simmer for about 15 minutes.

Meanwhile cook 3 pounds of fresh spinach or 2 packages of frozen chopped spinach in boiling salted water until tender. Drain thoroughly. If the spinach is fresh, chop it well. Blend in 3 tablespoons of sour cream and a small clove of crushed garlic.

To Serve: Make a bed of the spinach on a hot serving dish. Arrange the slices of ham slightly overlapping on top of the spinach. Spoon the sauce over all and sprinkle with half a cup of shredded browned almonds. Serves 6.

HAM WITH SWEET AND SOUR SAUCE II

3 tablespoons butter
4 chicken livers
1 tablespoon brandy
1 small clove garlic, crushed
½ cup currants or raisins
¼ pound mushrooms, sliced
½ teaspoon tomato paste
3 teaspoons potato flour
salt, pepper
1½ cups stock

¼ cup muscatel or Marsala
¼ cup red wine
cayenne, chili pepper
2 teaspoons lemon juice
1 tablespoon papaya syrup or guava jelly
1 tablespoon coconut syrup or honey
1 tablespoon currant jelly or apple jelly

6 large slices cooked ham

Melt 1 tablespoon of butter in a large skillet over a brisk fire. When it is just turning color, put in 4 chicken livers and brown them quickly all over. Remove the livers from the pan. Lower the heat and add another 2 tablespoons of butter, 1 tablespoon of brandy and 1 small clove of crushed garlic; cook for ½ minute.

Add ½ cup of currants or raisins and ¼ pound of sliced mushrooms and cook another 5 minutes.

Stir in, off the fire, ½ teaspoon of tomato paste, 3 teaspoons of potato flour, salt and pepper. When well blended pour on 1½ cups of stock. Stir over the fire until the mixture comes to a boil. Add ¼ cup of Muscatel or Marsala and ¼ cup of red wine, a dash of cayenne and chili pepper, then 2 teaspoons of lemon juice and 1 tablespoon each of the three contrasting sweetnesses — papaya syrup, coconut syrup and currant jelly — or guava jelly, honey and apple jelly. Chop the chicken livers and return them to the sauce with 6 large slices of cooked ham. Heat thoroughly. Serve on a hot platter with the sauce poured over the ham. Serves 6.

OEUFS POCHÉS BENEDICT
(Poached Eggs Benedict)

POACHED EGGS
½ cup vinegar   4 eggs

HOLLANDAISE SAUCE

2 egg yolks	*1 tablespoon tarragon vinegar*
salt, cayenne	*1 tablespoon cream*
	¼ pound butter

4 slices cooked ham	*2 English muffins*
3 tablespoons butter	*1 small clove garlic, crushed*
	4 slices truffle, optional

Poached Eggs: Since eggs can be poached ahead of time and kept waiting in a bowl of warm water, they are the first step in this simple but excellent dish. Fill ¾ of the top of a double boiler with water, add ½ cup of vinegar and bring to a boil. Lower the heat to simmering and stir the water around with a wooden spoon, forming a whirlpool. Break an egg into a cup and slide it into the center of the whirlpool. Cook over low heat for 3 to 3½ minutes, then lift the egg out with a slotted spoon. Put it into a bowl of warm water — this removes any flavor of vinegar and keeps the egg warm without further cooking. Poach 4 eggs in this manner.

Hollandaise Sauce: Put 2 egg yolks into a small bowl with a little salt and cayenne. Beat in 1 tablespoon of tarragon vinegar with a wire whisk, then 1 tablespoon of cream. Put the bowl into a small skillet with an inch of gently boiling water in the bottom and continue beating until the mixture begins to thicken. Then beat in ¼ pound of butter a little at a time. Remove the pan from the fire. If the sauce is to stand for a while, cool the water in the skillet to lukewarm and cover the sauce with a piece of waxed paper or aluminum foil.

Ham: Cook 4 slices of ham in 1 tablespoon of butter until heated through and slightly browned; 2 tablespoons of sherry may be added.

English Muffins: Split 2 English muffins in half by pushing a fork into them all around the middle. Blend 2 tablespoons of softened butter with a small clove of crushed garlic and spread it on the muffin. Brown lightly under the broiler.

To Serve: Arrange the muffins on a hot ovenproof serving dish. Top with a slice of ham and a well-drained poached egg. Spoon Hollandaise sauce over the eggs and brown under the broiler. Each egg may be garnished with a slice of truffle. Allow 1 or 2 per serving.

Note: Cooked tongue may be substituted for the ham.

TOMATOES STUFFED WITH HAM

4 large firm tomatoes	*2 teaspoons lemon juice*
1 small avocado pear, diced	*salt*
4 slices bacon, cooked and diced	*coarsely ground black pepper*
1 cup chopped cooked ham	*4 tablespoons melted butter*

GARLIC TOMATO SAUCE

2 tablespoons butter	*2 teaspoons potato flour*
1 small clove garlic, crushed	*1 cup light stock or water*
2 tablespoons tomato paste	*salt*
½ teaspoon meat glaze	*freshly cracked black pepper*

Cut the tops off 4 large tomatoes and scoop out the inside pulp with a spoon. Chop the pulp coarsely, discarding as many of the seeds as possible. Peel and dice an avocado and combine with 4 slices of diced cooked bacon, 1 cup of chopped cooked ham, 2 teaspoons of lemon juice, 4 tablespoons of the chopped tomato pulp, salt and coarsely ground black pepper. Fill the tomatoes and pour 4 tablespoons of melted butter over the tops. Bake in a moderate oven at 350° for 25 minutes. Meanwhile prepare the following sauce.

Garlic Tomato Sauce: Melt 1 tablespoon of butter. Add a small clove of crushèd garlic and cook for 1 minute. Blend in, off the fire, 2 tablespoons of tomato paste, ½ teaspoon of meat glaze and 2 teaspoons of potato flour. Pour on 1 cup of light stock or water. Season with salt and freshly cracked black pepper. Stir over the fire until the sauce comes to a boil. Simmer for at least 5 minutes or until ready to serve. Just before serving beat in 1 tablespoon of butter, bit by bit.

To Serve: Remove the tomatoes and place them on a hot serving dish. Pour the hot sauce over and around them. Serves 4.

POACHED EGGS AND HAM IN ASPIC

ASPIC

6 cups cold clear stock	*¼ cup sherry*
6 tablespoons gelatine	*3 tablespoons tomato paste*
½ cup dry white wine	*4 egg whites, stiffly beaten*

6 thin slices cooked ham	*2 cups finely ground cooked ham*
2 or 3 truffles	*½ cup creamed butter*
6 poached eggs	*½ cup whipped cream*
1 tablespoon tomato paste	

Aspic: Put 6 cups of cold clear stock (cold water and meat glaze can be used), 6 tablespoons of dry gelatine, ½ cup of dry white wine, ¼ cup of sherry and 3 tablespoons of tomato paste into a large deep saucepan. Stir well and add 4 stiffly beaten egg whites. Beat with a large wire whisk over a slow fire, using an up and down motion when beating rather than a circular one. As soon as the mixture boils up remove the pan from the fire and let stand for 15 minutes. Then strain through a damp dishcloth placed over a large strainer. Put ¼ of the aspic into a shallow cake tin and into the refrigerator to set for the garnish. Stir the rest over a bowl of ice until on the point of setting.

Fill the bottom of a large ring mold with a ½-inch layer of aspic. Chill until set — it only takes a few minutes. Cut 6 thin slices of cooked ham into 1½-inch rounds, cut small rounds from the center of each piece and fill with a thin slice of truffle. Arrange evenly around the bottom of the mold and cover with a thin layer of aspic. Chill. Place 6 poached eggs on top of the ham slices and cover them with aspic. Chill. Mix together 2 cups of ground cooked ham, ½ cup of creamed butter, ½ cup of whipped cream and 1 tablespoon of tomato paste. Taste for seasoning. Make a layer of this in the mold and on top of that a final layer of aspic. Leave in the refrigerator for at least 2 hours.

To Serve: Run a small sharp knife around the outside and inside edge of the mold and invert it on a silver dish. Garnish with chopped set aspic and finely chopped truffle. Serves 6.

Note: See page 182 for instructions on poaching eggs. After they are cooked place them in a bowl of cold (not warm) water.

Aspic can be left to set for a few minutes in a freezer, but if left for any length of time it gets cloudy.

JAMBON AU PORTO
(Ham with Port)

6 *large slices cooked ham*	1 *teaspoon tomato paste*
1 *tablespoon butter*	½ *cup port wine*
2 *teaspoons potato flour*	½ *cup heavy cream*

Cut 6 large even slices from a cooked ham and have them at room temperature rather than straight from the refrigerator. Melt 1 tablespoon of butter in a small saucepan. Blend in, off the fire, 2 teaspoons of potato flour and 1 teaspoon of tomato paste. Add ½ cup of port wine and stir over the fire until the mixture comes to a boil. Slowly add ½ cup of heavy cream. Taste for seasoning.

Arrange the slices of ham slightly overlapping on a hot ovenproof serving dish. Cover with the sauce and leave in a moderate oven at 350° for 10 minutes to heat the ham. Serves 6.

HAM AND ASPARAGUS WITH MORNAY SAUCE

8 thin slices boiled ham   *24 stalks cooked asparagus*

MORNAY SAUCE

3 tablespoons butter	*salt, white pepper*
3 tablespoons flour	*1 cup heavy cream*
1 cup milk	*4 tablespoons grated Parmesan cheese*

Drain the asparagus well and trim neatly. Place 3 stalks on each slice of ham and roll the ham around them. Place the rolls close together in a lightly buttered shallow baking dish that can be used for serving; or place 2 rolls each on 4 individual baking dishes.

Mornay Sauce: Melt 3 tablespoons of butter. Blend in 3 tablespoons of flour. Add 1 cup of milk, salt and white pepper, and stir over the fire until the mixture comes to a boil. Add ½ cup of heavy cream and 2 tablespoons of grated Parmesan cheese. Whip the remaining ½ cup of cream and fold it into the sauce. Adding whipped cream to a sauce is a trick invented by Louis Diat to make sauces brown evenly, and it is a fine one.

Spoon the sauce carefully over the ham. Sprinkle with the remaining 2 tablespoons of cheese. Bake in a moderate oven at 350° for 10 to 15 minutes to heat the ham and finish with a minute or two under the broiler to lightly brown the top. Serve in the baking dish. Serves 4.

MUSHROOMS STUFFED WITH HAM

12 large white mushrooms	*2 tablespoons bread crumbs*
1 tablespoon finely chopped onion	*¼ cup chicken stock or cream*
4 tablespoons butter	*1 tablespoon finely chopped parsley*
1 cup minced or ground cooked ham	*½ cup grated Parmesan cheese*

Remove the mushroom stems and chop them finely. Cook the mushroom stems and 1 tablespoon of finely chopped onion in 2 tablespoons of butter over a slow fire for about 5 minutes, until soft but not brown. Blend with 1 cup of minced or ground cooked ham, 2 tablespoons of bread crumbs, ¼ cup chicken stock or cream and 1 tablespoon of finely chopped parsley. Taste for seasoning. Fill the mushroom caps, rounding the tops with a spoon. Sprinkle with ½ cup of grated Parmesan cheese and dot with 2 tablespoons of butter. Place in a shallow ovenproof serving dish and bake in a moderate oven at 350° for 15 minutes. Serves 4.

AUBERGINE FARCIE
(Stuffed Eggplant)

2 medium-size eggplants	½ pint sour cream
6 tablespoons olive oil	½ cup bread crumbs
1 large yellow onion	2 tablespoons chopped parsley
1 pound boiled ham, ground, or	salt, pepper
2 cups ground leftover ham	4 thin slices Cheddar cheese
1 large clove garlic, crushed	1 tablespoon butter

Cut the eggplants in half lengthwise. Make crisscross incisions ½ inch deep on the cut surface and run a knife around the edges ¼ inch from the skin. Sprinkle well with salt and let stand for ½ hour. Drain off any liquid that accumulates. Put the eggplants in a baking dish, pour 4 tablespoons of olive oil over them and bake for 40 minutes in a moderate oven at 350°.

Meanwhile peel 1 large yellow onion and chop it finely. Cook very slowly in 2 tablespoons of olive oil for about 10 minutes until soft and lightly browned. Put into a large mixing bowl 2 cups of ground cooked ham, 1 large clove of crushed garlic, ½ pint of sour cream, ½ cup of bread crumbs, 2 tablespoons of finely chopped parsley and the cooked onion. Season with salt and pepper and blend well.

Remove the eggplants from the oven and scoop out the pulp, leaving a ½-inch shell. Chop the pulp and add it to the ham mixture. Fill the shells with the stuffing and place them on an ovenproof serving dish. Top each half with a thin slice of Cheddar cheese and dot with 1 tablespoon of butter. Bake in a moderate oven at 350° for 20 to 30 minutes; if the tops aren't nicely browned by then, finish off with a minute or so under the broiler. A garlic tomato sauce (see page 183) may be served separately. Serves 4.

ARTICHAUTS À LA BARIGOULE
(Stuffed Artichokes)

4 globe artichokes	*2 tablespoons chopped parsley*
2 tablespoons lemon juice	*½ cup bread crumbs*
6 tablespoons butter	*4 slices bacon*
1 cup finely chopped mush-	*½ cup white wine*
rooms	*½ cup stock*
1 cup shredded cooked ham	*1 tablespoon sherry*
2 small onions, finely chopped	*2 tablespoons flour*
2 teaspoons tomato paste	*salt, cayenne*

1 small clove garlic, crushed

Cook 4 globe artichokes uncovered in 2 quarts of boiling salted water with 2 tablespoons of lemon juice until tender, about 45 minutes, more or less; when one of the large bottom outer leaves pulls off readily, the artichokes are done. Remove and drain well. Pull out the small center leaves, leaving the outer ones as a shell. Scoop out the choke with a spoon.

Melt 2 tablespoons of butter in a skillet and cook 1 cup of finely chopped mushrooms and 1 cup of shredded cooked ham over a moderate fire for about 5 minutes. Add 2 small chopped onions, 1 teaspoon of tomato paste, 1 tablespoon of chopped parsley and ¼ cup of bread crumbs and cook another 2 to 3 minutes. Fill the center of the artichokes with this mixture. Sprinkle the tops with ¼ cup of bread crumbs and 2 tablespoons of melted butter. Wrap a slice of bacon around the outside of each artichoke and secure it with a piece of string.

Place the artichokes in a greased ovenproof dish. Combine ½ cup of white wine, ½ cup of stock, 1 tablespoon of sherry and 1 teaspoon of tomato paste and pour into the dish. Cover the

artichokes with waxed paper and bake in a moderate oven at 350°
for 40 minutes. Remove from the oven, drain off the pan juices
(reserving them) and return the artichokes to the oven with the
heat off to keep warm.

Melt 2 tablespoons of butter. Blend in, off the fire, 2 tablespoons
of flour, salt and cayenne. Strain the pan juices into the roux,
then stir over the fire until the mixture comes to a boil. Add
1 clove of crushed garlic and simmer about 5 minutes.

To Serve: Pour the sauce over the bottom of a hot serving
dish. Remove the bacon from the artichokes, arrange them in
the dish and sprinkle with 1 tablespoon of parsley. Serves 4.

HAM AND MUSHROOM CASSEROLE

1 pound mushrooms, sliced	*1 cup light cream*
4 tablespoons butter	*4 tablespoons sherry*
3 tablespoons flour	*3 cups diced cooked ham*
1 cup chicken stock or milk	*4 hard-boiled eggs*

Remove the stems and thinly slice the caps of 1 pound of mushrooms. Sauté in 2 tablespoons of butter until lightly browned.
Melt another 2 tablespoons of butter in the pan. Blend in 3 tablespoons of flour, off the fire. Add 1 cup of chicken stock or milk
and 1 cup of light cream. Stir over the fire until the sauce comes
to a boil. Add 4 tablespoons of sherry and taste for seasoning.
Cut enough cooked ham in small ½-inch dice to make 3 cups and
cut 4 hard-boiled eggs into pieces about the same size. Mix with
the sauce. Put into a lightly greased casserole or large, shallow,
ovenproof serving dish. Bake for about 30 minutes in a moderate
oven at 350° until the top is nicely browned. If you wish to delay
serving this dish, just cover it and turn the heat down to 250°.
Serve in the casserole or baking dish. Serves 6.

LENTIL SOUP

1 pound lentils (2 cups)	*1 medium-size onion, chopped*
1 ham bone	*2 stalks celery, chopped*
4 tablespoons olive oil	*1 tablespoon chopped parsley*
2 tomatoes	

We have the Italians to thank for this version of the perennially popular lentil soup. Soak 1 pound of lentils overnight in plenty of cold water — they will swell, so make allowances for it. Drain. Put into a large saucepan with the ham bone and 2 quarts of cold water. Bring slowly to a boil. Cover and simmer until the lentils are very soft, about 1½ to 2 hours. Remove and put through a strainer.

In the meantime heat 4 tablespoons of olive oil. Add a medium-size finely chopped onion, 2 chopped stalks of celery and 1 tablespoon of finely chopped parsley. Cook over a moderate fire until lightly browned. Skin 2 tomatoes, remove the seedy pulp and cut the rest into shreds. Add to the vegetables and simmer for 10 to 15 minutes.

Reheat the strained lentil soup and add the tomato mixture. Taste for seasoning. Simmer for at least 15 minutes or until ready to serve. Serve with croutons. This makes at least 6 generous servings.

JAMBALAYA

½ pound link sausage
1 large onion, finely chopped
1 green pepper, diced
1 pound raw smoked ham, diced
1 large clove garlic, crushed
1½ cups rice
½ cup chopped tomatoes

3 cups stock or water
salt, pepper
2 sprigs fresh thyme or ½ teaspoon dried thyme
1 tablespoon chopped parsley
1 dozen oysters or 1 cup cooked shrimp — or both

Cook ½ pound of sausage in a deep heavy saucepan until well browned. Remove from the pan and cut in half. Add to the pan 1 large finely chopped onion, 1 diced green pepper and 1 pound of raw smoked ham cut into small dice. Cook over a moderate fire until lightly browned, stirring often to brown evenly. Add 1 clove of crushed garlic and cook for 1 minute. Add 1½ cups of rice and ½ cup of chopped tomatoes and cook another minute or so. Pour on 3 cups of stock or water and bring to a boil. Season with salt, pepper, 2 sprigs of fresh thyme or ½ teaspoon dried thyme and 1 tablespoon of chopped parsley. Put back the sausage.

Cover and cook over a very slow fire for 30 to 35 minutes, until the rice is tender but not soft. Just before serving add a dozen oysters or 1 cup of cooked shrimp — or both — and cook only until the edges of the oysters curl.

Serve in a hot casserole. Serves 6 to 8.

Note: Diced cooked chicken may be added to this dish. And if the stock is chicken it will give the rice an excellent flavor.

GLAZED HAM

1 slice precooked ham, ¾ inch thick, weighing about 1½ pounds
whole cloves
½ cup brown sugar
1 cup red wine
1 teaspoon Dijon mustard

Slash the fat around the edge of the ham and stick it with cloves at 1-inch intervals. Put the ham in a shallow baking dish with 1 cup of red wine. Bake in a moderate oven at 350° for 20 minutes. Blend together 1 teaspoon of Dijon mustard, ½ cup of brown sugar and 2 to 3 tablespoons of the pan juices. Spread over the ham. Raise the oven temperature to 425° and cook the ham until the top is glazed, another 15 to 20 minutes. Baste several times with the pan juices. Serve on a hot platter and spoon the gravy over the top. Serves 4.

VEAL AND HAM LOAF

2 pounds ground ham and veal
1 tablespoon butter
1 small onion, finely chopped
salt, pepper
1 green pepper, finely chopped
1 egg
⅓ cup sherry

Use either equal proportions of ham and veal — in other words, 1 pound of each — or 1½ pounds of ham and ½ pound of veal. Melt 1 tablespoon of butter in a small skillet. Add a small finely chopped onion and a finely chopped green pepper and cook slowly until soft but not brown. Put the meat, onion and pepper, and 1 egg into a large mixing bowl. Bring ½ cup sherry to a boil in the skillet and pour it in with the meat. Season with salt and pepper. Work until thoroughly blended with one hand which has been dipped into cold water. Place on a cookie sheet and shape into a loaf. Bake in a moderately hot oven at 400° for 45 minutes. Carefully transfer the meat loaf to a hot serving dish and garnish with small mounds of fresh cooked vegetables such as carrots, lima beans, corn, asparagus and zucchini. Serves 6.

CROWN ROAST OF PORK

crown roast pork, 16 ribs   *2 tablespoons chopped parsley*
1 large clove garlic, crushed   *½ teaspoon dried thyme*
salt, pepper   *1 cup dry white wine*
½ cup chopped onion   *1 bunch celery*
½ cup chopped celery   *1 teaspoon meat glaze*
3 tablespoons butter   *1 bunch carrots*
1 pound lean ground pork   *2 teaspoons potato flour*
3 tablespoons applesauce   *1½ cups stock or water*

Have the butcher prepare a 16-rib crown of pork. He will remove the back or chine bone to facilitate carving, French the ends of the ribs — that is, remove the fat and meat leaving the bones bare — and then form the meat into a crown with the meat inside and the bones on the outside. Season with a large clove of crushed garlic, salt and pepper. Place in a roasting pan and put the following filling into the center. Cook ½ cup of chopped onion and ½ cup of chopped celery in 1 tablespoon of butter until soft but not brown. Blend with 1 pound of lean ground pork, 3 tablespoons of applesauce, 1 tablespoon of chopped parsley and ½ teaspoon of dried thyme. Make ridges in the top of the stuffing with a fork. Tie a small piece of aluminum foil around the end of each rib to prevent the bones from charring. Pour 1 cup of dry white wine into the pan. Roast in a moderate oven at 350° for 30 to 35 minutes to the pound, or until a meat thermometer registers 185°. Baste occasionally with the pan juices.

Meanwhile cut 1 bunch of celery into 1½-inch pieces and cook until tender in boiling water with 1 teaspoon of meat glaze. Cut 1 bunch of carrots into small even pieces and cook until tender in boiling salted water. Drain and blend with 2 tablespoons of melted butter and 1 tablespoon of chopped parsley.

To Serve: Remove the pork from the oven and place on a hot serving dish. Put a paper cutlet on each rib. Let stand for about 15 minutes. Skim any fat in excess of about 3 tablespoons off the pan juices, leaving all the good brown juices. Blend in 2 teaspoons of potato flour. Pour on 1½ cups of stock or water and stir over the fire until the gravy comes to a boil. Arrange small alternate piles of celery and carrots around the pork. Serve the gravy in a separate bowl. Serves 8.

ROAST PORK WITH GLAZED APPLES

1 piece loin of pork, 4 to 5 pounds
salt, pepper
1 large clove garlic, crushed
½ pound sausage meat
1 large yellow onion, finely chopped

2 hard-boiled eggs, finely chopped
2 tablespoons chopped parsley
1 cup white wine
1 cup water

GLAZED APPLES

4 apples
¾ cup water
juice and shredded rind of 1 orange

juice of 1 lemon
few drops red vegetable coloring

Bone the pork or have the butcher do it. Spread it out on a board. Season with salt, pepper and a clove of crushed garlic. Cook ½ pound of sausage meat and a large finely chopped onion over a brisk fire for 3 to 4 minutes. Add 2 chopped hard-boiled eggs and 2 tablespoons of chopped parsley and spread this mixture on top of the pork, leaving a 1-inch margin around the edge. Roll and tie with string at 2-inch intervals. Place in a shallow roasting pan with ½ cup of white wine. Roast in a moderate oven at 350° for about 30 minutes to the pound, or until a meat thermometer registers 185°. Baste every 15 minutes or so, using 1 tablespoon of wine until it is gone, then the pan juices.

Glazed Apples: Skin the top halves of 4 apples and remove the cores. Cook ¾ cup of sugar, ¾ cup of water, the juice and finely shredded rind of 1 orange and the juice of 1 lemon to a light thread, 225°. Add a few drops of red vegetable coloring. Put the apples in a baking dish, cover with the syrup and cook in a moderate over at 350° until they are soft but not broken. Baste occasionally, and the cooking time will be about 20 to 30 minutes.

To Serve: Remove the pork from the pan, cut off the strings and carve as many slices as needed for one meal. Arrange them slightly overlapping on a hot serving dish, with the uncut piece at one end. Add 1 cup of water to the pan juices and bring to a boil. Spoon a little of this gravy over the meat and serve the rest in a gravy bowl. Garnish with the glazed apples. Serves 6 to 8.

Note: Use additional apples if you are planning to serve more than 4 people.

ROAST LOIN OF PORK

1 piece loin of pork, 4 to 5 pounds   *1 clove garlic, crushed*
salt, pepper   *1 cup red wine*
8 medium-size onions

LIMA BEAN PURÉE

2 packages frozen baby lima beans   *salt, pepper*
2 to 3 tablespoons sour cream

BROILED TOMATOES

4 tomatoes   *½ cup grated Parmesan cheese*
½ cup bread crumbs   *salt, pepper*

2 tablespoons butter   *½ teaspoon meat glaze*
2 tablespoons flour   *1½ cups water*

Bone the loin of pork or have the butcher do it. Season with salt, pepper and 1 clove of crushed garlic. Roll and tie with string at 2-inch intervals. Place in a shallow roasting pan and pour in ½ cup of red wine. Put the bones in the pan to add flavor. Roast in a moderate oven at 350° for 30 minutes to the pound, or until a meat thermometer registers 185°. Baste every 15 minutes, adding 1 to 2 tablespoons of wine each time until it is gone, then use the pan drippings. When the meat has cooked for 1 hour put 8 medium-size onions into the pan.

Lima Bean Purée: Cook 2 packages of frozen baby lima beans in boiling salted water until very tender. Drain well and put through a strainer. Season lightly with salt and pepper and blend in 2 to 3 tablespoons of sour cream. Reheat in a double boiler.

Broiled Tomatoes: Cut the tomatoes in half. Sprinkle with ½ cup of bread crumbs, ½ cup of grated Parmesan cheese, salt and pepper. Dot with 2 tablespoons of butter and broil until golden brown.

When the meat is done, remove it and the onions from the pan and let stand for the few minutes it takes to make the gravy. Bring the pan juices to a boil. Blend in, off the fire, 2 tablespoons of flour and ½ teaspoon of meat glaze. Pour on 1½ cups of water and stir over the fire until the gravy comes to a boil. Taste for seasoning. Simmer for a few minutes.

To Serve: Cut the strings off the pork and carve as many slices as needed for one meal. Make a bed of lima bean purée on a hot serving dish. Place the slices of pork slightly overlapping over the purée with the uncut piece at one end. Strain the gravy over all. Garnish with broiled tomatoes and the onions placed alternately around the edge of the dish. Serves 6 to 8.

PORK WITH PINEAPPLE

8 slices cooked roast pork	1 green pepper, diced
1 teaspoon crushed garlic	½ teaspoon tomato paste
1 tablespoon flour	1 teaspoon meat glaze
4 tablespoons butter	2 teaspoons potato flour
8 slices fresh or canned pine-apple	1 cup stock
	1 tablespoon red currant jelly
4 chicken livers	2 tablespoons sherry

salt, pepper

Rub 8 slices of cooked roast pork with ½ teaspoon of crushed garlic, dust lightly with 1 tablespoon of flour and brown quickly on both sides in 2 tablespoons of hot butter. Remove the pork from the pan. Put another tablespoon of butter in the pan and brown 8 slices of fresh or canned pineapple on each side. Arrange the pineapple slightly overlapping on a hot serving dish. Place the pork slices on top. Put in a very slow oven to keep warm while you prepare the following sauce.

Heat the remaining tablespoon of butter in the same pan and quickly brown 4 chicken livers. Remove them from the pan. Add ½ teaspoon of crushed garlic and a diced green pepper to the pan and cook for 2 to 3 minutes. Stir in, off the fire, ½ teaspoon of tomato paste, 1 teaspoon of meat glaze and 2 teaspoons of potato flour. When blended pour on 1 cup of stock and stir over the fire until the sauce comes to a boil. Add 1 tablespoon of red currant jelly, 2 tablespoons of sherry, salt and pepper and simmer for about 10 minutes. Add sliced chicken livers to the sauce, pour over the pork and pineapple and serve. Serves 4.

PORK TENDERLOIN WITH LEEK PURÉE

6 slices pork tenderloin   *5 tablespoons butter*

LEEK PURÉE

2 bunches leeks   *5 tablespoons flour*
salt, pepper   *1 cup milk*
4 tablespoons butter   *½ cup leek stock*

Pork tenderloin is the tenderest and most expensive pork cut but has no waste. Buy 6 slices of tenderloin about 1½ inches thick. Put them between 2 pieces of waxed paper and beat them lightly with a wooden mallet. Melt 3 tablespoons of butter in a heavy skillet and slowly brown the tenderloins on both sides. When well browned, cover the pan and cook another 20 minutes or so. Meanwhile prepare the leek purée.

Leek Purée: Remove the green tops from 2 bunches of leeks and slice the white part. Cook in boiling salted water until very tender. Drain, reserving the water, and put the leeks back on a low fire until all the liquid has evaporated. Then put them through a strainer. Boil the cooking water down to ½ cup. Make a thick white sauce. Melt 4 tablespoons of butter. Blend in 5 tablespoons of flour, off the fire. Add 1 cup of milk and the ½ cup of leek stock and stir over the fire until the sauce comes to a boil. Add all but 2 tablespoons of the leek purée and season with salt and pepper.

To Serve: Make a bed of the leek purée on a hot serving dish. Arrange the pork tenderloins on top of the purée. Melt another 2 tablespoons of butter in the same pan the tenderloins were cooked in and add the 2 tablespoons of leek purée. Pour this over the tenderloins. Serves 6.

ROAST SUCKLING PIG

1 suckling pig, about 10 pounds	*3 cups soft bread crumbs*
2 large onions, finely chopped	*salt, pepper*
about 2 cups butter	*thyme*
6 chicken livers	*2 tablespoons chopped parsley*
1 cup chopped mushrooms	*2 eggs*
1 cup chopped apples	*watercress*
2 tablespoons flour	

Have the butcher clean the pig thoroughly. Sauté 2 large finely chopped onions in 3 tablespoons of butter until soft but not brown. Put them into a large mixing bowl. In the same pan quickly brown the pig's liver and 6 chicken livers in 1 tablespoon of butter over a very hot fire. Remove them from the fire and when cool enough to handle, chop them coarsely. Add to the onions with 1 cup of chopped raw mushrooms, 1 cup of chopped apples, 3 cups of soft bread crumbs, 1 cup of melted butter, salt, pepper, thyme, 2 tablespoons of chopped parsley and 2 eggs. Blend thoroughly. Put this stuffing into the pig and secure with skewers and string.

Put the pig's front feet forward and the hind ones backward and skewer them into place. Put a piece of wood the size of a small apple into the pig's mouth to keep it in position for an apple after it is cooked. Cover the ears with aluminum foil so they will not get burned. Season the pig with salt and pepper and rub the entire surface with softened butter. Place in a roasting pan and pour in 1 cup of boiling water. Roast in a moderate oven at 350° for 3 to 3½ hours, until thoroughly done. Baste every 15 minutes with the pan juices.

Meanwhile simmer the pig's heart in 4 cups of water seasoned with a little celery, onion, salt and pepper. When it is tender drain, reserving the stock, and chop the heart finely for the gravy.

To Serve: Remove the pig from the roasting pan and place it on a bed of watercress on a large hot platter. Rub the skin with butter to make it shine. Take the wood out of its mouth and put in an apple. Place cranberries or raisins in the eyes and a wreath of holly or cranberries around the neck. The pig may be garnished with glazed apples (see page 193). Skim any excess fat off the pan juices and blend 2 tablespoons of flour into them. Add the strained heart stock and stir over the fire until the gravy comes to a boil. Add the chopped heart and taste for seasoning. Serve the gravy in a separate bowl.

To carve a suckling pig, first remove the legs as you would with a turkey. Run the carving knife down both sides of the backbone. Then carve into rib chops at right angles to the backbone. A 10-pound pig will serve 10 to 12 people.

STUFFED PORK CHOPS

4 double loin pork chops	*½ cup soft bread crumbs*
1 medium-size onion, finely chopped	*salt, pepper*
	⅛ teaspoon ground nutmeg
2 tablespoons butter	*1 tablespoon chopped parsley*
	1 egg

The chops should be cut 1 to 1½ inches thick with a pocket in each one. Sauté 1 medium-size finely chopped onion in 2 tablespoons of butter until soft but not brown. Add ½ cup of soft bread crumbs, salt, pepper, about ⅛ teaspoon of ground nutmeg and 1 tablespoon of chopped parsley. Remove from the fire and blend in 1 egg. Put the stuffing into the pockets and secure with skewers or toothpicks. Place the chops in a shallow baking dish and bake in a moderate oven at 350° for about 1 hour, or until well browned. Serve on a hot serving dish. Serves 4.

PORK CHOPS WITH MUSHROOMS

4 large pork chops	½ pound mushrooms, sliced
2 tablespoons olive oil	2 tomatoes
1 large clove garlic, crushed	3 tablespoons white wine
1 green pepper, diced	salt, pepper

Trim 4 large pork chops of any excess fat. Brown them rather slowly in 2 tablespoons of olive oil in a large skillet. Remove the chops from the pan. Add 1 large clove of crushed garlic, a diced green pepper and ½ pound of sliced mushrooms and cook until they are lightly browned. Skin 2 tomatoes, remove the seedy pulp and shred the rest. Put back the chops with the tomatoes and 3 tablespoons of white wine. Season with salt and pepper. Cover and simmer about 20 to 30 minutes, or until the chops are tender. Serve the chops on a hot serving dish surrounded with the vegetables. Serves 4.

PORK CHOPS WITH WHITE WINE

4 large pork chops	3 tablespoons butter
½ teaspoon dry mustard	1 medium-size yellow onion, sliced
1 teaspoon salt	1 teaspoon tomato paste
¼ teaspoon pepper	½ cup white wine
¼ cup brandy, optional	

Season 4 large pork chops with ½ teaspoon of dry mustard blended with 1 teaspoon of salt and ¼ teaspoon of pepper. Brown them quickly on both sides in a large skillet in 1 tablespoon of hot butter. Remove the chops from the pan. Add another 2 tablespoons of butter to the pan and sauté a medium-size thinly sliced yellow onion until soft but not brown. Blend in 1 teaspoon of tomato paste. Add ½ cup of white wine and return the chops to the pan. Cover and simmer until the chops are tender, about 40 to 50 minutes. Serve on a hot platter. To serve the chops flaming, heat ¼ cup of brandy in a small pan, ignite and pour over the chops. Serves 4.

PORK CHOPS WITH APPLES

4 thick pork chops	*8 small white onions*
salt, pepper	*4 apples*
2 tablespoons butter	*½ cup water*
1 tablespoon sugar	

Season 4 pork chops with salt and pepper. Heat 1 tablespoon of butter in a shallow casserole and quickly brown the chops on both sides. Remove the chops. Put another tablespoon of butter in the pan and brown 8 small white onions. Pare, quarter and core 4 apples. Lift the glaze in the pan with ½ cup of water and put back the chops. Surround the chops with the apples and onions and sprinkle them lightly with 1 tablespoon of sugar. Cover and cook in a moderate oven at 350° for about 45 minutes, until the chops are tender. Serve in the casserole. Serves 4.

PORK CHOPS WITH MUSTARD SAUCE

4 large pork chops	*1 teaspoon French mustard*
2 tablespoons butter	*salt, pepper*
2 tablespoons vinegar	*½ cup cream*
1 to 2 tablespoons finely chopped parsley or chives	

Cook the chops slowly in a large skillet in 2 tablespoons of butter until well browned on both sides. Pork always needs ample cooking and it will take 30 to 40 minutes to thoroughly cook and brown the chops. Remove the chops, arrange them in a hot serving dish and keep warm. Lift the glaze in the pan with 2 tablespoons of vinegar. Add 1 teaspoon of French mustard, salt and pepper. Blend in ½ cup of cream and stir until the mixture comes to a boil. Let simmer for 2 to 3 minutes. Pour over the chops, sprinkle with 1 to 2 tablespoons of finely chopped parsley or chives and serve immediately. Serves 4.

SPARERIBS WITH PINEAPPLE

3 pounds spareribs	1 cup pineapple juice
salt, pepper	½ cup vinegar
2 tablespoons butter	1 teaspoon paprika
1 medium-size onion, finely chopped	1 teaspoon chili powder
2 cloves garlic, crushed	1 teaspoon sugar
	1 teaspoon dry mustard
1 cup crushed pineapple	

Cut the spareribs into serving pieces. Season both sides with salt and pepper. Place in single layers in shallow baking dishes. Bake in a hot oven at 400° for about 1½ hours, or until they are well browned. Meanwhile prepare the following sauce.

Melt 2 tablespoons of butter in a saucepan. Cook 1 medium-size finely chopped onion until soft but not brown. Put 2 cloves of crushed garlic in the pan and cook another 1 to 2 minutes. Pour on 1 cup of pineapple juice and ½ cup of vinegar and bring to a boil. Add 1 teaspoon each of paprika, chili powder, sugar and dry mustard. Season with salt and pepper and simmer for 20 to 30 minutes.

When the spareribs are browned, pour off all the fat in the pan. Spread 1 cup of crushed pineapple over the spareribs and pour the sauce into the pans. Cook for another 20 to 30 minutes, basting the spareribs often with the sauce.

To Serve: Arrange the spareribs on a hot serving dish. Spoon a little of the sauce over them and serve the rest in a sauce bowl. Serves 6.

CHOUCROUTE GARNIE
(Sauerkraut Garnished)

4 pounds sauerkraut	salt, peppercorns
1 pound bacon	2 cups dry white wine
1 large carrot	4 cups water
1 onion stuck with 1 clove	12 medium-size potatoes
1 pound sausage	1 to 2 tablespoons butter
1 cottage ham	1 tablespoon chopped parsley

Drain the sauerkraut well. Put ⅓ of the bacon on the bottom of a deep casserole or baking dish. Cover with half the sauerkraut. Put in 1 large carrot, 1 onion stuck with a clove, a pound of sausage, a cottage ham and another third of the bacon. Cover with the rest of the sauerkraut and top with the remaining bacon. Season with salt and peppercorns. Pour into the pan 2 cups of dry white wine and 4 cups of water. Cover and cook in a moderately slow oven at 325° for 4 hours.

An hour or so before serving time peel 12 medium-size potatoes, or if they are new they can be left in their jackets. Cook until just tender in boiling salted water. Drain and put them back in the pan and over a slow fire for a few minutes to dry out. Mix with 1 to 2 tablespoons of melted butter and 1 tablespoon of chopped parsley.

To Serve: Make a neat mound of the sauerkraut on a hot serving dish. Cut the ham into thin slices and arrange them slightly overlapping on top of the sauerkraut. Place the sausages around the sides of the dish and pile the potatoes at each end. Serve with mustard. Serves 6 to 8.

PIEDS DE PORC À LA SAINTE MENEHOULD
(Grilled Pigs' Feet)

4 pigs' feet	*2 sprigs parsley*
1 carrot, sliced	*1 bay leaf*
1 onion, sliced	*3 or 4 cloves*
1 clove garlic	*salt, peppercorns*
1 sprig fresh thyme	*about 2 tablespoons melted butter*
	bread crumbs

Grilled pigs' feet have an appetizing flavor and appearance. Plain boiled pigs' feet may taste good, but that is more than can be said for the way they look.

Buy 4 prepared pigs' feet and wash them well. Prepare a court bouillon with 1½ quarts of water, 1 sliced carrot, 1 sliced onion, 1 clove of garlic, 1 sprig of thyme, 2 sprigs of parsley, 1 bay leaf, 3 or 4 cloves, salt and peppercorns. Bring to a boil and simmer for half an hour. Add the pigs' feet and let them simmer for 4 to 5 hours, until very tender. Cool them in the liquid. If you wish to keep the skin from breaking, tie each foot tightly in cloth before cooking.

Brush the pigs' feet with melted butter and roll in fine dry bread crumbs. Then either broil them slowly until golden brown all over or roast them in a hot oven at 450° until well browned. Serve with strong mustard. Serves 4.

ENGLISH PORK PIE

PASTRY

2 cups flour	1½ sticks butter (¼ pound each)
1 teaspoon salt	1 egg yolk
1 teaspoon baking powder	¼ cup ice water

FILLING

1 pound sausage meat	¼ pound tongue, cut in strips
½ pound cooked ham, cut in strips	2 hard-boiled eggs

STUFFED EGGS

4 hard-boiled eggs	1 tablespoon tomato paste
3 ounces cream cheese	salt, pepper
2 ounces creamed butter	dash Tabasco

1 egg, beaten   aspic
watercress

Pastry: Sift 2 cups of flour, 1 teaspoon of salt and 1 teaspoon of baking powder together on a pastry board or marble slab. Make a well in the center and in it put 1½ sticks of butter, 1 egg yolk and ¼ cup of ice water. Work the center ingredients to a smooth paste. Then work in the flour with the heel of your hand. Wrap in waxed paper and chill in the refrigerator for 1 to 2 hours. Then roll out half the pastry about ¼ inch thick and line a raised pie mold. Put in the filling (below); brush the edge of the dough with beaten egg. Roll the rest of the dough a little thicker than the bottom crust. Cover the top and trim the edges neatly. Make a small hole in the center and cover it with a flower made with small rounds of pastry. Brush the top with beaten egg. Chill in the refrigerator for at least an hour. Then bake in a moderate oven at 350° for about an hour or until golden brown. Remove and cool. Take off the center flower and pour into the hole 1 cup of aspic on the point of setting (see index for aspic recipes). Chill in the refrigerator for 2 to 3 hours or until ready to use.

Filling: Use ⅛ of the sausage to make a layer in the bottom. Cover it with half the ham, cut in strips. Then another layer of sausage, the tongue cut in strips, sausage, sliced hard-boiled eggs, sausage, the rest of the ham and a final layer of sausage.

Stuffed Eggs: Cut 4 hard-boiled eggs in half lengthwise. Remove yolks and strain them. Blend with 3 ounces of cream cheese, 2 ounces of creamed butter, 1 tablespoon of tomato paste, salt, pepper and a dash of Tabasco. Put into a pastry bag with a large rose tube and pipe into the whites.

To Serve: Carefully unmold the pie and place it on a serving dish. Garnish with the stuffed eggs, chopped set aspic and watercress. Serves 6 to 8.

SAUSAGE WITH WHITE WINE

1 pound link sausage	*1 small onion, finely chopped*
¼ cup water	*2 teaspoons chopped parsley*
butter	*1 tablespoon flour*
1 cup dry white wine	

Try to get nice thick sausages which have a large proportion of meat to fat. Some of the small link sausages shrink to almost nothing when they are cooked. Put them in a large skillet with ¼ cup of water. Bring to a boil, cover and steam over a low fire for 5 minutes or so, until the water has evaporated. Remove the cover, turn up the heat a little and brown the sausages all over. Remove them from the pan and keep warm. If there is not about 3 tablespoons of fat in the pan, add butter to make that amount. Sauté a small finely chopped onion and 1 teaspoon of chopped parsley until lightly browned. Blend in 1 tablespoon of flour, off the fire. Add 1 cup of dry white wine and stir over the fire until the sauce comes to a boil. Taste for seasoning and simmer for a few minutes.

Place the sausages on a hot serving dish and strain the sauce over them. Sprinkle with the remaining 1 teaspoon of parsley. Serves 4.

SAUSAGE SOUFFLÉ

6 slices white bread	2 eggs, beaten
1 tablespoon butter	1 teaspoon dry mustard
1 pound sausage meat	salt
¼ pound Cheddar cheese, grated	2 cups milk

This is a simplified version of a soufflé. Remove the crusts from 6 slices of white bread. The bread should be at least a day old, and it is better if it is older than that. Butter the bread very lightly with 1 tablespoon of butter. Cook 1 pound of sausage meat until browned. Put alternate layers of bread, sausage and grated cheese in a greased soufflé dish or casserole. Mix together 2 beaten eggs, 1 teaspoon of dry mustard and a little salt. Add 2 cups of milk and beat until blended. Pour into the baking dish. Let stand for at least 4 hours before cooking. It can be made the night before and placed in the refrigerator; just remove it an hour or two before baking. Bake in a moderate oven at 375° for about 45 minutes, until puffed and nicely browned. Serve immediately in the baking dish. Serves 4 to 6.

MACARONI WITH SAUSAGE

1 pound link sausage	1 can tomato paste (6 ounces)
¼ cup olive oil	salt, pepper
1 large clove garlic, crushed	pinch oregano
1 medium-size yellow onion, sliced	1 bay leaf
	2 cups water
1 pound mushrooms, sliced	1 pound macaroni
½ cup grated Parmesan cheese	

Cut the sausages into 1-inch pieces and cook over a slow fire until well browned. In another pan heat ¼ cup of olive oil. Add a large clove of crushed garlic and cook 1 minute. Put a medium-size yellow onion and a pound of sliced mushrooms into the pan and cook until the onion is soft but not browned. Add the sausage, 1 can of tomato paste, salt, pepper, a pinch of oregano, 1 bay leaf and 2 cups of water. Cover and simmer for about 1 hour.

In the meantime cook 1 pound of macaroni in plenty of boiling salted water. Drain and place in an ovenproof serving dish or casserole. Add the sausage mixture and blend lightly with 2 forks. Sprinkle with ½ cup of grated Parmesan cheese and bake in a moderate oven at 350° until heated through and lightly browned, about 15 to 20 minutes. Serve in the dish it was baked in. Serves 6.

HEAD CHEESE

1 pig's head	2 bay leaves
salt	1 tablespoon butter or pork fat
½ lemon	2 sprigs fresh thyme
3 onions	¼ teaspoon powdered cloves
1 carrot, sliced	pepper
1 stalk celery, sliced	1 teaspoon grated lemon rind
peppercorns	½ cup sherry or Madeira

VINAIGRETTE SAUCE

1 teaspoon salt	½ cup olive oil
½ teaspoon coarsely cracked black and white peppercorns	1 teaspoon lemon juice
few grains cayenne	¼ teaspoon crushed garlic
4 tablespoons tarragon vinegar	1 tablespoon finely chopped onion
½ cup salad oil	1 tablespoon finely chopped parsley
	1 finely chopped hard-boiled egg

Quarter a pig's head. Remove the ears, brains, eyes, tongue and most of the fat. Soak in cold water to cover for several hours to remove all traces of blood, changing the water occasionally. Put the head, tongue and ears in a wide shallow saucepan. Add enough water to just cover the meat, bring to a boil and skim. Add salt, ½ lemon, 1 sliced onion, 1 sliced carrot, a sliced celery stalk, peppercorns and 2 bay leaves. Simmer for about 4 hours, until the meat is falling from the bones. Cool in the stock. Drain, reserving the stock, separate the meat from the bones and cut it into small dice. Cook the brains in a little of the stock for 15 minutes, dice them and the tongue and ears.

Finely chop 2 large onions and cook until soft but not brown in 1 tablespoon of butter or pork fat. Add 2 sprigs of fresh thyme, ¼ teaspoon powdered cloves, a little pepper and the strained stock. Simmer for 10 minutes. Then add 1 teaspoon of grated lemon rind and ½ cup of sherry or Madeira and simmer another 20 minutes. Put the meat into a loaf pan and cover with the stock. Cover with a cloth and cool. Then put a heavy weight on the top and chill for 5 to 6 hours. Meanwhile make the following vinaigrette sauce.

Vinaigrette Sauce: Put into a large screw-top jar 1 teaspoon of salt, ½ teaspoon of coarsely cracked black and white peppercorns, a few grains of cayenne, 4 tablespoons of tarragon vinegar, ½ cup of salad oil, ½ cup of olive oil, 1 teaspoon of lemon juice, ¼ teaspoon of crushed garlic, 1 tablespoon of finely chopped onion and 1 tablespoon of finely chopped parsley. Shake until well blended. Just before serving add 1 finely chopped hard-boiled egg.

To Serve: Turn out the head cheese. Cut into thin slices and arrange them slightly overlapping on a cold serving dish. Serve the vinaigrette sauce separately. One loaf pan will make 12 to 15 slices.

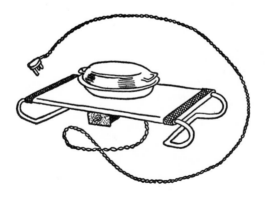

CHICKEN

There is an almost infinite number of ways of preparing chicken and the following recipes are just a few of the possibilities. It has a delicate flavor but one that is still strong enough to hold its own with other definite flavors. That is one of the reasons why chicken is such a versatile bird and lends itself readily to a variety of uses, in combination with many varied foods, herbs and spices, at home with the expensive truffle or the common garden onion.

Chickens are easy to purchase. Generally speaking there are only two kinds, young and old. Young chickens may only weigh as much as 1½ pounds, and then they are roasted whole. Slightly larger chickens, from 2 to 3½ pounds, have fine flavor and are used in many of the following recipes. Broilers weigh from 2 to 3 pounds, while fryers are slightly larger, weighing as a rule from 3 to 3½ pounds. The 4 to 5 pound young chickens are generally roasted, and are also often used instead of the so-called fowls when a stewing chicken is wanted. Their flavor is excellent for roasting, but although they are more tender than fowl and therefore cook more quickly, sometimes their flavor is so delicate it is almost lost when they are stewed — that is, cooked in water. Fowl or stewing chickens, as they are now usually called, are birds over a year old and tougher. They weigh from 5 to 6 pounds and are good only for stewing, requiring a relatively long period of cooking submerged in water to bring them to a desirable tenderness. If you have a fowl that isn't too old and tough, you will get fine flavor. A few old toms will never get tender no matter how long you cook them, but it is rare that they reach a reputable market.

Chickens are usually sold already dressed, that is with the head, feet and insides removed. All you need do is pull out any pin feathers with tweezers, feel the inside to be sure the lung is removed and cut out the little oil sac above the tail piece. You can wash the chicken quickly in cold water, although this isn't necessary unless it is bloody. But never leave it soaking in water unless you want to lose some of the flavor.

Some of the following recipes call for tying up the chicken, which is done to keep it in shape while it cooks. Many butchers do this for you, but it only takes a few seconds to do it yourself. Use a soft white twine and cut a piece about 20 inches long. Place the chicken on a flat surface with its feet towards you. Push the legs back close to the body of the chicken. Put the center of the twine across the end of the legs and bring it around and up between them forming a figure 8. Then put the string between the legs and breast, turn the chicken over and put the twine through the wings, fold the neck flap over the vent and tie the string in a bow over it.

Chickens are always tied when they are cooked whole. If they are stuffed, put 3 or 4 small skewers across the vent to hold the stuffing in and close it by lacing the skewers together with twine. There are special small stainless-steel skewers for this purpose which you can get at any dime store. This is far simpler and quicker than sewing the vent.

Some of these recipes start with browning the whole chicken on top of the stove, and this may be a new idea to some cooks. The chicken is tied up and put into a deep heavy saucepan with the breast side down, and slowly both the breast and then the legs and back are browned. Putting a wooden spoon in the center cavity makes it easy to turn the chicken whenever it needs it. It takes about 30 minutes to brown the chicken all over. The chicken isn't fully cooked then, just browned on the outside, and it is usually cut up before it finishes cooking. Chickens can have this preliminary browning in a moderate oven rather than on top of the stove. But heat all around the chicken rather than on just the particular spot that is being browned tends to dry out the chicken more than the top-of-the-stove method. The top of the stove only takes a few minutes longer, and requires just a little attention to see when the chicken should be turned. The advantage of this technique is that the skin doesn't shrink away from the flesh as it does when you cut up the meat before browning, and browning it whole keeps it tender and juicy.

To cut a browned chicken into serving pieces, grasp one leg and pull it and the thigh out from the body, and with a sharp knife cut the thigh bone that attaches it to the body. Separate the leg and thigh. With a pair of kitchen scissors cut off the rather un-attractive-looking bone at the end of the leg. Do the second leg and thigh. Then cut each side of the breast and the wing off in one piece, and if the breast is large enough, cut it in half crosswise. This will give you either 6 or 8 pieces of chicken plus the carcass. The oysters are the only meat worth speaking of on the carcass, but these do have flavor so put them in the pan with the rest of the chicken when you finish cooking it. In finishing cooking put the thighs and legs in the pan first, skin side down, since they require the longest cooking, then the breast with the carcass on top. The advantage of cutting up a chicken in this manner is that you have neat pieces of meat to serve, without a lot of unappeal-ing-looking bone.

When you are cooking a chicken in water — that is, stewing it — it is important to flavor the water with onion, carrot and celery. Also the water should not boil, but merely simmer with the water barely moving. There is a mistaken notion that the harder something boils the quicker it will cook. Boiling meat hard not only does not hasten the cooking time, but it toughens rather than tenderizes the meat. So after the water comes to a boil, lower the heat and keep it low. If the chicken can cool in the cooking liquid, it will help retain juiciness and prevent shrinkage. The cooking liquid is of course excellent stock and should always be kept and used. If you want a more concentrated stock, it can be boiled down after the chicken is removed. Any stock not im-mediately needed can be kept for a few days in the refrigerator or frozen.

There are several recipes for dishes using just the breasts of the chicken. This isn't quite the problem it may sound. In many localities there are poultry-in-parts shops where you can buy any section of the chicken you want as well as chicken livers and chicken fat. Chicken in parts is also almost universally avail-able frozen. If you have to use whole chickens, many of the re-cipes calling for chicken breasts may be used with the whole chicken instead; if the breasts are essential, there are always many uses for the rest of the chicken.

One more word about chickens — please don't overcook them. This doesn't apply as much to stewing, but it does apply to all other cooking methods. A properly cooked chicken is full of flavor and is tender and juicy. Overcooking dries it out, eventually making it rather stringy with far less flavor than it should have. There are two ways of testing when a chicken is done: when the meat and skin on the leg start shrinking back from the bone; or when you pierce the thickest part of the leg and the juice that runs out is clear with no trace of pink.

Chicken livers are a great delicacy and fortunately available frozen if fresh ones are scarce. For the maximum flavor and tenderness brown them over high heat in a very little fat, which only takes 2 to 3 minutes. If they are to have further cooking, be sure there is some additional liquid to keep them from getting hard and dry.

POULET RÔTI PRINTANIÈRE
(Roast Chicken with Fresh Vegetables)

1 roasting chicken, 4 to 5 pounds	1 pound asparagus
salt and pepper	½ pound mushrooms
1 clove garlic	2 tomatoes
7 tablespoons butter	3 tablespoons bread crumbs
¼ cup white wine	3 tablespoons grated Parmesan cheese
3 carrots, scraped and cut into thin strips	3 tablespoons flour
1 pound peas	½ teaspoon tomato paste
	1½ cups stock or water

Sprinkle the inside of the chicken with salt. Place the liver, heart, cut-up gizzard and a peeled clove of garlic in the cavity. Tie up the chicken. Spread with 2 tablespoons of softened butter. Put in a roasting pan with ¼ cup dry white wine. Roast in a moderate oven at 350° for 1 to 1¼ hours, or until the skin is well browned and the chicken is tender. Baste occasionally with melted butter, using 2 more tablespoons, and the pan juices.

While the chicken is cooking, prepare the vegetables. Place the carrots, 1 pound peas and 1 pound of asparagus in cold water and bring to a boil, using separate saucepans. Drain and put each vegetable in a piece of aluminum foil with a little butter and seasoning. Wrap up well, put in a shallow pan and cook in a moderate oven with the chicken for 20 to 30 minutes. Sauté ½ pound of mushroom caps in 1 tablespoon of butter. Halve 2 tomatoes, sprinkle with 3 tablespoons of bread crumbs and 3 tablespoons of grated Parmesan cheese, season, dot with 1 tablespoon of butter and broil until golden brown.

To Serve: Remove the chicken and carve it into serving pieces. Arrange on a hot serving dish and keep warm. Blend 3 tablespoons of flour and ½ teaspoon tomato paste into the pan juices. Add 1½ cups stock or water and stir over the fire until the gravy comes to a boil. Taste for seasoning and simmer for 2 to 3 minutes. Spoon a little of the gravy over the chicken and serve the rest in a sauce bowl. Place the sautéed mushroom caps at each end of the dish, with the broiled tomatoes next to them. At each side put little mounds of peas, carrots and asparagus. Serves 4.

POULET RÔTI FARCI
(Roast Stuffed Chicken)

1 3½ to 4 pound chicken	1 tablespoon chopped parsley
2 tablespoons butter	¼ teaspoon dried thyme
½ large yellow onion	salt, pepper
¼ pound mushrooms	⅔ cup white wine
½ pound sausage meat	sprig fresh tarragon
1 small clove garlic	shoestring potatoes
5 chicken livers, sautéed	1 bunch watercress

Melt 1 tablespoon of butter in a small skillet and cook ½ a finely chopped large yellow onion and ¼ pound of finely chopped mushrooms over a slow fire for 5 minutes. Put ½ pound sausage meat in a mixing bowl and add the cooked onion and mushrooms, 1 small clove of garlic, crushed, 5 sautéed chopped chicken livers, 1 tablespoon chopped parsley, ¼ teaspoon dried thyme, salt and pepper. Stuff the chicken with this mixture and close the opening with skewers and string. Rub the skin with 1 tablespoon softened butter. Put into a roasting pan with ⅓ cup white wine and a sprig of fresh tarragon. Cook in a moderate oven at 350° for 1 to 1¼ hours, until tender, basting every 15 minutes or so with a little of the remaining ⅓ cup of wine.

To Serve: Place the chicken on a hot serving dish and garnish with shoestring potatoes and watercress. Put ½ cup of water into the roasting pan and bring to a boil. Serve this gravy in a separate gravy bowl. Serves 4.

ROAST INDIVIDUAL CHICKENS WITH BREAD SAUCE

4 small chickens, about 1½ pounds	*4 sprigs tarragon*
	7 tablespoons butter
4 small cloves garlic	*salt and pepper*
½ to 1 cup dry white wine	

BREAD SAUCE

6 cloves	*¾ cup soft fresh bread crumbs*
1 small white onion, peeled	*2 tablespoons butter*
1½ cups milk	*salt, white pepper*

Inside each chicken put 1 small clove of garlic, a sprig of fresh tarragon, 1 teaspoon of butter, salt and pepper. Tie up the chickens. Rub the breast and legs of each chicken with 1 tablespoon of softened butter. Place the chickens in a shallow roasting pan with ½ cup dry white wine. Roast in a moderate oven at 350° about 1 hour, or until tender. Baste occasionally with an additional 2 tablespoons of melted butter and then the pan juices. Meanwhile make bread sauce, a traditional English accompaniment to poultry with a pleasant if bland flavor.

Bread Sauce: Stick 6 cloves in 1 small whole peeled onion. Put 1½ cups of milk in a double boiler with the onion and heat very slowly for 20 to 30 minutes without letting the milk boil. Remove the onion. Add ¾ cup soft white bread crumbs with the crust removed, 1 tablespoon of butter, salt and pepper (preferably white). Raise the heat a little and cook for 10 to 15 minutes until the crumbs have absorbed all the milk, stirring frequently to keep the sauce smooth. Add another tablespoon of butter and serve at once; this sauce turns yellow if kept standing for any length of time.

To Serve: Remove chickens, cut off string and take out the garlic and tarragon. Arrange on a hot serving dish. Add ½ cup white wine or water to the juices in the pan and bring to a boil to dissolve the glaze. Taste for seasoning. Pour a little of this gravy over the chickens and serve the rest in a gravy boat. Serve the bread sauce in a separate sauce bowl. Serves 4.

CHICKEN WITH MUSHROOMS IN WHIPPED CREAM SAUCE

1 3½-pound chicken	*salt*
6 tablespoons butter	*freshly cracked black pepper*
¼ cup brandy	*1 cup heavy cream, whipped*
½ pound mushrooms	*½ cup dry white wine*

Cut the chicken into serving pieces, or have your butcher do it. Heat 4 tablespoons of butter in a large skillet, put in the pieces of chicken and brown slowly all over. Heat ¼ cup brandy in a small pan, ignite and pour over the chicken. Cover and cook slowly for 30 to 40 minutes, until the chicken is tender. Meanwhile slice ½ pound mushrooms thinly and sauté in 2 tablespoons of butter until lightly browned. Add to the chicken, with all the pan juices. Season with salt and pepper. Whip 1 cup of heavy cream in a metal bowl placed over a bowl of ice.

To Serve: When the chicken is tender, remove it from the pan and arrange it in a casserole. Keep warm. Pour ½ cup white wine into the pan and bring to a boil to dissolve the glaze. Slowly stir the whipped cream into the pan juices, using a moderate fire. Taste for seasoning and pour over the chicken. Serves 4.

POULET AUX FONDS D'ARTICHAUTS
(Chicken with Artichokes)

2 2½ to 3 pound chickens	2 tablespoons flour
salt, pepper	½ cup white wine
4 to 6 tablespoons butter	1 tablespoon Madeira
6 artichokes	1 cup cream
1 small onion, finely chopped	a little grated nutmeg
¼ cup apple brandy	4 thin slices white bread

Split the chickens down the back, as for broiling. Sprinkle with salt and pepper. Heat 4 tablespoons of butter in a heavy skillet and put the chickens in the pan, skin side up. After 5 minutes turn the chickens, and continue to turn every 5 minutes until the chickens are well browned, about 30 to 40 minutes in all.

Remove all the leaves and the chokes from 6 artichokes and cut the bottoms into quarters (canned artichoke bottoms may be used, if you wish — they will not need the following preliminary cooking). Cook for 5 minutes in boiling salted water. Drain and put into the pan with the chickens after they are browned; also add 1 small finely chopped onion. Cover and cook for another 15 minutes. Heat ¼ cup apple brandy in a small pan, ignite and pour over the chicken. Remove chickens from pan and keep them warm. Put another 2 tablespoons of butter in the pan. Blend in, off the fire, 2 tablespoons of flour. Add ½ cup white wine, 1 tablespoon of Madeira and 1 cup of cream. Stir over the fire until the sauce comes to a boil. Taste for seasoning, add a little grated nutmeg and simmer for a minute or so.

To Serve: Cut each chicken into 4 pieces. Place on a hot serving dish and spoon over the sauce. Garnish with triangles of bread which have been fried until golden brown in butter. Serves 8.

CHICKEN CREOLE

2 2 to 2½ pound chickens
2 cloves garlic, crushed
10 tablespoons butter
1 small onion, sliced
1 carrot, sliced
1 stalk celery, sliced
1 bay leaf
1 cup white wine
1 large yellow onion
1 cup rice
¼ cup raisins
2 cups stock or water
¾ cup sliced sautéed mushrooms

1 green pepper, shredded
½ cup blanched, split, browned almonds
salt and pepper
3 tablespoons grated Parmesan cheese
½ teaspoon meat glaze
1 teaspoon tomato paste
3 tablespoons flour
2 cups stock
3 tablespoons sherry
2 tomatoes
2 bananas

Put in the cavity of each chicken half a clove of crushed garlic, 1 teaspoon of butter, salt and pepper. Tie the chickens up and rub the skin of each with 1 tablespoon of softened butter. Place in a baking dish with the sliced onion, carrot, celery, a bay leaf and 1 cup of white wine. Roast in a slow oven at 325° for 50 to 60 minutes, until the chickens are tender, basting occasionally. Remove, cut off the breasts and with scissors cut out the entire breast-bone section. Fill the center of each chicken with the following rice pilaff, in the shape of the chicken's breast.

Rice Pilaff: Heat 2 tablespoons of butter in a skillet. Add 2 tablespoons of chopped onion and cook for 2 to 3 minutes to soften but not brown the onion. Add 1 cup of rice and 1 clove crushed garlic and cook for another 2 to 3 minutes, stirring constantly. Pour on 2 cups of stock or water and bring to a boil. Cover with waxed paper and a lid and bake in a moderate oven at 375° for 25 minutes. Combine with ¾ cup sautéed mushrooms, 1 shredded green pepper and ½ cup browned almonds. Season well and add 1 tablespoon of grated Parmesan cheese.

Sauce: Add ½ cup of water to the pan the chicken was cooked in and bring to a boil to lift the glaze. Strain and if there aren't 2 cups of stock, add enough wine or water to make that amount.

Melt 3 tablespoons of butter. Blend in, off the fire, ½ teaspoon of meat glaze, 1 teaspoon of tomato paste and 3 tablespoons of flour. Add the 2 cups of stock and stir over the fire until the sauce comes to a boil. Taste for seasoning and add 3 tablespoons of sherry. Simmer for 2 to 3 minutes, or until ready to use.

Broiled Tomatoes: Remove the cores of 2 tomatoes and cut them in half, leaving the skins on. On each half place a thin slice of onion, a teaspoon of grated Parmesan cheese and 1 teaspoon of butter. Brown under the broiler.

Fried Bananas: Cut 2 sliced bananas into thin slices, on the bias, and fry until golden brown in 1 tablespoon of butter.

To Serve: Place the chickens on a hot serving dish. Slice the chicken breasts very thin and arrange on top of the rice as follows: 1 slice of chicken and 1 slice of fried banana. Pour over half the sauce; serve the rest of the sauce in a separate gravy boat. Garnish with broiled tomatoes. Serves 5 or 6.

POULET EN CASSEROLE

1 chicken, 2½ to 3 pounds	*1 teaspoon tomato paste*
4 tablespoons butter	*3 teaspoons potato flour or*
½ cup sherry	*3 tablespoons flour*
12 small white onions	*1 cup chicken stock or water*
12 pieces of carrot	*¼ cup dry white wine*
12 pieces of turnip	*salt and pepper*
4 mushrooms, quartered	*1 bay leaf*
1 tablespoon finely chopped chives	

Tie up the chicken and brown slowly all over in 3 tablespoons of hot butter. Use a heavy deep saucepan and start breast side down. Heat ¼ cup sherry in a small pan, ignite and pour over the chicken. Remove chicken from pan. Add 1 tablespoon of butter to the pan and 12 small white onions, 12 pieces of carrot (cut into the shape of 1-inch baby carrots) and 12 pieces of white turnip (cut into the shape of 1-inch baby turnips). Cook briskly until browned, about 5 minutes. Add 4 quartered mushrooms and cook for 2 minutes. Blend in, off the fire, 1 teaspoon of tomato paste and 3 teaspoons of potato flour or 3 tablespoons of flour.

Add 1 cup of chicken stock or water, ¼ cup dry white wine and ¼ cup sherry. Stir over the fire until the mixture comes to a boil. Season with salt and pepper and simmer about 5 minutes.

Cut the chicken into serving pieces and put back into the pan, skin side down. Add a bay leaf. Cover with waxed paper and a lid and simmer for 30 to 35 minutes, or until the chicken is tender. Serve in a casserole, garnished with the liver which has been sautéed in a little hot butter. Sprinkle with a tablespoon of finely chopped chives. Serves 4.

POULET EN CASSEROLE BONNE FEMME

2 chickens, 2½ to 3 pounds	12 small pieces turnip
4 tablespoons butter	18 baby mushrooms, cut in half
3 tablespoons brandy	½ teaspoon tomato paste
½ pound salt pork, diced	3 teaspoons potato flour
4 chicken livers	2 cups chicken stock
12 small white onions	½ cup white wine
12 potato balls	4 truffles
12 small pieces carrot	1 to 2 tablespoons chopped parsley

Tie up the chickens. Heat 3 tablespoons of butter in a deep heavy saucepan and slowly brown the chickens all over. Heat 3 tablespoons of brandy in a small pan, ignite and pour over the chickens. Remove the chickens from the pan. Put another tablespoon of butter in the same pan and quickly brown the diced salt pork and 4 chicken livers. Remove the chicken livers and set them aside with the chickens.

Add to the salt pork 12 small white onions, 12 potato balls, 12 small pieces of carrot, 12 small pieces of turnip. Slowly brown all these vegetables, which will take 10 to 15 minutes. Add 18 small halved mushrooms and cook another 1 to 2 minutes. Blend in, off the fire, ½ teaspoon of tomato paste and 3 teaspoons of potato flour. Pour on 2 cups of chicken stock and ½ cup of white wine and stir over the fire until the mixture comes to a boil. Cut the chicken into serving pieces and put them back in the pan with 4 sliced truffles. Cover with waxed paper and a lid and simmer for about 35 minutes, or until the chicken is tender. Serve in a casserole, garnished with the chicken livers and 1 to 2 tablespoons of chopped parsley. Serves 4 to 6.

POULET SAUTÉ AU ROMARIN ET CITRON
(Chicken with Rosemary and Lemon)

2 2½-pound chickens	1½ cups light chicken stock
4 tablespoons butter	juice and grated rind of 1 large
3 tablespoons brandy	lemon
1 clove garlic, crushed	½ teaspoon rosemary
¼ teaspoon tomato paste	¼ cup dry white wine
2 teaspoons potato flour	salt, pepper

STUFFED TOMATOES

4 large firm tomatoes	1 tablespoon butter
1 large onion	1 clove crushed garlic
¼ pound mushrooms	½ cup bread crumbs
2 hard-boiled eggs, chopped	

Tie up the chickens. Brown slowly all over in 3 tablespoons of butter, using a large heavy pan; it will take at least ½ hour to brown the chickens evenly and well. Heat 3 tablespoons of brandy in a small pan, ignite and pour over the chickens. Remove chickens from the pan. Put another tablespoon of butter into the same pan and lightly brown 1 clove crushed garlic and the liver, heart and gizzard (cut up). Blend in, off the fire, ¼ teaspoon tomato paste and 2 teaspoons potato flour. Add 1½ cups chicken stock, the juice and grated rind of 1 lemon and ½ teaspoon rosemary and stir over the fire until the sauce comes to a boil. Add ¼ cup white wine and taste for seasoning. Cut up the chicken and put the pieces back into the sauce, cut side down. Cover with waxed paper and a lid and simmer for 30 to 40 minutes, until the chicken is tender.

Stuffed Tomatoes: Cut a slice off the top of 4 tomatoes and scoop out the seedy centers with a spoon. Peel and finely chop 1 large onion and finely chop ¼ pound mushrooms. Sauté for 5 minutes in 1 tablespoon of butter. Blend with 1 clove crushed garlic, ½ cup bread crumbs and 2 chopped hard-boiled eggs. Season and fill the tomato shells. Heat for 5 to 10 minutes in a moderate oven at 350°.

To Serve: Arrange the chicken on a hot serving dish and spoon the sauce over it. Garnish with the stuffed tomatoes. Serves 4.

ARROZ CON POLLO
(Chicken with Rice)

1 frying chicken, 3½ to 4 pounds	1 cup rice
½ cup olive oil	2½ cups chicken stock or water
2 tablespoons Marsala or sherry	pinch of saffron
1 large yellow onion, chopped	1 bay leaf
1 green pepper	salt, paprika
	3 tomatoes
	2 tablespoons butter

Cut the chicken into small serving pieces. Heat ¼ cup of olive oil in a large skillet and slowly cook the chicken until it is golden brown all over. Heat 2 tablespoons of Marsala or sherry in a small pan, ignite and pour over the chicken. Remove chicken from pan. Put in another ¼ cup of olive oil. Finely chop 1 large yellow onion, seed 1 green pepper and cut into small dice. Add the onion, green pepper and 1 cup of rice to the pan and cook about 5 minutes, stirring constantly; do not let the rice get brown. Add 2½ cups of chicken stock or water and a good pinch of saffron and bring to a boil. Butter a casserole or baking dish that can be used for serving and pour in the rice and stock. Put in 1 bay leaf and salt. Place the browned chicken on top and dust with paprika. Cover and cook in a moderate oven at 350° for an hour. By then all the liquid should be absorbed by the rice and the chicken should be tender.

Skin and slice 3 tomatoes and sauté until lightly browned in 2 tablespoons of hot butter. Just before serving arrange them on top of the dish. The tomatoes are really optional, but add a nice touch. Serves 4.

SAUTÉED CHICKEN WITH VEGETABLE GARNISH

2 2-pound chickens
7 tablespoons butter
¼ cup brandy
½ teaspoon tomato paste
3 tablespoons flour
1 cup stock
¾ cup sour cream
5 tablespoons grated Parmesan
    cheese

1 teaspoon grated lemon rind
salt and pepper
1 small cauliflower
4 tablespoons bread crumbs
1 hard-boiled egg, chopped
1 tablespoon chopped parsley
½ clove garlic, crushed
8 mushroom caps
1 teaspoon lemon juice

3 tomatoes

Tie up the chickens and brown slowly all over in 3 tablespoons of hot butter in a heavy saucepan. Heat ¼ cup brandy in a small pan, ignite and pour over the chickens. Remove chickens from pan. Blend in, off the fire, ½ teaspoon tomato paste and 3 table-spoons flour. Add 1 cup of stock and stir over the fire until the mixture comes to a boil. Slowly beat in ¾ cup of sour cream with a wire whisk. Add 2 tablespoons of grated Parmesan cheese, 1 teaspoon of grated lemon rind, salt and pepper. Cut chicken in serving pieces and return to the sauce, skin side down. Simmer for 30 to 40 minutes, or until the chicken is tender.

Meanwhile prepare the following vegetables: cauliflower Polonaise, sautéed mushrooms and broiled tomatoes.

Cauliflower Polonaise: Cook a small cauliflower in boiling salted water until tender, about 20 to 25 minutes. Drain and return to a slow fire for a minute or so to drain out any excess water. Melt 2 tablespoons of butter in a small pan, add 2 table-spoons of bread crumbs, 1 chopped hard-boiled egg, 1 tablespoon chopped parsley, ½ crushed clove of garlic, salt and pepper. Sauté slowly for 5 minutes. Pour over the cauliflower. Gently break into flowerets with 2 forks.

Mushrooms: Sauté 8 whole mushroom caps in 1 tablespoon of butter and 1 teaspoon of lemon juice.

Broiled Tomatoes: Cut 3 tomatoes in half, sprinkle with 2 table-spoons of bread crumbs and 3 tablespoons of grated cheese, dot with 1 tablespoon of butter, season and brown under the broiler.

To Serve: Arrange chicken in the center of a hot serving dish. Pour part of the sauce over the chicken and serve the rest in a gravy boat. Place cauliflower at each end of the dish, and tomatoes and mushrooms alternately along the sides. Serves 4 to 6.

CHICKEN TETRAZZINI

1 4-pound chicken	6 tablespoons butter
1 medium-size onion, sliced	3 tablespoons flour
1 carrot, sliced	1½ cups chicken stock
1 stalk celery, sliced	½ cup cream
salt, pepper, cayenne	1 egg yolk
1 bay leaf	2 tablespoons sherry
½ pound mushrooms	½ pound thin spaghetti
1 cup grated Parmesan cheese	

Tie up the chicken and place in a heavy saucepan with the sliced onion, carrot, celery, salt, pepper and a bay leaf. Just cover the chicken with cold water and bring slowly to a boil. Simmer covered for 1 to 1¼ hours, until tender. Remove the chicken, reserving the stock, take the meat off the bones and cut into thin strips.

Slice ½ pound mushrooms and cook in 2 tablespoons of butter 10 minutes over a moderate fire, until lightly browned. In another pan melt 3 tablespoons of butter. Off the fire blend in 3 tablespoons of flour, salt and a pinch of cayenne pepper. Add 1½ cups chicken stock and stir over the fire until the sauce comes to a boil. Beat ½ cup cream and 1 egg yolk lightly with a fork and add to the sauce; stir until the sauce is hot but do not let it boil again. Add 2 tablespoons sherry, the chicken and mushrooms.

Meanwhile boil ½ pound thin spaghetti in 3 to 4 quarts of boiling salted water until tender, following the manufacturer's directions for cooking time. Drain in a colander and rinse quickly with warm water. Make a ring of spaghetti around a buttered casserole or baking dish that can be used for serving. Place the chicken mixture in the center. Sprinkle with 1 cup grated Parmesan cheese and dot with 1 tablespoon of butter. Bake in a moderate oven at 350° for 20 to 30 minutes; if the top isn't nicely browned, finish with a few seconds under the broiler. Serves 4 to 6.

Note: This dish may be prepared hours ahead of time and placed in the refrigerator. Let stand at room temperature for ½ hour and bake at least 30 to 40 minutes to be sure it is thoroughly heated through. It can be kept in the oven longer than the specified time if dinner is delayed; just put a cover on it.

POULET SAUTÉ AU MIREPOIX
(Chicken with Diced Vegetables)

1 3½ to 4 pound chicken	*1 stalk celery, diced*
4 tablespoons butter	*1 leek, diced*
1 bay leaf	*½ cup green beans, diced*
1 clove garlic	*½ cup shelled peas*
½ cup dry white wine	*salt and pepper*
2 carrots, diced	*¼ cup cream*
1 white turnip, diced	*¾ cup skinned white grapes*

Place 1 tablespoon of butter, a bay leaf and 1 clove of garlic inside the chicken. Tie up. Spread 2 tablespoons of softened butter over the breast and legs. Place in a small baking dish and add ½ cup dry white wine. Roast for 50 to 60 minutes, or until tender, in a moderate oven at 375°, basting several times. Remove chicken and carve into 4 serving pieces. Keep warm.

Meanwhile put 2 diced carrots, 1 diced turnip, 1 stalk diced celery, 1 diced leek, ½ cup diced beans and ½ cup peas into a saucepan. Cover with cold water, bring to a boil and drain. Melt 1 tablespoon of butter in a heavy saucepan, add the blanched vegetables, salt and pepper. Cover with waxed paper and a lid and simmer until the vegetables are tender, approximately 30 minutes.

To Serve: Make a bed of the vegetables on a hot serving dish. Arrange the chicken over the vegetables and place in a very slow oven to keep warm. Strain the gravy in the pan and season. Add ¼ cup of cream and bring to a boil. Add ¾ cup skinned white grapes and simmer for 4 to 5 minutes. Pour over the chicken and serve at once. Serves 4.

POULET SAUTÉ AU CITRON
(Chicken with Lemon Cream Sauce)

1 4-pound chicken	*2 teaspoons lemon juice*
5 tablespoons butter	*salt and freshly ground pepper*
¼ cup sherry	*1 cup heavy cream*
¼ cup white wine	*½ cup grated Parmesan cheese*
grated rind of 1 lemon	*4 thin lemon slices*

Cut the chicken into serving pieces, or have your butcher do it. Cook until brown all over in 4 tablespoons of hot butter. Cover the pan and continue sautéing over a slow fire until the chicken is tender, about 30 to 40 minutes. Remove chicken. Stir ¼ cup sherry and ¼ cup white wine into the pan and bring to a boil to lift the glaze. Add the grated rind of 1 lemon, 2 teaspoons of lemon juice and season with salt and pepper. Slowly add 1 cup of heavy cream over a fairly brisk fire. Put back the chicken and simmer for 5 to 10 minutes.

To Serve: Arrange the chicken on an ovenproof serving dish. Spoon the sauce over it. Sprinkle with ½ cup grated Parmesan cheese, put 4 thin slices of lemon on top, dot with 1 tablespoon of butter and brown under the broiler. Serves 4 or 5.

COQ AU VIN I
(Chicken with Wine)

1 3½ to 4 pound chicken	*½ cup white wine or sherry*
4 tablespoons butter	*salt, pepper*
¼ cup brandy	*1 small clove of garlic, crushed*
3 tablespoons flour	*¼ pound salt pork*
1½ cups red wine	*12 small white onions, peeled*
½ pound mushrooms, sliced	

This recipe and the one that follows for Coq au Vin are quite similar, the main difference being in the use of either bacon or salt pork. This classic French dish is one of the easiest to make, and one of the most delicious.

Tie up the chicken and brown slowly in 3 tablespoons of hot

butter. Heat ¼ cup of brandy in a small pan, ignite and pour over the chicken. Remove the chicken from the pan and cut into serving pieces. Add 1 tablespoon of butter to the pan. Blend in, off the fire, 3 tablespoons of flour. Pour on 1½ cups red wine and ½ cup white wine or sherry (all red wine may be used, if you wish). Stir until the sauce comes to a boil. Season with salt and pepper, and add 1 small clove of crushed garlic. Put back the chicken, cover the pan and simmer for 45 minutes, or until the chicken is tender.

Meanwhile cut ¼ pound salt pork into small dice and cook slowly until the pork bits are brown. Remove them with a slotted spoon and put on absorbent paper to drain. Brown 12 small white onions in the pork fat and put them into the pan with the chicken. Cook ½ pound sliced mushrooms in the pork fat until lightly browned, and add them to the chicken too.

Serve in a casserole, with the browned pork bits sprinkled over the top. The chicken may be cooked in a heat-resistant casserole and served right in the dish it was cooked in. Serves 4.

Note: Coq au Vin may be made ahead of time and reheated; in fact, if anything, the flavor is improved. Just do not fully cook the chicken; let it simmer about half an hour, and finish cooking later in a moderate oven at 350° for another half hour or so.

COQ AU VIN II

2 2½-pound chickens	*3 teaspoons potato flour or 3*
¼ pound lean bacon	*tablespoons flour*
¼ cup brandy	*1½ cups Burgundy*
1 tablespoon butter	*½ cup dry white wine*
12 small white onions	*salt, pepper*
¼ pound mushrooms, sliced	*1 large clove garlic, crushed*
1 sprig fresh parsley or tarragon	

Dice ¼ pound lean bacon and cook slowly in a heavy saucepan until nicely browned. Remove bacon pieces with a slotted spoon and reserve. Tie up chickens and brown them all over in the bacon fat. Heat ¼ cup of brandy in a small pan, ignite and pour over the chickens. Remove chickens. Put 1 tablespoon butter into the pan and quickly brown 12 small peeled white onions. Add ¼ pound mushrooms, sliced, and cook 1 minute longer. Off the fire stir in 3 teaspoons potato flour, or 3 tablespoons flour. Blend in 1½ cups Burgundy and ½ cup dry white wine. Stir over the fire until the sauce comes to a boil. Add salt, pepper and 1 large clove garlic, crushed. Cut up chickens and put them back into the sauce, with a sprig of fresh parsley or tarragon. Cover the pan and cook slowly for about 45 minutes, until the chickens are tender. Remove the parsley or tarragon and add bacon pieces. Serve in a casserole, garnished with the chicken liver which has been sautéed in a little hot butter. Serves 4.

POULET SAUTÉ LOUISETTE
(Sautéed Chicken with Mushrooms and Ham)

2 2½-pound chickens	½ teaspoon meat glaze
6 to 7 tablespoons butter	3 tablespoons flour
1 small onion, thinly sliced	½ cup dry white wine
salt, freshly ground pepper	1 cup stock or water
¼ pound mushrooms, sliced	¼ pound cooked ham

4 slices white bread, ½ inch thick

Tie up the chickens and brown slowly all over in 4 tablespoons of hot butter. Put 1 sliced onion on top of the chickens, season with salt and pepper, cover and sauté slowly for 30 to 40 minutes, or until tender. Remove chickens. Put 1 tablespoon of butter in the pan, then the ¼ pound sliced mushrooms and sauté about 5 minutes, until lightly browned. Blend in, off the fire, ½ teaspoon of meat glaze and 3 tablespoons of flour. Pour on ½ cup dry white wine and 1 cup of stock or water and stir over the fire until the mixture comes to a boil. Shred ¼ pound cooked ham and add it to the sauce; simmer about 5 minutes.

Meanwhile cut the chickens in half, discarding the backbone. Put them back into the sauce and simmer for 5 to 10 minutes, until the chicken is heated through. Cut 4 slices of bread, ½ inch thick, into rounds or triangles and fry until golden brown in 1 to 2 tablespoons of butter.

To Serve: Arrange chicken on a hot serving dish. Spoon over the sauce and garnish with fried bread. Serves 4.

POULET AUX DENTS DU CHAT
(Chicken with Cat's Teeth)

1 4-pound chicken	*1 tablespoon tomato paste*
5 tablespoons butter	*3 tablespoons flour*
¼ cup sherry	*1½ cups light stock or water*
1 clove garlic, crushed	*¼ cup shredded almonds*
2 tablespoons finely chopped onion	*salt and pepper*
	1 bay leaf
5 skinned tomatoes	*¾ cup sour cream*

½ cup grated Gruyère

Tie up the chicken and brown slowly all over in 4 tablespoons of butter. Heat ¼ cup sherry in a small pan, ignite and pour over the chicken. Remove chicken from pan and add 1 clove crushed garlic, 2 tablespoons chopped onion and 3 skinned and sliced tomatoes. Cook for 2 to 3 minutes. Blend in, off the fire, 1 table-spoon of tomato paste and 3 tablespoons of flour. Pour on 1½ cups of stock or water and stir over the fire until the mixture comes to a boil. Add ¼ cup shredded almonds, salt and pepper and 1 bay leaf. (The almonds are the "cat's teeth.") Put back the chicken, breast side down. Cover and cook slowly for 45 to 50 minutes, until the chicken is tender, turning it once or twice. Remove the chicken and cut it into serving pieces. Arrange in a shallow ovenproof serving dish.

Slowly stir ¾ cup sour cream into the sauce. Add 2 skinned and sliced tomatoes and 1 tablespoon grated cheese. Simmer 2 to 3 minutes and pour over the chicken. Sprinkle with remaining grated cheese, dot with 1 tablespoon of butter and brown under the broiler. Serves 4.

POULET SAUTÉ À LA MAINTENON
(Sautéed Chicken with Mushrooms)

2 chickens, 2½ to 3 pounds each
4 tablespoons chicken fat or butter
salt and pepper
2 chicken livers
5 tablespoons butter
½ pound mushrooms, finely sliced

1 cup shredded cooked tongue
½ teaspoon dry thyme
8 rounds white bread
½ cup white wine
½ cup water

2 tablespoons chopped parsley

Split the broilers. Spread with 2 tablespoons chicken fat or softened butter; chicken fat gives a delicious flavor and if not on hand can often be procured at poultry-in-parts stores. Season with salt and pepper and broil slowly on both sides, brushing occasionally with an additional 2 tablespoons of chicken fat or butter. It takes about 30 to 40 minutes to cook and brown a broiler.

Meanwhile sauté 2 chicken livers very quickly in 1 tablespoon of butter. Remove and slice. Add 2 tablespoons of butter to the pan, then ½ pound sliced mushrooms, 1 cup shredded cooked tongue, ½ teaspoon dry thyme, salt and pepper. Cook slowly for 10 minutes. While this is cooking, fry 8 rounds of white bread about ½ inch thick until golden brown on both sides in 2 tablespoons of butter.

To Serve: Spread each round of bread with the mushroom mixture, dividing it evenly, and arrange on a hot serving dish. Cut the broilers into quarters and put one piece on each bread round. Put ½ cup white wine and ½ cup water in the pan the chickens were cooked in, bring to a boil, taste for seasoning and pour over the chicken. Garnish with slices of liver and chopped parsley. Serve immediately, while the bread is still crisp. Serves 8.

POULET VIEILLE FRANCE
(Chicken with Mushrooms and Pâté)

1 2½ to 3 pound chicken
2 tablespoons butter
salt and pepper
1 small truffle, finely chopped

¼ pound mushrooms, sliced
¼ cup sherry or dry white wine
1½ cups heavy cream
2 tablespoons pâté or liverwurst

Cut the chicken into small serving pieces, separating the wings from the breast and the legs from the second joints. Heat 2 tablespoons of butter in a deep heavy saucepan and when the butter is on the point of turning color, put in the chicken. Brown slowly all over. Season with salt and pepper. Add a finely chopped truffle (optional) and ¼ pound of sliced mushrooms and cook for another 5 minutes. Pour over ¼ cup of sherry or dry white wine, being careful that each piece gets a little. Continue cooking for 3 to 4 minutes while the wine soaks in. Add 1½ cups of heavy cream and heat to the boiling point. Cover and simmer for 30 to 40 minutes, until the chicken is tender, stirring several times.

To Serve: Remove the chicken and arrange it on a hot serving dish. Add 2 tablespoons of pâté or liverwurst to the sauce and beat until thoroughly blended with a wire whisk. True pâté de foie gras is hard to obtain and expensive; however, there are good tinned domestic pâtés, and liverwurst is an acceptable substitute. Spoon the sauce over the chicken and serve immediately. Serves 4.

POULET SAUTÉ À LA VICHY
(Chicken with Carrots)

1 3½-pound chicken	½ cup red wine
6 tablespoons butter	1 cup stock
1 bunch young carrots	1 bay leaf
1 onion, thinly sliced	1 sprig tarragon or parsley (optional)
salt and pepper	
½ teaspoon meat glaze	1 teaspoon lemon juice
½ teaspoon tomato paste	2 tablespoons white wine or sherry
3 tablespoons flour	2 tablespoons chopped parsley

3 tablespoons sour cream

Tie up the chicken and brown all over in 3 tablespoons of hot butter, starting with the breast side down. Remove from the pan. Put 1 tablespoon of butter in the pan, then 1 thinly sliced carrot, 1 sliced onion, salt and pepper. Cook slowly for 5 minutes. Blend in, off the fire, ½ teaspoon meat glaze, ½ teaspoon tomato paste and 3 tablespoons flour. Add ½ cup red wine and 1 cup of stock and stir over the fire until the sauce comes to a boil. Put back the chicken with a bay leaf and a sprig of tarragon or parsley. Cover and cook for 35 to 40 minutes, or until the chicken is tender.

Meanwhile scrape remaining carrots and cut into thin slices. Cover with cold water, bring to a boil and drain. Put in a small saucepan with 2 tablespoons of butter, 1 teaspoon of lemon juice, 2 tablespoons of white wine or sherry, salt and pepper. Cover and cook until just soft, about 10 minutes. Add 2 tablespoons of chopped parsley and 3 tablespoons of sour cream.

To Serve: Remove the chicken and cut it into serving pieces. Make a smooth bed of the carrot mixture on a hot serving dish and arrange the chicken on top. Strain the sauce and spoon it over the chicken. Serves 4.

POULET À LA VALLÉE D'AUGE
(Chicken with Celery and Apples)

1 3½ to 4 pound chicken	4 apples
5 tablespoons butter	3 or 4 stalks celery
3 tablespoons brandy	3 tablespoons flour
1 small onion, sliced	1½ cups chicken stock
1 stalk celery, sliced	salt, freshly cracked pepper
1 cup heavy cream, whipped	

Tie up the chicken and brown slowly all over in 3 tablespoons of hot butter. Heat 3 tablespoons of brandy in a small pan, ignite and pour over the chicken. Remove chicken and cut into serving pieces. Put another 2 tablespoons of butter in the same pan, then 1 small sliced onion, 1 stalk celery and 2 sliced apples which have been cored but not peeled. Cook slowly until soft, about 10 to 15 minutes. Blend in, off the fire, 3 tablespoons of flour. Add 1½ cups of stock and stir over the fire until the mixture comes to a boil. Season with salt and pepper. Put back the chicken and simmer until tender, about 40 minutes. Meanwhile prepare the garnish.

Core 2 apples, cut into rings and fry in butter until golden brown. Cut 3 or 4 stalks of celery into small matchsticks, tie into small bundles and cook until just tender in boiling salted water.

To Serve: Remove the chicken, arrange on a hot serving dish and keep warm. Strain the sauce, pushing through as much of the vegetables as possible. Bring slowly to a boil. Add 1 cup of heavy cream, whipped, a little at a time. Spoon the sauce over the chicken and garnish the top with the fried apple rings and the bundles of celery. Serves 4 or 5.

POULET WESTPHALIENNE
(Chicken with Westphalian Ham)

1 3½ to 4 pound chicken	*1 cup dry white wine*
4 tablespoons butter	*salt, pepper, cayenne*
1 medium-size onion, sliced	*½ pound medium noodles, cooked*
1 carrot, sliced	*3 tablespoons flour*
1 stalk celery, sliced	*1½ cups stock*
1 bay leaf	*½ cup cream*
¼ pound cooked ham, diced	

Tie up the chicken and place in a small shallow baking dish. Rub the breasts and legs with 1 tablespoon of softened butter. Put a sliced onion, carrot and stalk of celery in the pan with a bay leaf. Pour in ½ cup white wine. Season with salt and pepper. Bake for 1 hour in a moderate oven at 350° or until the chicken is tender. While the chicken is baking, cook ½ pound of noodles, drain in a colander and keep warm over a little boiling water.

When the chicken is tender, cut it into serving pieces and arrange them on top of hot buttered noodles on a hot platter. Put the platter in a very slow oven at 250° to keep warm while preparing the sauce.

Put ½ cup white wine into the pan the chicken was cooked in and bring it to a boil to dissolve the glaze. Strain, and if there isn't 1½ cups of stock, add water to make that amount. Melt 3 table-spoons of butter. Blend in, off the fire, 3 tablespoons of flour. Pour on 1½ cups of stock and stir over the fire until the sauce comes to a boil. Season with salt and a little cayenne pepper. Add

½ cup cream and ¼ pound diced cooked ham. Spoon over the chicken and serve immediately. Serves 4.

Note: If Westphalian ham is available, by all means use it. But it is a European delicacy, not always procurable in the United States, and any good cooked ham can be substituted if necessary.

POULARDE ANDALOUSE
(Chicken with Suprême Sauce and Green Peppers)

1 4 to 4½ pound chicken	1 stalk celery, sliced
1 small onion, sliced	1 bay leaf
1 small carrot, sliced	salt and pepper

EGGPLANT

4 slices eggplant, ½ inch thick   1 large clove garlic, crushed
¼ cup olive oil

STUFFED PEPPERS

4 small green peppers	4 small garlic sausages, chopped
¼ cup olive oil	¾ cup rice
¼ cup chopped onion	1½ cups chicken stock

SUPRÊME SAUCE

3 tablespoons butter	1 cup chicken stock
3 tablespoons flour	½ cup cream
2 pimentos, minced	

2 tablespoons chopped chives   paprika

Tie up chicken and place it in a heavy saucepan with the sliced onion, carrot and celery. Just cover with cold water and bring slowly to a boil. Add bay leaf, salt and pepper and simmer for 1 to 1¼ hours, or until tender. Meanwhile prepare the eggplant, stuffed pepper garnish and the sauce.

Eggplant: Sprinkle 4 slices of eggplant about ½ inch thick with salt and let stand for ½ hour. Dry slices, dust lightly with flour and spread with 1 large clove crushed garlic. Sauté until golden brown on both sides in ¼ cup hot olive oil. Keep warm.

Stuffed Peppers: Cover 4 small green peppers with cold water, bring to a boil, simmer for 5 minutes and drain. Cut off the caps, remove all seeds and fill with the following mixture. Heat ¼ cup olive oil in a skillet. Add ¼ cup chopped onion and 4 small chopped garlic sausages and cook 3 to 4 minutes. Add ¾ cup rice and cook another 2 to 3 minutes. Cover with 1½ cups chicken stock, bring to a boil and season with salt and pepper. Cover and cook for 20 minutes over a very slow fire.

Suprême Sauce: Melt 2 tablespoons of butter. Blend in, off the fire, 3 tablespoons of flour. Add 1 cup of strained chicken stock and stir over the fire until the sauce comes to a boil. Add ½ cup cream, 2 minced pimentos and 1 tablespoon of butter, bit by bit.

To Serve: Remove chicken, reserving stock. Carefully take off skin and cut into serving pieces. Arrange on a hot serving dish and cover with the sauce. Surround with slices of eggplant topped with stuffed peppers. Sprinkle with chives and paprika. Serves 4.

POULET AUX TRUFFES
(Chicken with Truffles)

1 4-pound chicken
6 to 8 thin slices of truffle
1 egg white
½ pound ground raw veal
3 tablespoons sour cream
salt
freshly ground black pepper
6 chicken livers
1 tablespoon butter

1 teaspoon finely chopped thyme
1 small truffle, finely chopped
2 slices cooked ham, ¼ inch thick
1 small onion, sliced
1 small carrot, sliced
few sprigs fresh tarragon
¼ cup white wine

CREAM TARRAGON SAUCE

4 tablespoons butter
3 tablespoons flour
1½ cups chicken stock
fresh tarragon leaves

cayenne pepper
1 egg yolk
½ cup cream

Bone the chicken, taking out back and breast bones but leaving the leg bones in. Spread on a board or slab skin side down. Carefully lift up from the skin and slide 6 to 8 thin slices of truffle underneath. Beat 1 unbeaten egg white into ½ pound raw ground veal, then beat in 3 tablespoons of sour cream. Season with salt and pepper. Sauté 6 chicken livers, 1 teaspoon chopped thyme and 1 finely chopped truffle. Place sliced ham on top of the chicken and spread with the veal mixture, leaving a 1-inch margin all around the edge. Arrange the chicken livers over the veal. Roll up and sew with thread. Wrap in a long piece of cheesecloth with about 8 extra inches at each end. Tie these ends, close to the chicken. Place in a saucepan with the ends pulled through handles on each side so that the chicken is suspended. Barely cover with cold water and bring to a boil. Add sliced onion, carrot, 1 or 2 sprigs of tarragon and ¼ cup white wine. Season with salt and pepper. Simmer for 1¼ to 1½ hours. Remove chicken, reserving stock, unwrap and keep warm while preparing the sauce.

Cream Tarragon Sauce: Melt 3 tablespoons of butter. Blend in, off the fire, 3 tablespoons of flour. Add 1½ cups strained chicken stock and stir over the fire until the sauce comes to a boil. Season with cayenne pepper; taste to see if salt is needed. Add 1 tablespoon butter, bit by bit, then 1 egg yolk mixed with ½ cup cream; lastly, a few fresh tarragon leaves.

To Serve: Place the chicken on a hot serving dish, spoon the sauce over it and serve immediately. Serves 5 or 6.

CHICKEN WITH CUCUMBERS

1 chicken, 3½ to 4 pounds	*3 tablespoons flour*
5 tablespoons butter	*1 teaspoon tomato paste*
1 cucumber	*½ teaspoon meat glaze*
¼ pound mushrooms	*1 cup stock*
¼ cup sherry	*¾ cup sour cream*
4 chicken livers	*salt, freshly ground pepper*
1 small clove garlic, crushed	*1 sprig fresh parsley or tarragon*
½ cup grated Parmesan cheese	

Tie up the chicken and slowly brown all over in 3 tablespoons of hot butter. While chicken is browning, peel 1 cucumber, cut into slices, cover with cold water, bring to a boil and drain. Slice ¼ pound mushrooms.

When chicken is browned, heat ¼ cup sherry in a small pan, ignite and pour over the chicken. Remove chicken from pan. Put 1 tablespoon butter in the same pan, brown 4 chicken livers quickly and remove them from pan. Add the cucumber, mushrooms and 1 small clove of crushed garlic and cook for 2 minutes. Blend in, off the fire, 3 tablespoons flour, 1 teaspoon tomato paste and ½ teaspoon meat glaze. Pour on 1 cup stock and stir over the fire until the mixture comes to a boil. Still stirring constantly, slowly add ¾ cup sour cream. Season with salt and pepper. Cut the chicken into serving pieces and put back into the sauce with a sprig of fresh parsley or tarragon. Cover with waxed paper and a lid and cook slowly for about 35 minutes, or until the chicken is tender.

To Serve: Remove chicken and arrange on an ovenproof serving dish. Chop the chicken livers, add to the sauce and pour it over the chicken. Sprinkle with ½ cup grated Parmesan cheese, dot with 1 tablespoon butter and brown under the broiler. Serves 4.

POULARDE CARDINAL
(Chicken with Broiled Tomatoes)

1 4 to 4½ pound chicken	*1 tablespoon tomato paste*
1 small onion, sliced	*1 cup chicken stock*
1 small carrot, sliced	*1 tomato, skinned, seeded and*
1 stalk celery, sliced	*shredded*
1 bay leaf	*½ cup cream*
salt and pepper	*4 tomatoes*
5 tablespoons butter	*½ cup bread crumbs*
3 tablespoons flour	*½ cup grated Parmesan cheese*

Tie up chicken and place it in a heavy saucepan with 1 small sliced onion, 1 small sliced carrot and 1 stalk sliced celery. Just cover with cold water and bring slowly to a boil. Add bay leaf, salt and pepper and simmer slowly for 1 to 1¼ hours, until tender. Remove chicken from pan, reserving stock. Carefully take off skin and cut into serving pieces. Arrange on a hot serving dish and keep warm while you prepare the sauce and garnish.

Sauce: Melt 2 tablespoons of butter. Blend in, off the fire, 3 tablespoons of flour and 1 tablespoon of tomato paste. Add 1 cup strained chicken stock and stir over the fire until the sauce comes to a boil. Add 1 shredded tomato, ½ cup cream and 1 tablespoon of butter, bit by bit.

Broiled Tomatoes: Remove cores of 4 tomatoes and cut in half. Sprinkle with ½ cup bread crumbs, ½ cup grated Parmesan cheese, season, and dot with 2 tablespoons of butter. Broil until nicely browned.

To Serve: Spoon the sauce over the chicken and surround with broiled tomatoes. Serves 4.

POULET EN DEMI–DEUIL
(Chicken in Half Mourning)

1 3½ to 4 pound chicken	*1 small carrot, sliced*
1 large truffle	*1 stalk celery, sliced*
1 small onion, sliced	*1 sprig fresh tarragon and parsley*

SUPRÊME SAUCE

½ pound mushrooms, sliced	*1¼ cups chicken stock*
4 tablespoons butter	*1 egg yolk*
3 tablespoons flour	*½ cup cream*

Very carefully loosen the skin from the breast and legs on each side of the chicken and place 4 slices of truffle on each side. The black and white effect is what gives the dish its name demi-deuil, meaning half mourning. Tie up the chicken and place it in a deep heavy saucepan. Barely cover with cold water and bring slowly to a boil. Skim off any scum. Add the sliced onion, carrot and celery, the tarragon and parsley, and season with salt and pepper. Cover and simmer for 1 to 1¼ hours, until the chicken is tender. Remove from the pan, cut into serving pieces, place on a hot serving dish and keep warm. Reduce the liquid it was cooked in to 1½ cups.

Suprême Sauce: Slice ½ pound mushrooms and sauté for 5 minutes in 3 tablespoons of butter. Blend in 3 tablespoons of flour, off the fire. Add 1¼ cups strained chicken stock and stir over the fire until the sauce comes to a boil. Beat 1 egg yolk lightly with ½ cup of cream. Add to the sauce and stir until it thickens but does not boil. Then beat in 1 tablespoon of butter, bit by bit.

To Serve: Spoon the sauce over the chicken and serve immediately. Serves 4.

Note: In the restaurant in Lyon which made this dish famous it is not served with a sauce but served whole with just the natural stock and coarsely ground salt. I would suggest trying it both ways, and maybe you will agree that the suprême sauce is an excellent addition.

POULET MARENGO
(Chicken with Lobster and Fried Eggs)

2 2-pound chickens	*1½ cups chicken stock or water*
6 tablespoons butter	*salt, pepper*
3 tablespoons sherry	*½ pound mushrooms*
1 small clove garlic, crushed	*1 lobster, 1 to 1½ pounds, cooked*
4 skinned sliced tomatoes	*4 fried eggs*
1 teaspoon tomato paste	*4 triangles of bread*
3 teaspoons potato flour	*2 to 3 tablespoons salad oil*
1 to 2 tablespoons finely chopped parsley	

Tie up the chickens and brown them slowly all over in 3 tablespoons of hot butter. When browned, put another 3 tablespoons of butter into the pan, cover and sauté the chickens over a slow fire until tender, about 30 to 40 minutes. Remove chickens from the pan and keep them warm. Put 3 tablespoons of sherry into the pan and bring to a boil to dissolve the glaze. Add 1 clove of crushed garlic and 4 skinned sliced tomatoes and cook for 2 minutes. Blend in, off the fire, 1 teaspoon of tomato paste and 3 teaspoons of potato flour. Pour on 1½ cups of chicken stock or water and stir over the fire until the mixture comes to a boil. Season with salt and pepper and simmer for 5 minutes or until ready to use.

Meanwhile sauté the mushrooms, half of which are left whole, the rest thinly sliced. Remove the lobster meat from the shell and slice it. Fry 4 eggs and 4 triangles of bread until golden brown on both sides in 2 to 3 tablespoons of salad oil.

To Serve: Cut the chickens in half, discarding the backbone. Arrange them on a hot serving dish. Add the sliced sautéed mushrooms to the sauce and spoon it over the chickens. Top with alternate slices of lobster and sautéed whole mushrooms. Garnish the edge of the dish with fried eggs and triangles of bread. Serves 4.

POULET MAJORCA
(Chicken with Oranges and Peppers)

1 4-pound chicken	*3 teaspoons potato flour*
6 tablespoons butter	*1½ cups chicken stock*
3 tablespoons brandy	*shredded rind of 1 orange*
1 clove garlic, crushed	*2 pounds old potatoes*
1 cup sliced mushrooms	*salt, pepper*
½ green pepper, diced	*2 oranges, sectioned*
½ red pepper, diced	*2 tomatoes, skinned, seeded and*
½ teaspoon tomato paste	*shredded*
4 sautéed mushroom caps	

Tie up the chicken and brown it slowly all over in 2 tablespoons of hot butter. Heat 3 tablespoons of brandy in a small pan, ignite and pour over the chicken. Remove the chicken from the pan. Put another tablespoon of butter and 1 clove of crushed garlic in the same pan and cook 1 minute. Add 1 cup of sliced mushrooms, ½ a diced green pepper and ½ a diced red pepper and cook briskly for 2 to 3 minutes. Blend in, off the fire, ½ teaspoon of tomato paste and 3 teaspoons of potato flour. Add 1½ cups of chicken stock and stir over the fire until the mixture comes to a boil. Put in the shredded rind of 1 orange and taste for seasoning. Cut up the chicken and put it back into the sauce. Cover with waxed paper and a lid and cook gently for 40 to 50 minutes, or until the chicken is tender. Meanwhile make the noisette potatoes.

Noisette Potatoes: Pare 2 pounds of old potatoes and cut into balls with a potato baller. Sauté in 3 tablespoons of butter until golden brown, about 20 to 30 minutes over a slow fire, shaking the pan occasionally to brown the potatoes evenly. Season with salt and pepper just before serving.

To Serve: Arrange the chicken on a hot serving dish. Add the sections of 2 oranges and 2 shredded tomatoes to the sauce and spoon it over the chicken. Top with 4 sautéed mushroom caps and pile noisette potatoes at each end of the dish. Serves 4.

CHICKEN PAPRIKA

2 2½-pound chickens	3 tablespoons flour
5 tablespoons butter	1 tablespoon tomato paste
1 small onion, sliced	salt, pepper
1 small carrot, sliced	1¾ cups chicken stock
1 stalk celery, sliced	½ cup sour or sweet cream
2 tablespoons paprika	3 tablespoons grated Parmesan cheese

Tie up the chickens. Brown all over slowly in 3 tablespoons of butter in a heavy saucepan. Remove chickens from pan. In the same pan put 1 tablespoon butter, 1 small sliced onion, 1 small sliced carrot and 1 stalk sliced celery and cook slowly for 5 to 10 minutes. Add 2 tablespoons paprika and cook another 3 minutes. Off the fire blend in 3 tablespoons flour, 1 tablespoon tomato paste, salt and pepper. Pour on 1¾ cups stock and stir over the fire until the mixture comes to a boil. Simmer for 10 to 15 minutes, then strain.

Cut the chickens in half and put back into the pan, cut side down, with the strained sauce. Cover and cook slowly for 35 to 40 minutes, until chicken is tender.

To Serve: Arrange chicken on an ovenproof serving dish. Add ½ cup sour or sweet cream and 1 tablespoon grated Parmesan cheese to the sauce and spoon it over the chicken. Sprinkle with 2 tablespoons cheese, dot with 1 tablespoon butter and brown under the broiler. Serves 4.

PAELLA

1 chicken, 3 to 3½ pounds	1½ cups rice
½ cup olive oil	1 tablespoon hot water
½ pound cooked ham	3 cups chicken stock or water
1 green pepper	salt, pepper
1 large yellow onion	about ¼ teaspoon Spanish saffron
1 tomato	1 pound raw shrimps

Cut the chicken into small serving pieces, as for frying, or have the butcher do it. Heat ½ cup of olive oil in an ovenproof casserole; the Spanish use an earthenware casserole called a *paella.* When the oil is hot, put in the chicken and brown slowly all over. When it is browned on one side, turn it and put in the pan ½ pound of cooked ham, cut in small dice; 1 green pepper, seeded and diced; and 1 large yellow onion, finely chopped. Continue cooking until the chicken is browned on the other side, stirring the vegetables often to brown them evenly. Peel 1 tomato, chop it and put it in the pan. Add 1½ cups of rice, which need not be washed, and cook for a minute or two. Dissolve about ¼ teaspoon of Spanish saffron in 1 tablespoon of hot water; saffron has a very pronounced flavor and a little goes a long way, so do not think you will improve the dish by increasing the amount of saffron. Add it to the pan with 3 cups of chicken stock or water. Bring to a boil and season with salt and pepper.

Cover and bake in a moderate oven at 350° for 1 hour. Shell and remove the veins from 1 pound of raw shrimps and when the chicken has cooked ½ hour, put the shrimps in with it.

Serve the paella right in the dish it was cooked in. The shellfish can be varied, using clams or mussels instead of shrimps or with them. They will only need about 15 minutes cooking to steam open. Serves 4 to 6.

Note: Chicken stock can be made with the back, neck and gizzard. Just remember to start it at least 2 hours before you begin making the paella.

POULET À LA RÉGENCE
(Chicken with Olives)

2 3½-pound chickens	2 cups stock
6 tablespoons butter	salt and freshly ground pepper
¼ cup brandy	1 bay leaf
½ teaspoon meat glaze	3 slices bacon
1 teaspoon tomato paste	½ pound firm white mushrooms
3 teaspoons potato flour or	18 stoned green olives
3 tablespoons flour	18 stoned ripe olives

Tie up the chickens and brown them all over in 5 tablespoons of hot butter. Start them off breast side down and use a large deep saucepan. Heat ¼ cup brandy in a small pan, ignite and pour over the chickens. Remove chickens from pan. Add another tablespoon of butter to the pan. Blend in, off the fire, ½ teaspoon of meat glaze, 1 teaspoon of tomato paste and 3 teaspoons of potato flour or 3 tablespoons of flour. Pour on 2 cups of stock and stir over the fire until the mixture comes to a boil. Season with salt, pepper and a bay leaf. Put the chickens back into the pan, breast side down, cover and cook slowly for 40 to 50 minutes, or until tender, turning occasionally.

Meanwhile dice 3 slices of bacon and cook until well browned and crisp. Remove with a slotted spoon and drain on absorbent paper. Slice ½ pound of mushrooms and sauté about 5 minutes in the bacon fat, until lightly browned.

To Serve: Remove the skin from 1 chicken. Take the breasts from each side and cut in half lengthwise. Cut the remaining meat in fine shreds and combine it with the cooked bacon and mushrooms, 18 stoned green olives and 18 stoned black olives; mix lightly. Make a bed of this mixture on a hot flat serving dish.

Place the whole chicken on top. Put the breasts of chicken on each side. Pour over half the sauce and serve the rest in a separate gravy boat. Serves 5 or 6.

CHICKEN À LA KING

1 4 to 4½ pound chicken, cooked, or 3 cups cooked chicken or turkey	1 cup chicken stock
	salt, white pepper
	2 egg yolks
4 tablespoons butter	½ teaspoon paprika
½ pound mushrooms, thinly sliced	1 cup cream
½ green pepper, shredded	2 to 3 tablespoons sherry
2 tablespoons flour	1 piece pimento, shredded

Cut the chicken into thin strips. Melt 4 tablespoons butter. Add sliced mushrooms and green pepper and sauté for 5 minutes. Blend in 2 tablespoons of flour, off the fire. Add 1 cup of chicken stock and stir over the fire until the sauce comes to a boil. Season with salt and a little white pepper. Beat 2 egg yolks and ½ teaspoon paprika lightly with a fork. Slowly beat in 1 cup of cream. Add to the sauce and cook until the sauce is thickened but do not let it boil again. Add the chicken and heat thoroughly. Just before serving add 2 to 3 tablespoons of sherry and 1 piece shredded pimento. Chicken à la King can be served in patty shells (to make your own see Vol au Vent on page 265) or in a hot serving dish or chafing dish, garnished with triangles of thin toast. Serves 4 to 6.

Note: This dish can wait almost indefinitely in a double boiler, over simmering water; add the sherry and pimento just before serving.

GALANTINE OF CHICKEN
(Boned Stuffed Chicken)

1 4-pound chicken	1 chicken liver
½ pound sausage meat	1 truffle
2 slices cooked ham, ¼ inch thick	¼ cup pistachio nuts
4 slices liverwurst	chives
3 hard-boiled eggs	fresh dill

CHAUD-FROID SAUCE

3 tablespoons salad oil	½ cup chicken stock
3 tablespoons flour	½ cup creamy milk
2 teaspoons gelatine	3 tablespoons cream

ASPIC

3½ cups cold clear stock	5 tablespoons gelatine
1 tablespoon tomato paste	¼ cup sherry
3 egg whites, stiffly beaten	

Wash the chicken in lemon juice and water and dry well on a cloth. Cut off the neck, big wing joints and top of the leg joints. With a sharp knife slit the skin down the center of the back. Cut the chicken away from the back and breast bone, removing the entire center carcass — take care not to split the skin. Remove the leg bones and little wing bones. Spread out on a board, skin side down. Cover with ½ pound sausage meat, leaving an inch-wide margin all around the edge. Place 2 slices of ham over the sausage, 4 slices of liverwurst in the center, with 2 shelled hard-boiled eggs over them. Top with 1 raw chicken liver, 1 truffle, sliced, and ¼ cup pistachio nuts. Roll up chicken, folding each end over snugly, and sew together with a needle and thread. Wrap in a long piece of cheesecloth which has about 8 extra inches at each end. Tie the ends close to the chicken. Place in a deep saucepan with the ends pulled through handles at each side so that the chicken is suspended. Cover with cold water, bring slowly to a boil, cover and simmer for 1½ hours. Let chicken cool in the cooking water.

Remove, place in a large loaf pan and put a brick on top to press the chicken down well. Chill in the refrigerator for several hours. Unwrap, remove thread and place on a cake rack with a pan underneath. Spoon chaud-froid sauce over it all. Decorate with a hard-cooked egg, chives and fresh dill. Cover with aspic on the point of setting and return to the refrigerator to chill for at least another hour, or as long as you wish.

Chaud-Froid Sauce: Heat 3 tablespoons of a bland salad oil (not olive oil, which is too strong). Blend in, off the fire, 3 tablespoons of flour and 2 teaspoons of dry gelatine. Add ½ cup chicken stock and ½ cup creamy milk and stir over the fire until it just comes to a boil. Remove and add 3 tablespoons of cream. Put the pan over a bowl of ice and stir until the sauce is just on the point of setting.

Aspic: In a deep saucepan put 3½ cups cold stock, 1 tablespoon of tomato paste, 5 tablespoons of dry gelatine, ¼ cup sherry and 3 stiffly beaten egg whites. Beat with a large wire whisk over a slow fire until the mixture just comes to a boil. Strain through a damp cloth which has been placed over a large strainer. Take ¼ of this aspic and stir over ice until on the point of setting to use for covering the galantine. Place the rest in 2 shallow cake tins and put in the refrigerator to set to be used for the garnish.

To Serve: Place on a silver platter and garnish with chopped set aspic. Serves 4 to 6.

CHICKEN BREASTS WITH BROCCOLI PURÉE

4 half breasts chicken	*3 teaspoons potato flour*
5 tablespoons butter	*1½ cups stock*
3 tablespoons brandy	*salt, pepper*
1 clove garlic, crushed	*1 bay leaf*
½ teaspoon tomato paste	*1 large bunch broccoli*
1 teaspoon meat glaze	*1 tablespoon flour*
2 tablespoons sour cream	

HOLLANDAISE SAUCE

2 egg yolks	*salt, cayenne*
1 tablespoon vinegar	*1 tablespoon cream*
¼ pound butter	

Skin and bone the chicken breasts. Heat 3 tablespoons of butter in a heavy skillet and brown the chicken breasts slowly on both sides. Heat 3 tablespoons of brandy in a small pan, ignite and pour over the chicken. Remove chicken from the pan. Put another tablespoon of butter and a clove of crushed garlic in the same pan and cook ½ minute. Blend in, off the fire, ½ teaspoon of tomato paste, 1 teaspoon of meat glaze and 3 teaspoons of potato flour. Add 1½ cups of stock and stir over the fire until the mixture comes to a boil. Season with salt, pepper and a bay leaf. Put back the chicken breasts, cover the pan and cook slowly for 25 to 30 minutes.

Meanwhile cook the broccoli in boiling salted water until very tender. Drain and put through a strainer. Lightly brown 1 tablespoon of butter with 1 tablespoon of flour. Add to the broccoli with 2 tablespoons of sour cream and seasoning. Heat in a double boiler until ready to use. Also make the following Hollandaise sauce.

Hollandaise Sauce: Put 2 egg yolks and 1 tablespoon of vinegar in a small bowl and beat with a wire whisk. Beat in salt, cayenne and 1 tablespoon of cream. Place the bowl in a skillet of hot water and beat over a slow fire until the mixture begins to thicken. Then beat in ¼ pound of butter, bit by bit.

To Serve: Make a smooth bed of the broccoli on a hot serving dish. Arrange the chicken breasts on top, slightly on the bias, and strain the brown sauce over all. Spoon Hollandaise over each breast and brown lightly under the broiler. Serves 4.

CHICKEN WITH MAYONNAISE

4 half breasts chicken	*1 stalk celery, sliced*
1 medium-size onion, sliced	*salt, peppercorns*
1 carrot, sliced	*2 cups cold water*

MAYONNAISE

2 large egg yolks	*1 cup olive oil*
2 tablespoons tarragon vinegar	*1 tablespoon gelatine*
¼ teaspoon dry mustard	*¼ cup cold water*
salt, cayenne	*3 tablespoons cream*
4 small onions	*½ cup French dressing*
4 large tomatoes	*paprika*

Put the chicken breasts into a pan with the sliced onion, carrot, celery, salt, peppercorns and 2 cups of cold water. Bring slowly to a boil and simmer for about 20 minutes. Drain and cool. Remove skin and bones, leaving the small wing bone attached to the breast. Place on a cake rack in a shallow pan and carefully spoon mayonnaise over each breast. Chill at least 3 hours in the refrigerator.

Mayonnaise: Put 2 egg yolks, 2 tablespoons of tarragon vinegar, ¼ teaspoon of dry mustard, salt and cayenne into a bowl and beat until well blended. Slowly beat in 1 cup of olive oil (part salad oil may be used if you prefer a milder flavor). Dissolve 1 tablespoon of gelatine in ¼ cup of cold water and mix into the mayonnaise. Then add 3 tablespoons of cream.

Peel and thinly slice 4 small onions and separate into rings. Sprinkle well with salt and let stand ½ hour. Drain. Peel and slice 4 large tomatoes.

To Serve: Make a bed of tomatoes on a serving dish and cover with the onion rings. Sprinkle with ½ cup of French dressing. Arrange the chicken on top and sprinkle with paprika. Serves 4.

SUPRÊME DE VOLAILLE JEANNETTE
(Chicken Breasts with Aspic)

6 half breasts chicken	4 ounces foie gras (goose liver
1 truffle or large black olive	pâté) or liverwurst

CHAUD-FROID SAUCE

3 tablespoons salad oil	½ cup chicken stock
3 tablespoons flour	½ cup rich milk
2 teaspoons gelatine	3 tablespoons cream

ASPIC

3 cups water	2 tablespoons tomato paste
2 tablespoons meat glaze	3 tablespoons white wine or sherry
4 tablespoons gelatine	3 egg whites, stiffly beaten

RICE SALAD

3 tomatoes	1 cup diced green beans, cooked
1 cup rice, cooked	salt, pepper
1 cup diced carrots, cooked	¾ cup French dressing

Cook 6 half breasts of chicken (see preceding recipe). Meanwhile make a chaud-froid sauce and aspic.

Chaud-Froid Sauce: Heat 3 tablespoons of salad oil. Blend in, off the fire, 3 tablespoons of flour and 2 teaspoons of dry gelatine. Add ½ cup of chicken stock and ½ cup rich milk and stir over the fire until the sauce comes to a boil. Put the pan over ice and stir until the sauce begins to thicken. Blend in 3 tablespoons of cream.

Aspic: In a large saucepan put 3 cups of water, 2 tablespoons of meat glaze, 4 tablespoons of dry gelatine, 2 tablespoons of tomato paste, 3 tablespoons of white wine or sherry and 3 stiffly beaten egg whites. Beat with a large wire whisk over a slow fire until the mixture comes to a real boil. Remove and let stand for 10 minutes. Strain through a damp cloth placed over a large strainer. Put in a shallow cake tin and into the refrigerator to set for at least 1 hour.

Skin and bone the chicken breasts and cut them in half crosswise. Sandwich with pâté or liverwurst. Place on a cake rack in a pie plate. Carefully spoon chaud-froid sauce over the top and sides of each. Chill in the refrigerator for ½ to 1 hour. Melt ¼ of the aspic very slowly, put the pan over ice and when on the point of setting, spoon the aspic over the chicken. Put a slice of truffle or black olive on each breast and chill again for ½ to 1 hour, or until ready to serve.

Meanwhile prepare a rice salad. Skin 3 tomatoes, remove seeds and pulpy part and shred the rest. Mix together cool cooked rice, finely diced cooked carrots and beans, and the shredded tomatoes. Season with salt and pepper and blend in ¾ cup of French dressing.

To Serve: Put the rice salad on one half of a silver platter and smooth with a spatula. Arrange chicken breasts on top of the rice salad. Chop the remaining aspic and place it on the other half of the platter. Serves 6.

CHICKEN BREASTS WITH BLACK CHERRIES

6 half breasts of chicken	*3 teaspoons potato flour*
4 tablespoons butter	*½ teaspoon meat glaze*
3 tablespoons brandy	*1¼ cups stock*
1 small clove garlic, crushed	*¼ cup white wine*
½ cup sliced mushrooms	*salt, pepper*
1 cup pitted black cherries	

HOLLANDAISE SAUCE

2 egg yolks	salt, cayenne
1 tablespoon tarragon vinegar	1 tablespoon cream

¼ pound butter

Carefully remove skin and bone from 6 half chicken breasts. Brown slowly on both sides in 3 tablespoons of hot butter. Heat 3 tablespoons of brandy in a small pan, ignite and pour over the chicken. Remove chicken from the pan. Put 1 tablespoon of butter and a small clove of crushed garlic in the same pan and cook ½ minute. Add ½ cup of sliced mushrooms and cook until lightly browned. Blend in, off the fire, 3 teaspoons of potato flour and ½ teaspoon of meat glaze. Pour on 1¼ cups of stock and ¼ cup of dry white wine and stir over the fire until the mixture comes to a boil. Add salt, pepper, 1 cup of pitted black cherries and the chicken breasts. Cover with waxed paper and a lid and simmer for 20 to 25 minutes, until the chicken is tender. Meanwhile make the following Hollandaise sauce.

Hollandaise Sauce: Put 2 egg yolks and 1 tablespoon of tarragon vinegar in a small bowl and beat with a wire whisk. Beat in a little salt, cayenne and 1 tablespoon of cream. Place the bowl in a skillet of hot water and beat over a slow fire until the mixture begins to thicken. Then beat in ¼ pound of butter, bit by bit.

To Serve: Arrange the chicken on a hot serving dish. Add the Hollandaise sauce to the sauce in the pan and spoon over the chicken. Brown lightly under the broiler. Serves 6.

POULET À LA KIEV
(Breasts of Chicken Kiev Style)

4 half chicken breasts	salt, pepper
⅛ pound sweet butter	about ½ cup flour
1 clove garlic, crushed	1 egg, beaten
2 teaspoons finely chopped chives or marjoram	about ½ cup bread crumbs
	salad oil for deep-fat frying

1 bunch watercress

Skin the chicken and remove the breast bones. Cut off the wing tips, leaving the small wing bones attached to the meat as a handle.

Place each chicken breast between 2 pieces of waxed paper, skin side down. Beat with a wooden mallet until about ¼ inch thick, starting in the center. Remove the paper. In the middle of each breast place a small finger of firm cold butter, a bit of garlic, ½ teaspoon chopped chives or marjoram, salt and pepper. Roll up, tuck in each end. Dust lightly with flour, brush with beaten egg and roll in bread crumbs. Fry in deep hot fat (350°) for 3 to 4 minutes, until golden brown. Remove and drain on absorbent paper. Put paper cutlet frills on the wing bone, if available (butchers will usually give these to you). Serve on a hot platter and garnish with watercress. Serves 4.

Note: All of the preparations except the last-minute frying can be done ahead of time. Although frozen chicken breasts may be used in most of the chicken breast recipes in this book, do not use them for Chicken Kiev.

CHICKEN BREASTS WITH SOUR CREAM

4 half breasts of chicken	*½ teaspoon tomato paste*
5 tablespoons butter	*1 cup stock or water*
3 tablespoons brandy	*1 cup sour cream*
¼ pound mushrooms, sliced	*salt*
3 tablespoons flour	*freshly ground black pepper*
½ cup grated Parmesan cheese	

Skin and bone 4 half chicken breasts. Slowly brown on both sides in 3 tablespoons of hot butter. Heat 3 tablespoons of brandy in a small pan, ignite and pour over the chicken. Remove chicken from pan. Put 1 tablespoon of butter in the same pan and sauté the mushrooms about 5 minutes, until lightly browned. Blend in, off the fire, 3 tablespoons of flour and ½ teaspoon tomato paste. Stir in 1 cup stock or water and stir over the fire until the mixture comes to a boil. Add 1 cup sour cream, a little at a time. Season with salt and freshly ground black pepper. Put back the chicken, cover with waxed paper and a lid and cook gently for 25 minutes, or until the chicken is tender.

To Serve: Arrange the chicken breasts on an ovenproof serving dish. Cover with the sauce, sprinkle with ½ cup grated Parmesan cheese and dot with 1 tablespoon of butter. Brown under the broiler. Serves 4.

CHICKEN CURRY

4 half chicken breasts
6 tablespoons butter
¼ cup white wine
salt, freshly ground pepper
1 tablespoon oil
1 small onion, sliced
1 small carrot, sliced
1 stalk celery, sliced
1 apple, peeled, cored and sliced
3 to 5 tablespoons curry powder
2 tablespoons flour

1 teaspoon tomato paste
1½ cups chicken stock
2 teaspoons lemon juice
2 tablespoons shredded coconut
1 tablespoon red currant jelly
cayenne pepper
few drops Tabasco sauce
1 bay leaf
1 cup rice, cooked
chutney

Skin and bone the chicken breasts. Brown slowly in 3 tablespoons of hot butter. Heat ¼ cup white wine, ignite and pour over chicken. Season with salt and pepper, cover and cook slowly for 20 minutes, adding a little more wine or butter if the pan gets dry. Meanwhile prepare the following Burma curry sauce.

Burma Curry Sauce: Melt 3 tablespoons of butter and 1 tablespoon of oil. Add 1 small sliced onion, 1 small sliced carrot, 1 stalk sliced celery and 1 sliced apple. Cook slowly for 8 to 10 minutes. Add 3 to 5 tablespoons of curry powder and cook another 5 to 6 minutes; the amount of curry powder depends on its strength and your preference for a mild or hot curry. Blend in, off the fire, 2 tablespoons of flour and 1 teaspoon of tomato paste. Add 1½ cups of chicken stock and stir over the fire until the mixture comes to a boil. Add 2 teaspoons lemon juice, 2 tablespoons shredded coconut and 1 tablespoon red currant jelly. Season with salt, cayenne, a few drops of Tabasco and a bay leaf. Cover and simmer about 20 minutes, then strain.

To Serve: Place chicken breasts on a hot serving dish. Lift the glaze in the pan chicken was cooked in with a little wine or water and add it to the sauce. Pour over the chicken. Serve with boiled rice and chutney — and condiments if you wish (see Lamb Curry on page 148). Serves 4.

Note: Curry sauces improve on standing, so the sauce may be made ahead of time and then reheated.

POULET AMANDINE
(Chicken Breasts with Almonds)

4 half breasts chicken	*1 mushroom, finely chopped*
4 tablespoons butter	*1 teaspoon potato flour*
3 tablespoons sherry	*½ cup dry white wine*
1 small clove garlic, crushed	*½ cup stock or water*
½ cup blanched split almonds	*salt and pepper*

Carefully skin and bone 4 half chicken breasts. Brown them slowly on both sides in 3 tablespoons of hot butter. Heat 3 tablespoons of sherry in a small pan, ignite and pour over the chicken. Remove chicken breasts from the pan. To the pan add 1 tablespoon butter, 1 clove crushed garlic, ¼ cup almonds and 1 finely chopped mushroom. Cook for 3 to 4 minutes, until lightly browned. Blend in, off the fire, 1 teaspoon potato flour. Add ½ cup white wine and ½ cup stock or water and stir over the fire until the sauce comes to a boil. Season with salt and pepper. Put back the chicken, cover with waxed paper and a lid and cook for 20 to 25 minutes, until the chicken is tender. While the chicken is cooking, brown the remaining ¼ cup almonds in a moderate oven at 350°.

To Serve: Arrange chicken breasts on a hot serving dish, pour the sauce over them and scatter browned almonds over the top. Serves 4.

SUPRÊME DE VOLAILLE ITALIENNE
(Chicken Breasts with Stuffed Eggplant)

1 large eggplant	*3 tablespoons sour cream*
salt, pepper	*½ cup bread crumbs*
½ cup salad oil	*½ cup grated Parmesan cheese*
1 large yellow onion	*7 tablespoons butter*
½ pound mushrooms	*4 half breasts chicken*
4 slices cooked ham	

HOLLANDAISE SAUCE

2 egg yolks
1 tablespoon vinegar
¼ pound butter

salt, cayenne
1 tablespoon cream

BROWN SAUCE

2 tablespoons flour
½ teaspoon tomato paste

½ teaspoon meat glaze
1½ cups stock

Cut the eggplant into quarters lengthwise. Place on a cookie sheet. Sprinkle with 1 teaspoon salt and ½ cup salad oil and bake in a moderate oven at 375° for 30 minutes. While the eggplant is cooking, peel and finely chop 1 large yellow onion. Save 4 large mushroom caps and slice the rest of the mushrooms. Sauté the onion and mushrooms in 2 tablespoons of butter over a slow fire until soft but not browned. Remove eggplant from the oven, scoop out the flesh — leaving the skin intact — and chop it. Combine it with the cooked onion, sliced mushrooms, 3 tablespoons of sour cream, salt and pepper. Place eggplant skins on an oven-proof serving dish and fill with the eggplant mixture. Sprinkle with 2 tablespoons of butter. Meanwhile cook the chicken breasts and make Hollandaise sauce.

Chicken: Skin and bone 4 half breasts of chicken. Make a slit in the middle and sandwich each breast with a slice of ham; trim off neatly. Brown slowly on both sides in 2 tablespoons of butter, taking about 30 minutes in all to thoroughly cook the chicken. Remove and keep warm.

Hollandaise Sauce: Put 2 egg yolks, 1 tablespoon of vinegar, salt and a little cayenne pepper into a small bowl and beat with a wire whisk. Beat in 1 tablespoon of cream. Put the bowl into a skillet of hot water and beat over simmering water until the mixture begins to thicken. Then beat in ¼ pound of butter, bit by bit.

Brown Sauce: Put another tablespoon of butter in the pan the chicken was cooked in. Blend in, off the fire, 2 tablespoons of flour, ½ teaspoon of tomato paste and ½ teaspoon of meat glaze. Add 1½ cups of stock and stir over the fire until the sauce comes to a boil; 1 to 2 tablespoons of brandy may be added.

To Serve: Brown eggplant under the broiler. Top each quarter with a breast of chicken. Spoon Hollandaise sauce over the chicken and broil again until nicely browned. Strain the brown sauce around the edge and garnish with sautéed mushroom caps. Serves 4.

POULET VÉRONIQUE
(Chicken Breasts with White Grapes)

6 half breasts chicken	*1½ cups stock*
4 tablespoons butter	*¼ cup dry white wine*
3 tablespoons sherry	*salt and pepper*
1 small clove garlic, crushed	*½ cup shredded cooked*
1 small onion, finely chopped	*ham*
¼ pound mushrooms, sliced	*½ cup skinned white grapes*
3 teaspoons potato flour or 3	*6 large mushroom caps,*
tablespoons flour	*sautéed*

HOLLANDAISE SAUCE

2 egg yolks	*1 tablespoon cream*
1 tablespoon tarragon vinegar	*salt, cayenne pepper*
¼ pound butter	

Remove skin and bone from 6 half chicken breasts. Brown slowly all over in 3 tablespoons of hot butter in a heavy saucepan. Heat 3 tablespoons of sherry in a small pan, ignite and pour over the chicken. Take chicken from the pan and in it put 1 tablespoon of butter, 1 clove of garlic, crushed, and 1 small onion, finely chopped. Cook very slowly for 5 minutes. Add ¼ pound mushrooms, sliced, and cook briskly for 2 minutes.

Blend in, off the fire, 3 teaspoons of potato flour. Pour on 1½ cups stock and stir over the fire until the sauce comes to a boil. Add ¼ cup dry white wine, salt and pepper, and ½ cup shredded cooked ham. Return the chicken to the pan, cover and simmer for 20 minutes, or until tender. Meanwhile make the following Hollandaise sauce.

Hollandaise Sauce: Put 2 egg yolks and 1 tablespoon of vinegar into a small bowl. Beat with a wire whisk. Beat in 1 tablespoon of cream and a little salt and cayenne pepper. Place in a skillet of hot water and beat over simmering heat until the mixture begins to thicken. Then beat in ¼ pound butter, bit by bit.

To Serve: Arrange chicken breasts on a hot ovenproof serving dish. Add ½ cup skinned white grapes to the sauce and pour it around the chicken. Spoon Hollandaise sauce over the chicken breasts and brown under the broiler. Garnish with sautéed mushroom caps. Serves 6.

SUPRÊME DE VOLAILLE AUVERGNATE
(Breasts of Chicken with Eggplant and Tomatoes)

3 or 4 dried mushrooms *3 tablespoons sherry*
2 tablespoons white wine *salt and pepper*
4 half chicken breasts *1 medium-size eggplant*
about 1 tablespoon flour *4 to 5 tablespoons salad oil*
3 tablespoons butter *3 tomatoes*

An hour or so before you start preparing this dish put 3 or 4 dried mushrooms to soak in 2 tablespoons of white wine.

Remove skin and bones from 4 half chicken breasts. Dust lightly with flour. Heat 3 tablespoons of butter in a skillet and when the butter is on the point of turning color, add the chicken and brown slowly on both sides. Heat 3 tablespoons of sherry in a small pan, ignite and pour over the chicken. Cover and cook slowly for 20 to 25 minutes, until the chicken is tender. Season with salt and pepper.

Meanwhile cut 1 eggplant into slices, sprinkle with salt and let stand for ½ hour. Drain off any juice and dry. Fry until golden brown on both sides in 3 to 4 tablespoons of hot oil. Skin and slice 3 tomatoes and sauté them in the same pan the eggplant was cooked in, adding more oil as necessary.

To Serve: Arrange the slices of eggplant on a hot serving dish, slightly overlapping. Put a layer of tomatoes over the eggplant and place the chicken on top. Finely chop the dried mushrooms and put them with the white wine into the pan the chicken was cooked in. Add ½ cup of water. Bring to a boil and pour over the chicken. Serves 4.

CHICKEN RICE MOLD WITH HOLLANDAISE SAUCE

6 half breasts chicken	*¼ cup dry white wine*
5 tablespoons butter	*salt, peppercorns*
¼ cup sherry	*1 bay leaf*
¼ cup stock or water	*1½ cups rice*

HOLLANDAISE SAUCE

2 egg yolks	*salt, cayenne*
1 tablespoon tarragon vinegar	*1 tablespoon cream*
¼ pound butter	

Remove skin and bones from 6 half breasts of chicken. Brown slowly all over in 2 tablespoons of hot butter. Heat ¼ cup of sherry in a small pan, ignite and pour over the chicken. Add ¼ cup stock or water and ¼ cup dry white wine, salt, peppercorns and bay leaf. Cover and simmer for 25 minutes, or until chicken is tender. Meanwhile cook rice and make Hollandaise sauce.

Boil 1½ cups of rice in plenty of boiling salted water about 13 minutes, or until the grains taste tender; do not overcook for risk of the rice getting mushy. Drain in a strainer and place the strainer over a little gently boiling water to steam the rice; be sure the water does not touch the bottom of the strainer. Stir the rice occasionally with a fork. It should steam 5 to 10 minutes and can be left almost indefinitely.

Hollandaise Sauce: Place 2 egg yolks, 1 tablespoon of vinegar, salt and a little cayenne pepper in a small bowl and beat until blended with a wire whisk. Beat in 1 tablespoon of cream. Place the bowl in a skillet with an inch of gently boiling water in the bottom. Beat until the mixture begins to thicken, then beat in ¼ pound of butter, bit by bit.

To Serve: Mix the rice with 3 tablespoons of melted butter, salt and pepper. Grease a ring mold with salad oil or vegetable shortening, fill with rice, pressing it down with a fork. Unmold on a round platter. Fill the center with chicken and pan gravy. Spoon Hollandaise sauce over the chicken and brown lightly under the broiler. Serves 6.

CHICKEN PIE

1 chicken, 4 to 4½ pounds	1½ cups chicken stock
1 small onion, sliced	½ cup light cream
1 carrot, sliced	¼ pound mushrooms, sliced and
1 stalk celery, sliced	sautéed
1 bay leaf	4 hard-boiled eggs
salt, peppercorns	1 tablespoon grated Parmesan
4 tablespoons butter	cheese
4 tablespoons flour	1 egg, slightly beaten

CRUST — QUICK PUFF PASTE

2 cups flour	1½ sticks butter (¼ pound each)
1 teaspoon salt	¼ cup ice water

Tie up the chicken and place it in a deep heavy saucepan. Barely cover with cold water and bring slowly to a boil. Skim. Add a sliced onion, carrot and stalk of celery, 1 bay leaf, salt and a few peppercorns. Cover and simmer about 1 to 1¼ hours, until the chicken is tender. If there is time, cool the chicken in the water it was cooked in. Meanwhile make the following crust.

Quick Puff Crust: Put 2 cups of flour on a board or marble slab. Make a well in the center and in it put 1 teaspoon of salt and 1½ sticks of butter. Work ¼ cup of ice water into the butter. Cover with the flour and work quickly together with the heel of your hand. Knead lightly for a few seconds. Wrap in waxed paper and chill in the refrigerator for at least ½ hour before rolling out.

Remove the chicken from the stock. Skin and bone it and cut the meat into coarse shreds. Melt 4 tablespoons of butter. Blend in 4 tablespoons of flour, off the fire. Add 1½ cups of the strained chicken stock and stir over the fire until the sauce comes to a boil. Add ½ cup of light cream and 1 tablespoon of grated Parmesan cheese. Taste for seasoning. Put all but ½ cup of the shredded chicken into the sauce with the sliced sautéed mushrooms and 4 hard-boiled eggs, cut into eighths. Place in a deep 9-inch pie plate. Put the ½ cup of chicken over the sauce — this keeps the sauce from coming into direct contact with the crust and prevents sogginess. Brush the edge of the dish with beaten egg. Roll out the crust and place over the filling. Decorate with small fluted rounds of crust. Pierce several times with a fork for steam to escape. Brush the top with beaten egg. Chill in the refrigerator for at least ½ hour if possible, or as long as you wish. Bake in a moderate oven at 375° for 30 to 35 minutes, until golden brown. Serve in the pie dish. Serves 5 or 6.

FRICASSEE OF CHICKEN

1 4 to 5 pound chicken	*salt and peppercorns*
1 medium-size onion, sliced	*¼ pound mushrooms*
1 carrot, sliced	*1 tablespoon butter*
1 bay leaf	*1½ cups rice or noodles, cooked*

CREAM SAUCE

3 tablespoons butter	*1½ cups chicken stock*
3 tablespoons flour	*¼ cup cream*
cayenne pepper	*1 egg yolk*

Tie up the chicken and place in a heavy saucepan with the sliced onion, carrot, a bay leaf, salt and 10 to 12 peppercorns. Just cover with cold water and bring slowly to a boil. Simmer covered for 1¼ to 1½ hours, or until tender. Remove chicken from pan, reserving the stock, and skin. Take all the meat from the bones and cut into shreds. Slice ¼ pound mushrooms and sauté in 1 tablespoon of butter for 5 minutes. Add with the shredded chicken to the following sauce.

Cream Sauce: Melt 2 tablespoons of butter. Off the fire stir in 3 tablespoons flour, salt and cayenne pepper. Add 1½ cups strained chicken stock and stir over the fire until the mixture comes to a boil. Add 3 tablespoons cream, then 1 tablespoon butter, bit by bit. Beat 1 egg yolk with 1 tablespoon cream and add to the sauce; cook until the sauce is thickened but do not let it boil after adding the egg yolk for risk of curdling.

To Serve: Serve on buttered rice or noodles, which can be cooked in the remaining chicken stock. Serves 4 to 6.

CHICKEN GUMBO

1 chicken, 4 to 5 pounds	salt, pepper
½ pound smoked ham	1 sprig thyme
4 tablespoons butter	½ green pepper, diced
1 pound okra	1 small red pepper, optional
1 medium-size onion, finely chopped	2 to 3 tablespoons chopped parsley
2 tablespoons flour	1 pint oysters or 1 pound shrimp, optional
1½ quarts water	
6 large tomatoes	2 to 3 teaspoons filé powder

Have the chicken cut up for stewing. Cut the ham into small dice. Heat 3 tablespoons of butter in a deep heavy saucepan and slowly brown the chicken and ham. Remove from the pan. Cut the okra into slices about ¼ inch thick and lightly brown them and a finely chopped medium-size onion. Remove from the pan. Melt another tablespoon of butter in the same pan and stir in 2 tablespoons of flour. Cook until this roux is brown, stirring all the while. Pour on 1½ quarts of water and stir over the fire until the mixture comes to a boil. Put back the chicken, ham, okra and onion. Add 6 large skinned and cut-up tomatoes, salt, pepper and a sprig of fresh thyme. Simmer until the chicken is very tender, about 1½ to 2 hours, depending on its age.

Take the chicken out of the gumbo and when it is cool enough to handle, skin and bone it. Dice the meat, put it back into the pan and heat to the boiling point. At this stage the gumbo can be kept simmering almost indefinitely or can cool and be reheated later. Before serving add half a diced green pepper and a diced small red pepper if available — be sure all the seeds are removed — and 2 to 3 tablespoons of chopped parsley. Simmer about 5 minutes. Then add either a pint of coarsely chopped oysters or 1 pound of shelled shrimps and cook another 5 minutes. Take the pan off the fire and stir in 2 to 3 teaspoons of filé powder; this must not cook.

Serve in a hot casserole or tureen, with plainly boiled rice. Serves 7 or 8.

JELLIED CHICKEN LOAF

1 fowl, about 5 pounds	1 bay leaf
1 small onion, sliced	1 sprig fresh parsley
1 stalk celery, sliced	salt, peppercorns
1 carrot, sliced	2 tablespoons gelatine
	parsley or watercress

Tie up the chicken and place it in a deep heavy saucepan. Add 6 cups of cold water and bring slowly to a boil. Skim carefully. Add 1 sliced onion, a sliced stalk of celery, a sliced carrot, 1 bay leaf, 1 sprig of parsley, salt and a few peppercorns. Cover and simmer until the chicken is very tender and starts falling off the bones, about 1½ hours — longer if the chicken is an old fowl. Remove the chicken. Strain the stock and if there is more than 4 cups (1 quart), reduce it to that amount. Soften 2 tablespoons of gelatine in ¼ cup of cold water, add it to the hot stock and stir until it is completely dissolved.

Skin the chicken, take all the meat off the bones and cut it into small dice. Combine the chicken and stock and taste for seasoning. Pour into a loaf pan and chill in the refrigerator until set, at least 2 to 3 hours, and much longer if you wish. Unmold on a silver platter. Garnish with parsley or watercress. A simple but very refreshing summer luncheon or supper dish. Serves 8.

POULET PAYSANNE
(Chicken with Vegetables)

1 5-pound stewing fowl	1 clove garlic, crushed
6 onions, sliced	2 slices bacon, diced
6 carrots, sliced	¼ cup red wine
1 stalk celery	2½ cups chicken stock
bouquet of herbs	1 teaspoon tomato paste
salt, pepper, peppercorns	3 tablespoons chopped fresh herbs
3 tablespoons butter	2 white turnips, sliced

Tie up the chicken and place in a deep heavy saucepan. Just cover with cold water and bring slowly to a boil. Skim. Add 1 sliced onion, 1 sliced carrot, 1 sliced stalk of celery, a bouquet of herbs, salt and peppercorns. Simmer for 1 hour. Remove the fowl and cool slightly. Melt 1 tablespoon of butter in a casserole and brown the chicken lightly. Remove the chicken. Add 1 sliced onion, 1 sliced carrot, 1 clove crushed garlic and 2 slices diced bacon. Cook for 2 to 3 minutes. Stir in ¼ cup red wine, 2 cups of stock, 1 teaspoon of tomato paste, salt, pepper and 2 tablespoons chopped herbs. Bring to a boil. Replace the chicken and braise covered in a moderate oven at 375° for 1 hour, or until the chicken is tender. Remove the chicken. Carve and keep warm. Strain the gravy and reduce it to half the quantity; keep warm.

Meanwhile melt 2 tablespoons of butter in a skillet. Add 4 sliced onions, 4 sliced carrots, 2 sliced turnips, salt, pepper and ½ cup of chicken stock. Cover with waxed paper and a lid. Simmer until the vegetables are tender, about 30 minutes.

To Serve: Arrange vegetables on a serving dish. Place chicken on top. Pour over a little of the gravy and serve the rest in a gravy boat. Sprinkle with 1 tablespoon of chopped fresh herbs. Serves 5 or 6.

CHICKEN MOUSSE

1 fowl, about 5 pounds	*salt*
3 egg whites	*3 cucumbers*
1½ cups light cream	*4 tablespoons butter*
freshly cracked black pepper	

HOLLANDAISE SAUCE

2 egg yolks	*salt, cayenne*
1 tablespoon vinegar	*1 tablespoon cream*
¼ pound butter	

Mousse: Skin the chicken and cut all the meat off the bones. Put this uncooked meat through a meat grinder. Beat in 3 unbeaten egg whites and put through a strainer. Then slowly beat in 1½ cups of light cream, a little at a time. Add salt to taste, which will thicken the mixture. Place in a ring mold greased with vegetable shortening and cover with waxed paper. Bake in a moderate oven at 375° for 20 to 30 minutes, or until firm to the touch.

Cucumbers: Peel and dice 3 cucumbers and boil for 5 minutes in salted water. Drain well, add 4 tablespoons of butter, salt and freshly cracked black pepper, and cook for about 10 minutes, or until the cucumbers are tender but not too soft.

Hollandaise Sauce: Place 2 egg yolks, 1 tablespoon of vinegar, salt and a little cayenne pepper in a small bowl and beat until blended with a wire whisk. Beat in 1 tablespoon of cream. Place the bowl in a skillet with an inch of boiling water in the bottom. Continue beating until the mixture thickens, then beat in ¼ pound of butter, bit by bit.

To Serve: Remove mousse from oven and let stand for 5 minutes. Unmold on a round serving dish. Spoon Hollandaise sauce over the top and fill the center with cooked cucumbers. Serves 7 or 8.

CÔTELETTES DE VOLAILLE VICOMTESSE
(Chicken Cutlets)

1 3-pound chicken	*2 mushrooms, chopped*
2 egg whites	*1 tablespoon butter*
1 cup light cream	*¼ cup finely diced cooked*
salt and cayenne	*ham or tongue*
1 teaspoon chopped parsley	

Skin the chicken and remove all the meat from the bones. Put through a meat grinder. Slowly beat in 2 unbeaten egg whites, then 1 cup of light cream. Season with salt and a little cayenne pepper. Grease cutlet molds with vegetable shortening. Fill them level with the chicken mixture. Make small holes in the center of the molds with a wet finger and fill with a teaspoon of the following stuffing. Sauté 2 chopped mushrooms in 1 tablespoon of butter for about 5 minutes, until lightly browned. Add ¼ cup diced ham or tongue, 1 teaspoon of chopped parsley, salt and pepper, and mix well.

Cover with a little more chicken mousse, rounding and smoothing the tops with a spoon. Drop molds into a pan of salted simmering water and let them poach gently, without boiling, until set. The cutlets will slide out of the molds and float to the top when done. Remove with a slotted spoon and place on a cloth to dry.

To Serve: Arrange the cutlets on a hot serving dish in the shape of a crown, spoon over either velouté sauce (see Chicken Timbales, the following recipe) or Hollandaise sauce (see Chicken Mousse, the preceding recipe). Fill the center of the crown with cooked peas or lima beans. Serves 4 to 6.

CHICKEN TIMBALES WITH SAFFRON RICE

3 whole breasts chicken	*¼ to ½ teaspoon saffron*
3 egg whites	*7 tablespoons butter*
1½ cups light cream	*3 tablespoons flour*
salt, cayenne pepper	*1 cup chicken stock*
1½ cups rice	*¾ cup cream*
2 egg yolks	

Skin the chicken breasts and carefully remove the meat from the bones. Put it through a meat grinder. Slowly beat in 3 unbeaten egg whites and put the mixture through a strainer. Then beat in 1½ cups of light cream, a little at a time. Season with salt and a pinch of cayenne. Place in timbale molds which have been well greased with vegetable shortening. Put molds in a baking dish with an inch of boiling water in the bottom. Cover with waxed paper and bake in a moderate oven at 350° for 20 to 25 minutes, or until firm to the touch. Meanwhile cook the saffron rice and velouté sauce.

Saffron Rice: Cook 1½ cups of rice in 2 to 3 quarts of boiling salted water for 13 minutes or until just tender. Drain in a large strainer and place the strainer over a little boiling water to steam the rice; 5 to 10 minutes will do, and it can be as much longer as you wish. Just before serving crush ¼ to ½ teaspoon of saffron in a little hot water and mix into the rice with 3 tablespoons of melted butter, salt and a little cayenne.

Velouté Sauce: Melt 3 tablespoons of butter. Blend in, off the fire, 3 tablespoons of flour, salt and cayenne. Add 1 cup of chicken stock (which can be made with the chicken bones) and stir over the fire until the sauce comes to a boil. Add ¼ cup of cream and 1 tablespoon of butter, bit by bit. Mix 2 egg yolks with ½ cup of cream, add to the sauce and stir until thickened but do not let it boil again.

To Serve: Make a bed of rice on the bottom of a hot serving dish. Turn the chicken timbales out of the molds and arrange them on top of the rice. Pour the sauce over the timbales and serve immediately. Serves 5 or 6.

CHICKEN SOUFFLÉ

1 cup ground cooked chicken	*¼ cup brandy or sherry*
3 tablespoons butter	*salt, white pepper*
3 tablespoons flour	*pinch dry mustard*
¾ cup milk	*4 egg yolks*
6 egg whites, stiffly beaten	

Carefully remove all skin, bone and gristle from some cooked chicken, preferably the white meat. Put it through the fine blade of a meat grinder twice, giving a total of 1 cup when it is done.

Melt 3 tablespoons of butter in a saucepan. Blend in, off the fire, 3 tablespoons of flour. Add ¾ cup of milk and stir over the fire until the mixture just comes to a boil. Remove and add ¼ cup brandy or sherry. Season with salt, white pepper and a pinch of dry mustard. Beat in 4 egg yolks, one at a time. Add the chicken. Stiffly beat 6 egg whites and fold them into the chicken mixture.

Butter a soufflé dish and tie a band of buttered waxed paper around the outside. Fill with the soufflé mixture. Bake for 40 to 50 minutes in a moderate oven at 350° until the top is lightly browned and the soufflé feels a little firm to the touch. Do not open the oven door until the soufflé has cooked at least 40 minutes or it may fall. Remove, carefully take off the waxed paper and serve immediately. A suprême sauce (see page 237) goes well with this soufflé, although it is not necessary. Serves 4 or 5.

Note: If a soufflé dish is not available, a regular glass casserole may be used. It should be large enough so that the soufflé mixture does not fill more than ¾ of the dish, and the waxed-paper band is not used. The advantage of soufflé dishes is the straight sides; the dish is filled with the soufflé mixture, which rises straight up from the dish into the protective waxed-paper band.

VOL AU VENT À LA REINE
(Puff Pastry Case with Creamed Chicken)

PUFF PASTE

2 cups flour	¾ cup ice water
1 teaspoon salt	½ pound butter

1 egg

CHICKEN FILLING

2 tablespoons butter	2 egg yolks
3 tablespoons flour	½ cup heavy cream
salt, cayenne	2 cups diced cooked chicken
1¼ cups chicken stock	½ pound mushrooms, sliced
¼ cup light cream	and sautéed

parsley

Puff Paste: Put 2 cups of flour on a marble slab or wooden board. Make a well in the center and in it put 1 teaspoon of salt. Work the flour into a paste with ¾ cup of ice water, adding just a little water at one time to a small quantity of flour. Roll into a square the size of a handkerchief. Put ½ pound of butter in the center and wrap the sides and ends around the butter, completely covering it. Place in the refrigerator for ½ hour. Remove and roll into a long narrow strip. Fold in three. Turn the dough around so that the folded edge is facing you and roll out again, then fold in three. Place in the refrigerator for ½ hour. Remove and repeat the two rolling-out and folding processes. Chill and roll out once more. All this should be done 24 hours before baking the puff paste.

The next day roll and fold again. Then roll out about ¼ inch thick and cut 2 rounds, 8 inches in diameter. With a round cutter, cut a round about 3 inches in diameter out of the center of one large round. Make diagonal cuts with a sharp knife on the small round. Brush a cookie sheet with cold water and place the whole round on it. Brush the edge of the round with cold water and place the second round on top of the first. Make diamond-shaped cuts on top of the second round and straight shallow cuts down the side. Brush the small round and the top of the second round with beaten egg. Bake in a hot oven at 400° for about 20 minutes, or until golden brown. Remove and fill with the following mixture. Serve on a hot platter and garnish with parsley.

Chicken Filling: Melt 2 tablespoons of butter. Blend in 3 tablespoons of flour, salt and cayenne pepper, off the fire. Add 1¼ cups chicken stock and stir over the fire until the mixture comes to a boil. Add ¼ cup of light cream, then 2 egg yolks which have been lightly beaten with ½ cup of heavy cream. Cook until the sauce has thickened but do not let it boil again. Add 2 cups diced cooked chicken and the sautéed mushrooms. Serves 6.

Note: Patty shells are made exactly the same way, except that the rounds are only about 2½ inches in diameter.

CHICKEN HASH

2 *cups diced cooked chicken*	1 *cup milk*
1 *cup heavy cream*	*salt and white pepper*
2 *tablespoons butter*	½ *cup grated Swiss or*
2 *tablespoons flour*	*Parmesan cheese*

DUCHESS POTATOES
6 *medium-size old potatoes*   1 *egg*
2 *tablespoons butter*

Put 2 cups of diced cooked chicken into a double boiler with 1 cup of heavy cream and cook until well heated and the cream has reduced a little. Add 1 cup of cream sauce made as follows. Melt 2 tablespoons of butter. Blend in, off the fire, 2 tablespoons of flour. Add 1 cup of milk, salt and white pepper and stir over the fire until the sauce comes to a boil. Blend into the chicken mixture and taste for seasoning. Cook for another 10 to 15 minutes. Meanwhile prepare duchess potatoes.

Duchess Potatoes: Pare 6 medium-size potatoes and cook in boiling salted water until tender, about 20 minutes. Drain well and return to a slow fire for a minute or two to dry out. Put through a potato ricer. Beat in 1 egg, 2 tablespoons of butter, salt and white pepper. Put into a pastry bag. Mashed potatoes used for piping have to be firmer than regular mashed potatoes, but if they seem too stiff, a little hot milk may be added.

To Serve: Pipe a border of duchess potatoes around an oval ovenproof serving dish. Place the hash in the center and sprinkle it with ½ cup grated Swiss or Parmesan cheese. Brown lightly under the broiler and serve immediately. This is chicken hash at its simplest — and many people think best. It can be made even simpler by omitting the cheese. Turkey may be used instead of chicken, and there is another hash recipe for either chicken or turkey on page 285 in the turkey section. Serves 4.

CRÊPES NIÇOISES
(Pancakes Stuffed with Chicken)

CRÊPES BATTER

4 tablespoons flour	1 tablespoon oil
1 egg	about ½ cup milk
1 egg yolk	salt
	cayenne pepper

CHICKEN FILLING

¼ pound mushrooms	2 hard-boiled eggs, chopped
1 tablespoon butter	1 teaspoon finely chopped
¾ cup shredded cooked	parsley
chicken	3 tablespoons sour cream
	salt, pepper

butter   ½ cup grated Parmesan cheese

Crêpes Batter: Place 4 tablespoons of flour, 1 whole egg, 1 egg yolk, 1 tablespoon of salad oil, 4 tablespoons of milk, salt and a little cayenne pepper in a small bowl and beat until smooth. Add enough milk to reduce to the consistency of heavy cream, using about ½ cup in all. Place in the refrigerator for ½ hour. Meanwhile prepare the following stuffing.

Chicken Filling: Slice ¼ pound mushrooms and cook over a slow fire in 1 tablespoon of butter for about 5 minutes, until lightly browned. Use the top of a double boiler over direct heat. Add ¾ cup shredded cooked chicken, 2 chopped hard-boiled eggs, 1 teaspoon of finely chopped parsley, 3 tablespoons of sour cream, salt and pepper. Place over boiling water to heat through and keep warm while the crêpes are being cooked.

Remove the batter from the refrigerator. If it has thickened a little, add more milk. Heat a heavy omelet pan or cast-iron skillet. Rub the hot pan with a little butter on a piece of waxed paper. Cover the bottom with a very thin coating of batter. Brown carefully on one side, turn and brown the other, using a wide spatula. Cook the remaining batter in the same way, stacking the cooked crêpes on a cake rack.

Place a spoonful of the filling in the middle of each pancake. Fold over and arrange overlapping on a hot ovenproof serving dish. Pour 3 tablespoons of melted butter over the top and sprinkle with ½ cup of grated Parmesan cheese. Brown under the broiler. Serves 4 to 6.

Note: Cooked veal, ham or tongue may be used instead of chicken. If you wish, the crêpes can be covered with a Mornay sauce (see page 186) instead of butter and cheese, and lightly browned under the broiler.

CHICKEN CROQUETTES

2 cups cooked chicken	*1 truffle, optional*
2 hard-boiled eggs	*about ¾ cup flour*
½ cup diced mushrooms	*1 egg*
¼ cup diced ham	*about ¾ cup bread crumbs*
1 tablespoon butter	*deep fat for frying*

CREAM SAUCE

4 tablespoons butter	*½ cup chicken stock and ½ cup milk*
5 tablespoons flour	*or 1 cup milk*
salt, cayenne	*2 tablespoons sour cream*
	1 teaspoon lemon juice

All the ingredients should be cold before the croquettes are shaped; and after they are shaped they should be chilled at least half an hour before they are cooked.

Chop enough cooked chicken to make 2 cups into very small dice with a sharp knife. The chicken can be put through a meat grinder but is nicer diced by hand. Chop 2 hard-boiled eggs finely. Sauté ½ cup diced mushrooms and ¼ cup diced ham in 1 tablespoon of hot butter. Chop the truffle finely.

Cream Sauce: Make a thick cream sauce. Melt 4 tablespoons of butter in a small pan. Blend in, off the fire, 5 tablespoons of flour, salt and a little cayenne pepper. Add ½ cup chicken stock and ½ cup milk, or 1 cup of milk, and stir over the fire until the sauce comes to a boil. Blend in 2 tablespoons of sour cream and 1 teaspoon of lemon juice. Pour on a plate and allow to get cold.

Mix together the sauce, chicken, hard-boiled eggs, mushrooms, ham and truffle. Taste for seasoning. Form into small cutlet shapes or into croquettes. Dust lightly with flour, brush with beaten egg and roll in bread crumbs. Place in the refrigerator at least ½ hour to give the egg time to coagulate and thus prevent the coating from bursting when the croquettes are cooked. Fry in deep hot fat at 350° until golden brown, or sauté in butter until brown all over.

To Serve: Arrange in a crown on a hot flat serving dish. Serve with velouté sauce (see page 263), Béarnaise sauce (see page 164), or sauce Bercy (see page 37). Serves 4.

CHICKEN LIVER RISOTTO

¾ *pound chicken livers*	*1½ cups rice*
4 tablespoons butter	*1 tablespoon tomato paste*
½ *pound bacon*	*1 teaspoon meat glaze*
1 large yellow onion	*3 cups stock*
2 cloves garlic, crushed	*3 tomatoes, skinned*
salt and pepper	*2 small cans cocktail sausages*
½ *pound mushrooms, sliced*	*1½ cups grated Parmesan cheese*

Heat 2 tablespoons of butter in a heavy skillet and when very hot, quickly brown ¾ pound chicken livers on both sides. Remove them from the pan and in it put ½ pound bacon, cut in small dice. Cook slowly until the bacon is brown and crisp. Remove the bacon bits with a slotted spoon and put them on absorbent paper to drain. Cut 1 large yellow onion into thin slices and put it in the same pan with 2 cloves of garlic crushed. Season with salt and pepper and cook slowly for about 5 minutes, until the onion is soft but not brown. Add ½ pound of sliced mushrooms and cook another 3 to 4 minutes. Add 1½ cups of rice and cook for 2 to 3 minutes, stirring constantly.

Mix in 1 tablespoon of tomato paste and 1 teaspoon of meat glaze. Pour on 2 cups of stock, cover and cook about 10 minutes, or until all the liquid is absorbed. Add another cup of stock and continue cooking for another 10 minutes or so, or until the rice is nearly tender. Slice 3 skinned tomatoes, the cooked chicken livers and 2 small cans of cocktail sausages. Blend them into the rice. Sprinkle the top of the risotto with ½ cup of grated Parmesan cheese and dot with 2 tablespoons of butter. Cover again and keep warm over a very slow fire or in a slow oven for at least ½ hour.

To Serve: Place in a casserole and put the bacon bits over the top. Serve a bowl of grated Parmesan cheese separately. Serves 5 or 6.

GNOCCHI PARISIENNE

1 cup water	*3 large eggs*
salt, cayenne	*½ teaspoon Dijon or dry mustard*
3 tablespoons butter	*4 tablespoons grated Parmesan*
1 cup flour	*cheese*

CHICKEN LIVER SAUCE

6 chicken livers	*2 tablespoons flour*
2 tablespoons butter	*1 teaspoon tomato paste*
1 small clove garlic	*1 teaspoon meat glaze*
3 mushrooms, sliced	*1½ cups stock*
2 tablespoons red wine	

FOR SERVING

1 tablespoon butter   *½ cup grated Parmesan cheese*

Gnocchi: Put 1 cup of cold water into a saucepan with ½ teaspoon of salt, a pinch of cayenne pepper and 3 tablespoons of butter. Bring slowly to a boil. When boiling, throw in 1 cup of flour, all at once, and stir until smooth and the mixture clears the sides of the pan. Remove from the fire and beat in 3 eggs, one at a time. Beat in ½ teaspoon of Dijon or dry mustard, 4 tablespoons of grated Parmesan cheese and a little more salt and cayenne.

Bring 2 quarts of salted water to a boil for the gnocchi to poach in. Lower the heat to simmering. Shape the mixture with 2 spoons into small egg shapes. Or put it into a pastry bag with a large plain tube and pipe out 1-inch lengths, cutting them off with a sharp knife right into the hot water. Simmer gnocchi until set — they float to the top when done — and the water must not boil or the gnocchi will disintegrate. Meanwhile make the following chicken liver sauce.

Chicken Liver Sauce: Sauté 6 chicken livers quickly on both sides in 1 tablespoon of very hot butter. Remove livers. Put another tablespoon of butter and 1 small clove of crushed garlic in the pan. Sauté 3 sliced mushrooms. Blend in, off the fire, 2 tablespoons of flour, 1 teaspoon of tomato paste and 1 teaspoon of meat glaze. Add 1½ cups of stock and 2 tablespoons of red wine and stir over the fire until the sauce comes to a boil. Slice the livers and add them to the sauce and simmer for about 5 minutes.

To Serve: Remove the gnocchi with a slotted spoon and place them on a hot serving dish. Dot with 1 tablespoon of butter and sprinkle with ¼ cup of grated Parmesan cheese. Spoon the chicken liver sauce evenly over the top and sprinkle with another ¼ cup of cheese. The cheese may be browned under the broiler if you wish. Serves 4 to 6.

CHICKEN LIVERS AND MUSHROOMS

1 pound chicken livers	*3 tablespoons flour*
4 tablespoons butter	*1 cup chicken stock or water*
1 pound mushrooms, sliced	*½ cup dry white wine*
	1 tablespoon lemon juice

Heat a heavy skillet. Put in 2 tablespoons of butter and when the butter is on the point of turning color, add 1 pound of chicken livers. Cook briskly until well browned all over. Remove the livers with a slotted spoon. Melt another 2 tablespoons of butter in the same pan and add 1 pound of sliced mushrooms. Lower the heat a little and cook for about 5 minutes, until the mushrooms are lightly browned. Blend in, off the fire, 3 tablespoons of flour. Pour on 1 cup of chicken stock or water and ½ cup of dry white wine. Stir over the fire until the sauce comes to a boil. Taste for seasoning; if you have used a well-seasoned chicken stock you may not need any. Add 1 tablespoon of lemon juice. Put back the chicken livers with any juice and cook for about 5 minutes until they are well heated. Serve in a casserole. Serves 4.

CHICKEN LIVER SAUCE FOR SPAGHETTI

1 pound chicken livers	5 tomatoes, skinned and
7 tablespoons butter	coarsely chopped
2 cloves garlic, crushed	1 tablespoon flour
2 large onions, finely chopped	½ teaspoon meat glaze
¼ pound mushrooms, finely	3 tablespoons tomato paste
chopped	1 cup stock
salt and pepper	1 tablespoon chopped mixed
pinch of dry mustard	fresh herbs
1 pound thin spaghetti	1½ cups grated Parmesan cheese

Heat a large skillet. Put in 2 tablespoons of butter and when the butter is on the point of turning color, put in 1 pound of chicken livers. Cook briskly until the chicken livers are well browned all over. Remove the livers. Put 2 tablespoons of butter and 2 cloves of crushed garlic in the same pan and cook for 1 minute. Add 2 large finely chopped onions and cook fairly quickly until they begin to brown. Add ¼ pound finely chopped mushrooms, turn down the heat and cook slowly for 5 or 6 minutes. Season with salt, pepper and a pinch of dry mustard. Add 5 skinned and coarsely chopped tomatoes and cook for 2 minutes.

Blend in, off the fire, 1 tablespoon of flour, ½ teaspoon of meat glaze and 3 tablespoons of tomato paste. Pour on 1 cup of stock and stir over the fire until the mixture comes to a boil. Simmer about 10 minutes. Chop the chicken livers and add to the sauce with 1 tablespoon of chopped fresh herbs. Simmer another 5 minutes or so.

Meanwhile cook 1 pound of thin spaghetti, unbroken, in 4 quarts of boiling salted water until tender. It usually takes about 10 to 12 minutes, but the only way to judge is by tasting since brands vary considerably. Drain well and mix with 3 tablespoons of melted butter.

To Serve: Place on a hot serving dish and cover with the sauce. Serve a bowl of grated Parmesan cheese separately. Serves 4 to 6.

CHICKEN LIVERS WITH CREAM SAUCE

1 pound chicken livers	*¼ cup sherry*
6 tablespoons butter	*salt, pepper*
2 tablespoons flour	*1 tablespoon chopped parsley*
1¼ cups light cream	*8 triangles of white bread*

Heat a heavy skillet. Put in 2 tablespoons of butter and when the butter is on the point of turning color, add the chicken livers. Cook quickly until well browned all over, about 3 minutes in all. Remove the livers with a slotted spoon. Melt another 2 tablespoons of butter in the same pan. Blend in, off the fire, 2 tablespoons of flour. Pour on 1¼ cups of cream and stir over the fire until the sauce comes to a boil. Add ¼ cup of sherry, salt and pepper. Put back the chicken livers with any juice and cook for 5 minutes or so, just to heat the chicken livers thoroughly.

To Serve: Place in a casserole. Sprinkle with 1 tablespoon of finely chopped parsley. Garnish with 8 triangles of bread which have been fried until golden brown in 2 tablespoons of butter. Serves 4.

PILAFF OF CHICKEN LIVERS

½ *pound chicken livers*
6 *tablespoons butter*
1 *green pepper, diced*
1 *large yellow onion, finely chopped*
1 *pound mushroooms*
salt, pepper
1½ *cups rice*
3 *tablespoons tomato paste*

6 *slices bacon*
4 *tomatoes*
1 *teaspoon meat glaze*
2 *tablespoons flour*
1½ *cups water*
½ *cup whole blanched almonds*
½ *cup shredded browned almonds*
½ *cup currants*

Brown the chicken livers quickly in 1 tablespoon of hot butter. Remove and slice them. In the same pan melt another 2 tablespoons of butter. In it put a diced green pepper and a finely chopped large yellow onion and cook slowly about 10 minutes, until lightly browned. Save 6 large mushroom caps and slice the rest of the mushrooms. Put them all into the pan and continue cooking for 5 minutes. Take out the whole mushrooms. Add the sliced chicken livers to the rest of the mixture and season with salt and pepper.

In the meantime cook 1½ cups of rice in 3 quarts of boiling salted water until tender, about 13 minutes. Drain and add 2 tablespoons of melted butter, 2 teaspoons of tomato paste, salt and pepper; toss with 2 forks. Butter a deep round baking dish and put ¾ of the rice into it. Press down well with a wooden spoon and hollow out a space in the center with the back of the spoon. Fill this space with the chicken liver mixture. Cover with the remaining rice. Bake in a moderate oven at 350° for 10 to 15 minutes to set.

While pilaff is baking, fry 6 slices of bacon until brown and crisp. Remove and sauté 4 peeled quartered tomatoes in the bacon fat. Make a brown sauce in the pan the livers were cooked in. Melt 1 tablespoon of butter. Off the fire blend in 1 teaspoon of tomato paste, 1 teaspoon of meat glaze and 2 tablespoons of flour. Add 1½ cups water and stir over the fire until the sauce comes to a boil. Season with salt and pepper.

To Serve: Remove the pilaff and invert on a large round platter. Pour brown sauce over the top. Surround with little mounds of almonds, currants and tomatoes. Garnish the top with broiled bacon and whole mushrooms. Serves 6.

CHICKEN LIVERS EN BROCHETTE

24 *chicken livers*	12 *slices bacon*
4 *tablespoons butter*	*salt*
24 *mushroom caps, medium*	*freshly cracked black pepper*
size	1½ *cups rice, cooked*
½ *cup brandy*	1 *bunch fresh watercress*

Preheat the broiler. Heat a heavy skillet. Put in 2 tablespoons of butter and when the butter is on the point of turning color, put in the chicken livers and brown them quickly on both sides. Remove the livers with a slotted spoon. Put another tablespoon of butter in the pan and quickly sauté 24 mushroom caps. Remove them from the pan. Pour ½ cup of brandy into the pan, bring to a boil, then let simmer to keep warm.

Cut 12 slices of bacon in half crosswise and wrap each chicken liver in half a slice. Thread the livers and mushrooms alternately on 4 shashlik sticks, putting 6 chicken livers and 6 mushrooms on each one. Spread with 1 tablespoon of softened butter and season with salt and freshly cracked black pepper. Place the shashlik sticks on a broiling pan about 3 inches away from the flame and broil about 6 minutes in all, until the bacon is done, turning once to brown both sides.

To Serve: Make a bed of hot, cooked, buttered rice on a hot serving dish. Arrange the shashlik sticks on top of the rice. If you prefer, the livers and mushrooms can be gently pushed off the sticks. Add the pan juices to the gravy and spoon a little over the chicken livers; serve the rest in a separate gravy bowl. Garnish with fresh watercress. Serves 4.

CHICKEN LIVER PÂTÉ

1 pound chicken livers	cayenne pepper
2 eggs	¾ cup milk
salt	3 tablespoons cream
freshly cracked black pepper	thin slices of bacon
2 tablespoons butter	2 whole chicken livers,
3 tablespoons flour	sautéed

about ¼ cup clarified butter

Put 1 pound of chicken livers through a meat grinder. Beat 2 eggs, add the ground livers, salt, freshly cracked black pepper and the following sauce. Melt 2 tablespoons of butter. Stir in, off the fire, 3 tablespoons of flour, salt and cayenne pepper. When well blended add ¾ cup of milk. Stir over the fire until the mixture comes to a boil. Add 3 tablespoons of cream. Blend into the chicken liver mixture and put through a strainer.

Line a small deep earthenware crock with thin slices of bacon. Put in the liver mixture. Place 2 whole sautéed chicken livers on top and cover with waxed paper. Put into a baking pan with an inch of boiling water in the bottom and bake in a very slow oven at 250° for 45 to 50 minutes. Remove and allow to get quite cold. Place a plate and a gentle weight on top.

If it is to be kept for any length of time, put a thin layer of clarified butter over the top.

CAPONS

Capons are castrated male chickens which grow to a large size for a chicken, from 7 to 10 pounds as a rule, and have tender, well-flavored meat which makes them fine for roasting.

ROAST CAPON

1 capon, 8 to 10 pounds	1 pound noodles
8 to 9 tablespoons butter	1 pound mushrooms
½ cup dry white wine	3 stalks celery

1 cup heavy cream

Tie up the capon and rub all over with 3 tablespoons of softened butter. Place in a shallow roasting pan with ½ cup of dry white wine. Cover with aluminum foil and roast in a moderate oven at 350° for about 18 minutes to the pound. Half an hour before the capon is due to be done, remove the aluminum foil so that the skin can brown and spread another tablespoon of butter on the breast and legs.

Meanwhile prepare the following dressing. Cook 1 pound of noodles in plenty of boiling salted water until tender; the cooking time varies with brands, so the only way to tell when it is tender is by tasting. Drain in a colander and rinse with a little warm water. Add 2 to 3 tablespoons of melted butter and keep warm over a very slow fire. Slice 1 pound of mushrooms and sauté in 2 tablespoons of butter until lightly browned. Dice 3 stalks of celery and cook in boiling salted water until tender, then drain. Add the sautéed mushrooms and drained celery to the noodles. Also add a cup of heavy cream and taste for seasoning.

To Serve: Remove the capon from the roasting pan and let stand for 5 minutes. Carefully cut off the whole breasts. Then take out the large breast bones. Place the capon on a hot serving dish and fill the center with the noodles dressing. Slice the breasts and arrange them on top of the noodles. Add 1 cup of water to the pan juices, bring to a boil and strain into a gravy bowl. Serves 6 to 8.

ROAST CAPON VÉRONIQUE
(Roast Capon with White Grapes)

1 ounce dried mushrooms	*1 large yellow onion*
1 capon, 7 to 8 pounds	*6 tablespoons butter*
½ lemon	*1½ cups muscatel wine*
1 egg white	*½ cup brandy*
½ pound finely ground veal	*3 cups skinned pitted white*
1 cup light cream	*muscat grapes*
salt	*2 teaspoons potato flour or 2*
freshly cracked black pepper	*tablespoons flour*

1 cup chicken or veal stock

Soak 1 ounce of dried mushrooms in cold water for 1 hour.

Wash the capon well inside and out. Rub with half a lemon. Fill with the following stuffing. Mix 1 egg white into ½ pound finely ground veal. Slowly beat in 1 cup of light cream, salt and freshly cracked black pepper. Drain the dried mushrooms and chop finely. Also finely chop a large yellow onion and sauté both mushrooms and onion in 2 tablespoons of butter until soft but not brown. Blend the mushrooms and onion into the veal mixture and put into the capon. Close the vent with skewers and string.

Place the capon in a roasting pan and spread the entire skin with 4 tablespoons of softened butter. Cover with aluminum foil and pour ½ cup muscatel into the pan. Roast in a moderate oven at 350° for about 2 hours, or until done. Baste every 15 minutes with a tablespoon of wine, using 1 cup in all. When the capon has cooked 1½ hours, remove the aluminum foil so that the skin can brown.

Remove the capon from the pan and place it on a hot serving dish; leave in the oven with the heat off while you make the gravy. Heat the pan until very hot and deglaze it with ½ cup of brandy. Add 3 cups of skinned and pitted white muscat grapes and cook slowly for 2 to 3 minutes. Stir in, off the fire, 2 teaspoons of potato flour or 2 tablespoons of flour. Add remaining ½ cup of wine and 1 cup of stock and stir over the fire until the gravy comes to a boil. Taste for seasoning and simmer for a few minutes.

To Serve: Place cutlet frills on the capon legs. Remove the grapes from the gravy with a slotted spoon and put a few of them on the capon. Spoon a little of the gravy over the capon and serve the rest in a gravy bowl. Garnish the capon with cork potatoes (see page 000), placed in little piles with 2 on the bottom and 1 on top. Alternate these piles with small mounds of grapes. Serves 6.

TURKEY

The days when growers supplied turkeys only for the winter holidays such as Thanksgiving and Christmas are gone. Now we can enjoy turkey the year round. It is a lovely bird, full of fine flavor whether you have a small or a large one. Small birds, around 8 to 10 pounds, are a good buy for small families. Large ones, from 15 pounds on up, have a large proportion of meat to bone; since it is as easy to roast a large turkey as a small one, they are the most economical and timesaving if you have a large family or a big party. Leftover turkey is generally no problem anyway, since turkey is as good cold as it is hot, is fine for sandwiches and salads, and can be used in many other ways.

Turkeys are now being bred for good-sized breasts, so in buying one, look for a bird that is compact in build with a well-developed breast, rather than the long rangy ones that are full of bone and short of meat.

Although young turkeys can be boiled — it is a better buy than chicken if you have to make countless sandwiches or a lot of salad for a party — by far the most usual way to cook turkey is to roast it. Butchers usually tie them up. If not follow the directions on page 210. Fill both the center cavity and the neck cavity with stuffing if you want plenty. Fold the neck flap over and slip it over the twine that ties up the turkey. Secure the center vent with skewers and string (see page 210). Put the turkey, breast side up, in a roasting pan and cover the breast and legs with softened butter. Put aluminum foil over the top and sides, but don't wrap the turkey up in it because then it will steam rather than roast. Aluminum foil not only helps keep the turkey moist and juicy but saves the nuisance of continual basting. About ¾ of an hour before the turkey is due to be done, remove the foil so that the top can brown evenly.

It is best to roast at an even temperature of 350° or even at 325° if the turkey is large, rather than first searing at a high temperature. There will be less loss and more even cooking. The cooking time depends to some extent upon the size and age of the bird, larger birds taking less time per pound than small ones. Most of the time charts for turkeys specify too much cooking time; 15 minutes per pound is usually ample for large birds and about 20 minutes for small ones. Overcooking just dries them out. There are several ways of gauging the cooking time. A meat thermometer inserted in the thickest part of the leg next to the body will register 190° when a turkey is done. Or you can pierce the leg and if the juice is clear with no trace of pink, it is done; never pierce the breast or you will lose valuable juices. The easiest test of all and a perfectly reliable one is to wiggle the leg, and when it moves up and down readily, the turkey is ready.

Let the turkey stand for 15 to 50 minutes before it is carved. Put it on a platter and into the oven with the heat off and the door open to keep it warm while you make the gravy. Although many meats are carved in the kitchen, a golden-crusted turkey is a beautiful sight and should be brought to the table whole. If anyone in your family is skillful enough to carve a turkey and reassemble it whole, then it can be done ahead of time. But turkeys are often served at festive, relaxed times, when everyone enjoys sitting around the table and watching the carver. Cold turkey is another matter, when there are large expanses of bare carcass which look rather unattractive. Then the carving should be done in the kitchen and the meat arranged on a platter. But unless it is a very formal occasion, let the hot turkey make its appearance as it is when it comes from the oven.

ROAST TURKEY
1 14 to 15 pound turkey

STUFFING

2 *quarts chestnuts*	1 *large yellow onion, finely*
1 *cup oil*	*chopped*
6 *cups chicken stock or water*	1 *teaspoon chopped parsley*
3 *slices white bread*	1 *teaspoon chopped chives*
½ *cup milk*	½ *teaspoon dried thyme*
1 *pound sausage meat*	*salt, pepper*

FOR ROASTING

2 tablespoons butter   ½ pound salt pork
1 cup port wine

ACORN SQUASH GARNISH

6 acorn squash   1 egg
4 tablespoons melted butter   4 tablespoons chopped ginger
2 cans yams   ½ cup grated Parmesan cheese

GRAVY

4 tablespoons flour   2 cups stock or water

Prepare the following stuffing for the turkey. Make a slit in the shell of each chestnut on the flat side with a sharp knife. Put into a shallow pan with 1 cup of oil and cook in a hot oven at 400° for 5 minutes. Remove and when cool enough to handle take off the shells and inner skin. Cook in 6 cups of chicken stock or water until soft, about 20 to 30 minutes. Soak 3 slices of bread in ½ cup of milk in a large mixing bowl. Cook 1 pound of sausage meat until browned. Remove with a slotted spoon and put into the bowl. Sauté 1 large finely chopped yellow onion. Drain the chestnuts and put through a strainer. Add to the sausage with the onion, sausage fat, 1 teaspoon of chopped parsley, 1 teaspoon of chopped chives, ½ teaspoon dried thyme, salt and pepper.

Put into the turkey and secure with small skewers and string. Spread 2 tablespoons of softened butter all over the turkey. Cover the breast and legs with thin slices of salt pork, place breast side up on a rack in a roasting pan and put some slices of salt pork over the back. Cover with aluminum foil. Roast in a moderate oven at 350° for about 15 minutes to the pound. An hour before the roast is due to be done, remove the aluminum foil. Put 1 cup of port wine into the pan and baste every 15 minutes with the pan juices. A turkey is done when the juice which follows a fork placed in the leg comes out clear, or when a meat thermometer inserted in the leg registers 190°. While the turkey is cooking prepare the acorn squash garnish.

Acorn Squash Garnish: Cut 6 acorn squash in half crosswise and remove the seeds. Brush with 2 tablespoons of melted butter and season with salt and pepper. Place on a cookie sheet and bake in a moderate oven at 350° until the flesh is soft, about 50 to 60 minutes. Remove and scoop out the flesh. Drain 2 cans of yams and put through a strainer with the squash. Beat in 1 egg and 4 tablespoons of finely chopped ginger. Fill the squash shells, sprinkle with ½ cup of grated Parmesan cheese, dot with 2 tablespoons of butter and brown under the broiler.

To Serve: Remove the turkey and let stand for 10 to 15 minutes while the gravy is prepared. Blend 4 tablespoons of flour into the pan juices. Add 2 cups of water and stir over the fire until the gravy comes to a boil. The giblets can be cooked in seasoned water with sliced onion, carrot and celery, and this stock used for the gravy, the chopped giblets added to it. Carve the turkey as desired. Spoon a little of the gravy over it and serve the rest in a gravy bowl. Place the squash around the platter. Serves 10 to 12.

TO ROAST HALF A TURKEY

Because large turkeys do have a high proportion of meat and usually cost less per pound than small birds, they are a better buy. If they pose the problem of too much meat, you can buy half a turkey. Place the stuffing on a greased piece of parchment paper or aluminum foil and mold it into the shape of the cavity of the turkey. Skewer the skin of the turkey to the breast meat on the breast bone edge so that it won't shrink. Tie the leg firmly to the tail. Place the turkey, skin side up, over the stuffing and rub it well with melted butter. Cover with aluminum foil and roast according to the preceding directions. Use a moderate oven at 350° and allow 15 to 20 minutes to the pound. When the turkey is done the paper permits you to lift it intact out of the roasting pan. Let it stand for 15 to 20 minutes, then carefully slide it onto a serving dish.

WILD RICE STUFFING

2½ cups wild rice
1 cup butter
1 cup diced celery
1 cup finely chopped onion
½ pound mushrooms, sliced

2 cups walnuts or pecans,
  coarsely chopped
salt, pepper
2 tablespoons chopped parsley
nutmeg
thyme

Wash the wild rice in several changes of water. Bring 6 quarts of water to a boil. Slowly add the rice and cook until it is tender, about 30 to 35 minutes. Drain and steam for 10 minutes or so. Meanwhile sauté 1 cup of diced celery and 1 cup of finely chopped onion in ½ cup of butter until soft but not brown. Add ½ pound of sliced mushrooms and cook another 2 to 3 minutes. Melt the remaining ½ cup of butter in the same pan. Blend together the wild rice, vegetables and butter, 2 cups of coarsely chopped walnuts or pecans, salt, pepper, 2 tablespoons of chopped parsley and a little nutmeg and thyme.

This is enough stuffing for a 16 to 18 pound turkey.

BROILED TURKEY

Have a 4 to 6 pound turkey split down the center and the backbone removed. Rub well with softened butter and season with salt and pepper. Place skin side down in a shallow baking dish or in the broiler pan without the rack. Have the pan about 5 inches from the flame or have the broiler flame as low as possible so that the turkey will not get too brown before it is cooked. After it has cooked for 20 to 30 minutes, turn it over. Baste often with plenty of butter and then the pan drippings. It will take 45 to 60 minutes in all and will serve 4 to 6 people, depending upon the size of the turkey.

TURKEY FRICASSEE

1 turkey, 8 to 10 pounds	*½ pound mushrooms, sliced*
1 onion, sliced	*5 tablespoons butter*
1 stalk celery, sliced	*4 tablespoons flour*
1 carrot, sliced	*¼ teaspoon grated lemon rind*
1 sprig parsley	*¼ teaspoon mace*
salt, peppercorns, pepper	*2 egg yolks*
	1 cup cream

Have the turkey cut up into the following pieces: 2 legs, 2 thighs, 2 wings, 4 pieces of breast. Put them into a deep heavy saucepan with the backbone (for flavor) and 6 cups of water. Bring slowly to a boil and skim. Add a sliced onion, a sliced stalk of celery, a sliced carrot, 1 sprig of parsley, salt and a few peppercorns. Cover and simmer until the turkey is tender, about 2½ to 3 hours.

Remove the turkey. Boil the stock down to 4 cups. Skin the turkey and bone it. Arrange the pieces on a hot platter and keep warm in a very slow oven while you make the sauce.

Cook ½ pound of sliced mushrooms in a tablespoon of butter with salt and pepper until lightly browned. Melt 4 tablespoons of butter. Blend in 4 tablespoons of flour, off the fire. Add the strained turkey stock and stir over the fire until the mixture comes to a boil. Add ¼ teaspoon of grated lemon rind, ¼ teaspoon of mace and taste for seasoning. Simmer about 5 minutes. Beat 2 egg yolks. Add 1 cup of cream. Blend a little of the hot sauce into the egg yolk mixture, then add the mixture to the sauce with the mushrooms. Cook until well heated but do not let the sauce boil after the egg yolks have been added.

To Serve: Spoon the sauce carefully over the turkey. Serves 8

TURKEY PAPRIKA

1 cooked turkey, 8 to 9 pounds	*8 tablespoons flour*
8 tablespoons turkey fat or butter	*2½ cups turkey stock*
3 tablespoons paprika	*1 cup rich milk*
	1½ cups cream

RICE RING

2½ cups rice, cooked	3 cups cooked peas
½ cup melted butter	1 jar pimento, diced

Cook the turkey until tender in boiling salted water, following the directions in the preceding recipe. Cool in the cooking water if time allows. Make the following paprika sauce.

Melt 8 tablespoons of turkey fat or butter in a large saucepan. Blend in 3 tablespoons of paprika and 8 tablespoons of flour, off the fire. Pour on 2½ cups of turkey stock, 1 cup of rich milk and 1½ cups of cream. Stir over the fire until the sauce comes to a boil. Taste for seasoning; it may need salt. Simmer for at least 15 minutes to cook the paprika; otherwise it will have a raw taste. Meanwhile skin and bone the turkey and cut the meat into small pieces. Add to the sauce and cook until the turkey is thoroughly heated, about 10 minutes. This dish can be kept waiting indefinitely if the pan is put into a saucepan of simmering water or if a double boiler is used. It can also be made ahead of time and reheated, with the flavor improved if anything.

Rice Ring: Cook 2½ cups of rice until just tender in boiling salted water. Drain and steam for 10 to 15 minutes. Blend with ½ cup of melted butter, 3 cups of cooked peas, a jar of diced pimento and some salt. Put into a large well-greased ring mold and bake in a moderate oven at 375° for 10 minutes.

To Serve: Run a sharp knife around the edge of the rice mold and invert it on a hot serving dish. Fill the center with some of the turkey mixture and put the rest around the edge of the rice ring. Serves 10.

TURKEY HASH WITH OYSTERS

1 pint oysters	1 cup light cream
5 to 6 tablespoons butter	salt, pepper
3 tablespoons flour	2 cups diced cooked turkey
6 slices thin white bread	

Put the oysters into a saucepan with 1 cup of water. Bring slowly to a boil and simmer until the edges of the oysters curl, about 2 to 3 minutes. Remove from the fire and drain, saving the liquid.

Melt 3 tablespoons of butter. Blend in 3 tablespoons of flour, off the fire. Add 1 cup of the oyster liquid and stir over the fire until the mixture comes to a boil. Slowly add 1 cup of light cream. Season with salt and pepper and simmer for a few minutes. Coarsely chop the oysters and add them to the sauce with 2 cups of diced cooked turkey. Cook until the mixture is piping hot.

Serve in a hot oval serving dish and garnish with triangles of bread which have been fried until golden brown in 2 to 3 tablespoons of hot butter. Serves 5 or 6.

DEVILED TURKEY

4 slices cooked turkey	*½ teaspoon dry mustard*
2 tablespoons melted butter	*salt, cayenne*
¾ cup bread crumbs	*½ teaspoon curry powder*
parsley or watercress	

SAUCE DIABLE

2 shallots or 1 small onion	*salt*
½ cup wine vinegar	*1 bay leaf*
8 to 10 peppercorns	*paprika*
½ teaspoon dry mustard	*1 cup brown or tomato sauce*

Cut 4 large neat slices of breast of turkey and have them at room temperature. Brush them well with melted butter. Mix together ¾ cup of fine bread crumbs, ½ teaspoon of dry mustard, salt, a pinch of cayenne and about ½ teaspoon of curry powder. Coat the slices of turkey evenly with this mixture. Broil until nicely browned on both sides; use either a low flame or have the turkey 3 to 4 inches away from the flame so that it will brown slowly.

Sauce Diable: Finely chop 2 shallots or 1 small white onion. Put into a pan with ½ cup of wine vinegar, 8 to 10 crushed peppercorns, 1 bay leaf, ½ teaspoon of dry mustard, salt and a little paprika. Simmer until reduced one half, then strain. Add to 1 cup of brown sauce (turkey gravy may be used) or tomato sauce and cook until throughly heated.

To Serve: Arrange the slices of turkey slightly overlapping on a hot serving dish. Garnish with parsley or watercress. Serve the sauce in a separate sauce bowl. Serves 4.

TURKEY CASSEROLE I

1 cup uncooked wild rice	*1½ cups heavy cream*
½ pound mushrooms, sliced	*2½ cups chicken stock*
4 tablespoons butter	*salt and pepper*
2 cups diced cooked turkey	*2 tablespoons chopped chives*
½ cup grated Parmesan cheese	

Wash 1 cup of wild rice in several changes of lukewarm water and then if time allows, soak it in cold water for 1 to 2 hours; this helps increase its bulk. Slice ½ pound of mushrooms and sauté them in 2 tablespoons of butter until lightly browned. Drain the rice and put it into a mixing bowl. Blend with 2 cups of diced turkey, 1½ cups of heavy cream, 1½ cups of chicken stock, salt and pepper, 2 tablespoons of finely chopped chives and the sautéed mushrooms. Grease a casserole with 1 tablespoon of butter. Add the turkey mixture. Cover and bake for 1 hour in a moderate oven at 350°. Add another cup of stock and continue cooking for at least 30 to 40 minutes, until the rice is tender.

To Serve: Remove cover. Sprinkle with ½ cup of grated Parmesan cheese and dot with 1 tablespoon of butter. Brown lightly under the broiler. Serves 4 to 6.

Note: Cooked chicken or duck may be used instead of turkey.

TURKEY CASSEROLE II

1 pound chestnuts	*3 tablespoons brandy*
½ cup salad oil	*½ pound small white mushrooms*
2½ cups stock	*½ teaspoon meat glaze*
12 small white onions	*½ teaspoon tomato paste*
1 pound Brussels sprouts	*3 teaspoons potato flour or 3 table-*
2 cups diced cooked turkey	*spoons flour*
6 tablespoons butter	*¼ cup dry white wine*
6 large croutons of bread	

With a sharp knife make a cut in the shell of each chestnut. Heat ½ cup of salad oil in a skillet, add the chestnuts and cook for 5 minutes, shaking the pan constantly. Remove chestnuts and cool. Take off the shells and inner skin. Cook in 1 cup of boiling stock for about 15 minutes, or until tender. Drain.

Peel 12 small white onions, put in a saucepan with cold water to cover, bring to a boil and simmer for about 5 minutes; drain. Put a pound of prepared Brussels sprouts in a saucepan with cold salted water to cover; bring to a boil and cook for 10 minutes.

Cut leftover turkey into small neat pieces, enough to make 2 cups, and brown them slowly all over in 3 tablespoons of hot butter. Heat 3 tablespoons of brandy in a small pan, ignite and pour over the turkey. Remove the turkey meat from the pan. Melt another 3 tablespoons of butter in the pan. Put in the chestnuts, onions, Brussels sprouts and ½ pound of quartered mushrooms. Cook for 8 to 10 minutes over a slow fire, until the onions are nicely browned. Blend in, off the fire, ½ teaspoon of meat glaze, ½ teaspoon of tomato paste and 3 teaspoons of potato flour (or 3 tablespoons of flour). Add 1½ cups of stock and ¼ cup dry white wine and stir over the fire until the mixture comes to a boil. Put back the turkey and simmer for a few minutes, or until ready to serve. Serve in a casserole and garnish with large croutons of bread. Serves 6.

AVOCADOS STUFFED WITH TURKEY

4 avocados	*1 cup cream*
salt, white pepper	*2 cups diced cooked turkey*
4 tablespoons butter	*¾ cup grated Parmesan cheese*
4 tablespoons flour	*paprika*
1 cup turkey or chicken stock	*watercress*

Use avocado pears that are not too soft and ripe. Cut them in half lengthwise, with the peel on, and remove the large pits. Sprinkle lightly with salt. Melt 4 tablespoons of butter. Blend in 4 tablespoons of flour, off the fire. Add 1 cup of turkey or chicken stock and 1 cup of cream and stir over the fire until the mixture comes to a boil. Season with salt and white pepper. Blend in 2 cups of diced cooked turkey and ¼ cup of grated Parmesan cheese. Fill the avocado pears, spreading the filling over the entire top and doming it up in the center. Sprinkle with the remaining ½ cup of grated cheese and a little paprika. Place on a cookie sheet and bake about 15 minutes in a moderate oven at 350°. If the tops are not lightly browned, finish off with a minute or two under the broiler.

To Serve: Arrange the stuffed avocados on a hot serving dish and garnish with watercress. Serves 8.

SCALLOPED TURKEY

8 small button mushrooms	*½ cup cream*
1 tablespoon finely chopped green pepper	*3 cups diced cooked turkey*
3 tablespoons butter	*¼ cup sherry*
1 tablespoon flour	*salt, white pepper*
½ cup turkey or chicken stock	*1 cup Hollandaise sauce*
	triangles of toast

Sauté 8 small button mushrooms and 1 tablespoon of finely chopped green pepper in 2 tablespoons of butter over a slow fire so that they will not brown. Add another tablespoon of butter. Blend in 1 tablespoon of flour, off the fire. Pour on ½ cup of turkey or chicken stock and ½ cup of cream and stir over the fire until the mixture comes to a boil. Add 3 cups of diced cooked turkey and ¼ cup of sherry and season lightly with salt and white pepper. Blend in 1 cup of Hollandaise sauce (see page 261 for recipe).

Serve in a hot oval serving dish and garnish with triangles of toast. Serves 4 to 6.

TURKEY RISOTTO

2 medium-size onions, finely chopped	*3 cups turkey or chicken stock*
5 tablespoons butter	*salt, pepper*
1 cup rice	*about ¼ teaspoon saffron*
½ cup dry white wine	*2 cups diced cooked turkey*
	1 cup grated Parmesan cheese

Lightly brown 2 medium-size finely chopped onions in 2 table-spoons of butter in a large skillet. Add 1 cup of rice and cook gently for 3 to 4 minutes, stirring the entire time to prevent the rice from burning. Pour on ½ cup of dry white wine and 2 cups of turkey or chicken stock. Season with salt and pepper and add about ¼ teaspoon of saffron. Bring to a boil, lower the heat to simmering and cover the pan. Simmer for about 30 minutes, adding another cup of stock when the original lot has all been absorbed.

When the rice is tender and dry, add 2 cups of diced cooked turkey, 1 cup of grated Parmesan cheese and 3 tablespoons of butter. Leave over a very slow fire for 10 to 15 minutes, until the turkey is heated through.

Serve in a casserole. Serves 4.

DUCK AND GOOSE

Ducks are plentiful in the markets the year around, and the growers, particularly on Long Island, have made a feature of producing large plump birds. They weigh about 5 to 7 pounds before they are taken in charge by the butcher and divested of their heads, feet and insides. Duck costs less per pound than other poultry, but it also has a large carcass and lots of fat, so the amount of meat in proportion to bone is less. A 5 or 6 pound duck, unless it is prepared in a very rich manner, will only serve 4 people adequately. At the Tour d'Argent in Paris they serve half a duck with one order of Caneton à l'Orange, but it takes a strong person with a robust appetite to eat it all.

Most of the meat is on the breast. The legs don't have much meat on them and the wings have almost none. Ducks are easy to roast because the fat covering the bird makes it self-basting. Although directions sometimes call for pricking the duck before it is cooked, it does not help release the fat any faster and if the skin is pricked deeply enough, meat juices are lost.

Goose is like duck with rich dark meat and even more fat, and is treated the same way. Geese weigh about 10 to 12 pounds and are found in the markets only for a limited time, from November to about April, with the largest supplies around the Christmas holidays.

CANETON À L'ORANGE
(Duck with Orange)

1 duck, 5 to 6 pounds
coarse salt
1 orange
1 clove garlic
2 bay leaves
1 cup red wine
½ large onion, finely chopped
¼ pound mushrooms, finely chopped

3 tablespoons duck fat
3 teaspoons potato flour or 3 tablespoons flour
½ teaspoon tomato paste
1 teaspoon meat glaze
1 cup stock
2 teaspoons shredded orange rind
skinned sections of 2 oranges
¼ cup brandy

CORK POTATOES

5 medium-size potatoes	flour
2 eggs	bread crumbs
2 tablespoons butter	fat for deep frying
2 tablespoons grated orange rind	salt, pepper

Rub the duck well with coarse salt. Stuff with 1 orange, cut in quarters, 1 clove of garlic and 2 bay leaves. Tie up. Roast for 1 to 1¼ hours in a moderately hot oven at 400° basting every 15 minutes with red wine, using ½ cup in all. Meanwhile make the sauce. Sauté the duck liver, ½ a large onion, finely chopped, and ¼ pound mushrooms, finely chopped, in 2 tablespoons of duck fat (taken from the roasting pan) for 5 minutes. Remove the liver. Add another tablespoon of fat. Blend in, off the fire, 3 teaspoons of potato flour (or 3 tablespoons of flour), ½ teaspoon of tomato paste and 1 teaspoon of meat glaze. Add 1 cup of stock and ½ cup of red wine and stir over the fire until the sauce comes to a boil. Add 2 teaspoons of shredded orange rind and taste for seasoning. Simmer until the duck is ready to be served. Just before serving add the skinned sections of 2 oranges.

Cork Potatoes: Pare and boil 5 medium-size potatoes in salted water until tender. Drain and return to a very slow fire for a minute or so to dry out. Put through a ricer and beat in 1 egg, 2 tablespoons of butter, seasoning and 2 tablespoons of grated orange rind. Form into small cork shapes, roll lightly in flour, brush with beaten egg and roll in bread crumbs. Fry in hot deep fat until golden brown. Remove with a slotted spoon and drain on absorbent paper.

To Serve: Cut the duck into serving pieces and arrange on a hot serving dish. Pile the cork potatoes at each end of the dish. Skim the fat off the top of the juices in the pan. Pour ¼ cup brandy into the pan and bring to a boil to dissolve the glaze. Pour this into the sauce. Spoon a little of the sauce over the duck and serve the rest in a gravy boat. Garnish with the sautéed liver. Serves 4 to 6.

BREAST OF DUCK WITH OLIVES

2 ducks, 4 to 4½ pounds	1 clove garlic, crushed
5 tablespoons butter	1½ cups chicken stock or
4 tablespoons brandy	water
8 mushrooms	4 slices cooked tongue,
½ teaspoon meat glaze	shredded
3 teaspoons potato flour or	12 pitted green olives
3 tablespoons flour	12 pitted ripe olives
1 truffle, finely chopped	

PEA PURÉE

3 pounds fresh peas or 2	2 tablespoons butter
packages frozen peas	2 tablespoons flour
salt, pepper	3 tablespoons sour cream

Cut the 4 breasts from the ducks and skin them (duck soup can be made with the rest of the carcass; see page 300 for recipe). Heat 3 tablespoons of butter in a heavy skillet and when the butter is on the point of turning color, put in the duck breasts and brown them slowly on both sides. Heat 4 tablespoons of brandy in a small pan, ignite and pour over the duck. Cover and cook slowly until tender, about 25 to 30 minutes.

Pea Purée: While the duck is cooking, make a pea purée. Cook 3 pounds of fresh peas, shelled, or 2 packages of frozen peas in boiling salted water until very tender. Drain and put the peas through a strainer. Melt 2 tablespoons of butter in a small pan. Blend in 2 tablespoons of flour and cook slowly until browned. Add to the strained peas, season and blend in 3 tablespoons of sour cream. If the pea purée has to be kept waiting, put it in a double boiler.

Sauce: When the duck breasts are tender, remove them from the pan with a slotted spoon and keep warm. Heat another tablespoon of butter in the pan and quickly brown the duck liver. Remove. Slice 4 mushrooms and leave 4 of them whole. Lower the heat a little, add another tablespoon of butter and sauté the mushrooms for 5 minutes or so, until lightly browned. Remove the whole mushroom caps. Blend in, off the fire, ½ teaspoon of meat glaze and 3 teaspoons of potato flour (or 3 tablespoons flour). Add 1 clove of garlic, crushed. Pour on 1½ cups of chicken stock (or water) and stir over the fire until the sauce comes to a boil. Add the shredded tongue, pitted green and black olives, the liver, also shredded, and a finely chopped truffle.

To Serve: Make a bed of pea purée on a hot serving dish. Place duck breasts on top of the purée and spoon the sauce over the duck. Garnish each breast with a whole mushroom cap. Serves 4.

DUCK WITH PINEAPPLE

1 duck, about 5 pounds
2 tablespoons butter
3 tablespoons brandy
1 cup cubed pineapple, fresh or canned
1 small clove garlic, crushed
¼ pound mushrooms, finely chopped
½ teaspoon tomato paste

1 teaspoon meat glaze
3 teaspoons potato flour or 3 tablespoons flour
½ cup red wine
½ cup pineapple juice
½ cup stock or water
salt, black pepper
1 tablespoon red currant jelly

6 slices pineapple, fried in butter

Tie up the duck. Heat 2 tablespoons of butter in a heavy deep saucepan and when on the point of turning color, put in the duck and brown slowly all over, starting breast side down. When the duck is browned, if there is too much fat in the pan remove all but 4 tablespoons. Heat 3 tablespoons of brandy in a small pan, ignite and pour over the duck. Remove the duck from the pan. Put 1 cup of cubed pineapple into the pan and sauté for a few minutes until lightly browned. Add 1 small clove of garlic, crushed, and ¼ pound of mushrooms, finely chopped; cook another 2 to 3 minutes. Blend in, off the fire, ½ teaspoon of tomato paste, 1 teaspoon of meat glaze and 3 teaspoons of potato flour (or 3 tablespoons of flour). Add ½ cup of red wine, ½ cup of pineapple juice and ½ cup of stock (or water) and stir over the fire until the sauce comes to a boil. Season with salt and black pepper and add 1 tablespoon of red currant jelly. Simmer for about 5 minutes.

Cut the duck into serving pieces and put it into the sauce, skin side down. Cover with waxed paper and a lid and simmer for 40 to 50 minutes, or until the duck is tender. Arrange the duck on a hot serving dish. Spoon the sauce around the duck. Garnish the top with overlapping slices of pineapple which have been fried golden brown on both sides in butter. Serves 4.

DUCK IN COINTREAU SAUCE

2 tablespoons butter
1 duck, 4 to 5 pounds
finely shredded rind of 1 orange
½ cup sliced mushrooms
1 small clove garlic, crushed
3 teaspoons potato flour
¼ cup dry sherry
¼ cup brandy
½ cup Cointreau
½ cup orange juice
1 tablespoon red currant jelly
1 tablespoon chopped truffle
salt, pepper
4 sautéed fluted or whole
  mushroom caps
2 oranges

Tie up the duck and roast until tender and browned in a moderate oven at 350°, allowing 20 to 25 minutes to the pound. Remove the duck when it is cooked. Pour off all the duck fat. Melt 2 tablespoons of butter in the pan and add the finely shredded rind of 1 orange, ½ cup of sliced mushrooms and a small clove of crushed garlic. Cook slowly for 2 minutes. Blend in, off the fire, 3 teaspoons of potato flour. Add ¼ cup of dry sherry, ¼ cup of brandy, ½ cup of Cointreau and ½ cup of orange juice. Stir over the fire until the sauce comes to a boil. Add 1 tablespoon of red currant jelly and 1 tablespoon of chopped truffle. Season with salt and pepper.

Cut the duck into serving pieces and put into the sauce until thoroughly heated. Arrange the pieces of duck on a hot serving dish and spoon the sauce over them. Garnish with sautéed mushroom caps and oranges which have been sliced with the skin on and fried until golden brown in butter and sugar. Serves 4.

DUCK WITH CHERRIES

4 *half breasts of duck*	2 *teaspoons potato flour*
3 *tablespoons butter*	1 *cup stock*
3 *tablespoons Marsala*	*salt, pepper*
1 *small clove garlic, crushed*	1 *cup pitted black cherries*
½ *cup sliced mushrooms*	1 *tablespoon red currant jelly*
1 *teaspoon meat glaze*	*sautéed duck liver*

HOLLANDAISE SAUCE

2 *egg yolks*	*salt, cayenne*
1 *tablespoon vinegar*	1 *tablespoon cream*
4 *tablespoons butter*	

Skin the breasts of duck and trim off the bone and any excess fat. (The rest of the duck may be used for duck soup; see page 300.) Brown them quickly in 1 tablespoon of hot butter. Heat 3 table-spoons of Marsala in a small pan, ignite and pour over the duck. Remove the duck from the pan. Put 1 tablespoon of butter and a small clove of crushed garlic in the pan, lower the heat and cook for 2 minutes. Add another tablespoon of butter and ½ cup of sliced mushrooms and sauté until the mushrooms are lightly browned. Blend in, off the fire, 1 teaspoon of meat glaze and 2 teaspoons of potato flour. Pour on 1 cup of stock and stir over the fire until the sauce comes to a boil. Season with salt and pepper. Return the breasts and simmer for 20 to 30 minutes, until they are tender. Meanwhile make the following Hollandaise sauce.

Hollandaise Sauce: Put 2 egg yolks, 1 tablespoon of vinegar, salt and a pinch of cayenne into a small bowl and beat until blended with a wire whisk. Beat in 1 tablespoon of cream. Place the bowl in a skillet with an inch of simmering water in the bottom and beat over a slow fire until the mixture begins to thicken. Then beat in 4 tablespoons of butter, bit by bit.

To Serve: Arrange the breasts on an ovenproof serving dish. Add to the sauce in the pan 1 cup of pitted black cherries, 1 table-spoon of red currant jelly and ¾ cup of Hollandaise sauce. Spoon over the duck and brown quickly under the broiler. Garnish with thin slices of sautéed liver. Serves 4.

CANARD ESPAGNOLE
(Roast Duck Spanish Style)

1 duck, 5 to 6 pounds	1 tablespoon Spanish paprika
salt and pepper	½ teaspoon tomato paste
1 medium-size yellow onion, finely chopped	3 tablespoons flour
	1 cup stock
4 tablespoons butter	½ cup sherry
½ pound mushrooms, sliced	2 tomatoes

Season the duck well with salt and pepper and tie it up. Place in a roasting pan and roast in a moderate oven at 350° for about 1½ hours, until well browned and tender. When the duck has been cooking for half an hour, start preparing the sauce. Finely chop a medium-size yellow onion and sauté it in 2 tablespoons of butter over a slow fire until golden brown. Add another 2 tablespoons of butter and ½ pound of sliced mushrooms and cook another 5 minutes or so. Blend in, off the fire, 1 tablespoon of Spanish paprika, ½ teaspoon of tomato paste and 3 tablespoons of flour. Pour on 1 cup of stock and ½ cup of sherry and stir over the fire until the sauce comes to a boil. Season with salt and pepper and let simmer for 15 to 20 minutes. Skin 2 tomatoes, quarter them, remove the seedy pulp and cut the rest into shreds. Add to the sauce with the strained pulp and simmer another 5 to 10 minutes.

To Serve: Cut the duck into serving pieces and arrange them on a hot serving dish. Pour all the fat out of the roasting pan, put ½ cup of water (or ¼ cup water and ¼ cup brandy) into the pan and bring to a boil to lift the glaze. Add this to the sauce. Spoon some of the sauce over the duck and serve the rest in a gravy bowl. Surround the duck with small, boiled, buttered potatoes. Serves 4.

BROILED DUCK

1 duck, 5 to 5½ pounds	about 1 teaspoon salt
2 teaspoons lemon juice	½ teaspoon ground ginger
1 tablespoon butter	

Have the butcher quarter the duck and remove the backbone and wing tips. Cut off all excess fat. Sprinkle with 2 teaspoons of lemon juice, about 1 teaspoon of salt and ½ teaspoon of ground ginger. Let stand about half an hour to absorb the seasoning. Place on a preheated broiler pan, skin side down, and put the pan 4 to 5 inches from the broiler heat. Broil for 20 to 25 minutes on one side, then turn and cook another 20 to 25 minutes.

Place the duck on a hot serving dish and brush with 1 table-spoon of melted butter. This is a simple way to serve duck but good and not too rich. Serves 4.

COLD DUCK WITH ORANGE

ASPIC

1 quart stock	*¼ cup red wine*
4 tablespoons gelatine	*2 oranges*
¼ cup sherry	*1 tablespoon tomato paste*

3 egg whites, stiffly beaten

1 duck, cold, roasted and cut into pieces	*few small bundles watercress*
1 truffle	*1 tomato, skinned, cut in rings and seeded*

Aspic: Put into a large saucepan 1 quart of cold clear stock (may be made with water and 2 to 3 teaspoons of meat glaze), 4 table-spoons of dry gelatine, ¼ cup of sherry, ¼ cup of red wine, the grated rind of 1 orange and the juice of 2 oranges, 1 tablespoon of tomato paste and 3 stiffly beaten egg whites. Slowly bring to a boil, beating all the while with a large wire whisk. After the mixture comes to a full boil, take the pan off the fire and let stand for 10 minutes. Then strain through a damp cloth placed over a large strainer. Add the grated rind of 1 orange to ⅔ of this aspic, pour it into small molds and place them in the refrigerator to set. Place the rest of the aspic into a pan over a bowl of ice and stir occasionally until it is on the point of setting.

Put the pieces of duck on a rack on top of a cookie sheet. Coat them with aspic on the point of setting and decorate with slices of truffle. Place in the refrigerator until set, or until ready to use.

To Serve: Arrange the duck on a cold serving dish, preferably silver. Turn out the small molds and place them around the duck. Garnish with small bundles of watercress which have been threaded through rings of tomato. Serves 4.

DUCK WITH SALMI SAUCE

1 cup rice	2 teaspoons meat glaze
3 tablespoons butter	1½ cups stock or water
1 small onion, finely chopped	1 tablespoon chopped parsley
2 tablespoons flour	1 to 1½ cups diced cooked duck

¼ cup claret or red wine

Cook 1 cup of rice in plenty of boiling salted water for about 13 minutes, or until just tender. Drain and place in a large strainer over an inch or so of boiling water to steam for 10 to 15 minutes. Put into a small buttered ring mold and cook in a moderate oven at 350° for 10 minutes or so. Meanwhile prepare the duck.

Melt 1 tablespoon of butter in a saucepan and cook a small finely chopped onion over a slow fire until soft but not brown. Put another tablespoon of butter in the same pan. Blend in, off the fire, 2 tablespoons of flour and 2 teaspoons of meat glaze. Add 1½ cups of stock or water and stir over the fire until the mixture comes to a boil. Add 1 tablespoon of chopped parsley, 1 to 1½ cups of diced cooked duck and ¼ cup of claret or red wine. Simmer for 5 to 10 minutes, or until ready to serve.

To Serve: Run a sharp knife around the edge of the ring mold and unmold the rice on a hot serving dish. Fill the center with the duck mixture. Serves 4.

WILD RICE TO BE SERVED WITH DUCK

½ cup raisins, soaked in ¼ cup brandy	2 bay leaves
	salt
½ cup white raisins, soaked in ¼ cup dry white wine	freshly cracked black pepper
	1 small clove garlic, crushed
6 slices bacon	2 tablespoons chopped chives
¼ cup finely chopped onion	½ cup grated Parmesan cheese
2 cups wild rice	½ cup melted butter
4 cups duck or chicken stock	½ cup blanched split almonds

Soak ½ cup raisins in ¼ cup brandy and ½ cup white raisins in ¼ cup dry white wine for half an hour. Dice 6 slices of bacon and cook slowly until crisp and brown. Remove bacon bits with a slotted spoon and reserve them. Sauté ¼ cup finely chopped onion in the bacon fat over a slow fire for about 5 minutes, until soft but not browned.

Wild rice is very dusty so wash it well in several changes of cold water, until the water is clear. Place in a pan with 4 cups of duck or chicken stock, 2 bay leaves, salt and freshly cracked black pepper, and bring slowly to a boil. Add 1 clove of garlic, crushed, the raisins (drained), the sautéed onion and 2 tablespoons of chopped chives. Cover with waxed paper and a lid and cook in a moderate oven at 350° for 40 to 50 minutes, or until the rice is tender. Remove from the oven. With a fork stir in ¼ cup of grated Parmesan cheese and ½ cup of melted butter. Then add ½ cup of blanched split almonds and the bacon bits. Place in a serving dish and sprinkle with another ¼ cup of grated Parmesan cheese. Serves 6 to 8.

Note: Soaking wild rice overnight in cold water to cover will give an increased volume of rice when it is cooked — an important factor considering its cost.

DUCK SOUP

bones and neck of 1 duck	*2 large carrots, chopped*
2 tablespoons duck fat or butter	*1 tomato, chopped*
1 large onion, finely chopped	*2 quarts water*
1 large clove garlic, chopped	*salt, peppercorns*
2 stalks celery, chopped	*1 sprig thyme or parsley*
½ cup rice	

This soup can be made with the neck and bones of any poultry such as chicken and turkey, as well as with duck. If the bones have some meat on them, all the better — it will then make a main-course luncheon or supper dish.

Try out 2 tablespoons of duck fat or use 2 tablespoons of butter. Melt in a large heavy saucepan. Add a large finely chopped onion, a large chopped clove of garlic, 2 stalks of chopped celery,

2 large chopped carrots and a chopped tomato. Cook over a moderate fire until lightly browned. Put in the duck bones and neck and 2 quarts of water. Bring slowly to a boil and skim. Season with salt, a few peppercorns and a sprig of thyme or parsley. Cover and simmer for about 2 hours. Remove from the fire, strain and let the soup stand until it is cold. Take off any fat that rises to the top. If there is any meat on the bones, cut it into small dice and put it into the soup. Bring to a boil again, taste for seasoning and add ½ cup of rice. Cook gently until the rice is soft, about 15 minutes.

Serve in a hot tureen. This will make 6 generous servings.

ROAST GOOSE ALSATIAN

1 goose, 10 to 12 pounds	*1 cup finely chopped celery*
1½ pounds sausage	*½ teaspoon freshly grated nut-*
½ pound ground ham	*meg*
½ pound ground tongue	*salt*
ground gizzard, heart and liver	*freshly cracked black pepper*
4 shallots or 2 onions, chopped	*1 cup port wine*

GARNISH

2 small green cabbages	*2 medium-size onions*
½ pound salt pork	*3 apples*
2 pounds old potatoes	

Stuff the goose with the following mixture. Blend together 1½ pounds of sausage, ½ pound of ground ham, ½ pound of ground tongue, the ground gizzard, heart and liver of the goose, 4 shallots or 2 onions, finely chopped, 1 cup of finely chopped celery, ½ teaspoon of freshly grated nutmeg, salt and freshly cracked black pepper. Secure the opening with skewers and string. Place the goose on a rack in a roasting pan. Pour ½ cup of port wine into the pan. Roast in a moderate oven at 350° uncovered for 20 minutes to the pound, basting every 10 to 15 minutes and each time adding a tablespoon of wine.

Garnish: The last hour the goose is cooking prepare the garnish. Quarter and core 2 small green cabbages, cover with cold water, bring to a boil and cook for 5 minutes, then drain. Dice ½ pound of salt pork and sauté in a heavy skillet for about 5 minutes. Peel 2 medium-size onions and peel and quarter 3 apples, removing the pits. Slice the cabbage and put it into the skillet with the salt pork, onions and apples. Season with salt and pepper. Cook slowly for 30 to 40 minutes. Meanwhile pare 2 pounds of old potatoes, cut into small olive shapes and steam until tender.

To Serve: Place the goose on a hot serving dish. Add 1 cup of water to the pan juice and bring to a boil. Strain a little over the goose and serve the rest in a gravy bowl. Place the cabbage garnish on each side of the goose and pile the potatoes at each end of the platter. A 10-pound goose will serve 6 people.

GOOSE WITH CELERIAC

4 large pieces cooked goose	*3 tablespoons flour*
2 to 3 tablespoons coarse salt	*1 cup stock*
freshly cracked black pepper	*1 pound celeriac (celery root)*
2 bay leaves	*2 teaspoons lemon juice*
¼ teaspoon thyme	*flour*
4 tablespoons sherry	*1 egg*
2 tablespoons blackberry jelly	*bread crumbs*
1 teaspoon meat glaze	*fat for deep-fat frying*

Cut 4 pieces of cooked goose, preferably from the breast, into even pieces, large enough for one to a serving. Coat both sides with coarse salt, freshly cracked black pepper, 2 crumbled bay leaves and ¼ teaspoon of dried thyme. Let stand overnight.

Brown quickly on both sides in rendered goose fat, using a heavy deep saucepan. Heat 4 tablespoons of sherry in a small pan, ignite and pour over the goose. Remove the goose from the pan. Blend in, off the fire, 2 tablespoons of blackberry jelly, 1 teaspoon of meat glaze and 3 tablespoons of flour. Pour on 1 cup of stock and stir over the fire until the mixture comes to a boil. Blend in 1 cup of sour cream, a little at a time, starting in the center of the sauce and using a small wire whisk. Taste for seasoning. Put the goose into the sauce and simmer for 15 to 20 minutes, or until ready to serve. Meanwhile prepare the celeriac garnish.

Celeriac: Pare 1 pound of celeriac and cut into fingers the size of French fried potatoes. Put into a saucepan with cold water to cover and 2 teaspoons of lemon juice. Bring slowly to a boil and simmer for 7 to 8 minutes. Drain and dry on a cloth. Dust with flour, coat with beaten egg and bread crumbs. Fry until golden brown in deep hot fat at 350°.

To Serve: Arrange the pieces of goose on a hot serving dish and strain the sauce over the top. Garnish each end of the dish with celeriac. Serves 4.

SQUAB

Squabs are young pigeons and appear in our markets only in a limited quantity and at luxury price. They are small, weighing only about a pound each, so one is allowed for each serving. Although expensive, they have a distinctive flavor and are fine for an occasional treat.

STUFFED SQUAB

2 squabs	salt, pepper
8 chicken livers	3 tablespoons brandy
6 tablespoons butter	½ teaspoon tomato paste
4 large mushrooms, sliced	1 teaspoon meat glaze
1 apple, sliced	2 teaspoons potato flour
4 ounces shredded cooked	¾ cup stock
ham or tongue	½ cup dry white wine

1 sprig tarragon

Remove the back and breast bones of the squabs, leaving the little leg bones intact. Stuff them with the following dressing. Sauté 8 chicken livers and the squab livers quickly in 2 tablespoons of hot butter. Remove the livers. Put another tablespoon of butter in the pan and sauté 4 sliced mushrooms and a sliced apple until lightly browned. Slice the livers and put them in the pan with the mushrooms. Also add the shredded ham or tongue and season with salt and pepper. Fill the boned squabs. Sew the backs up with a needle and fine thread. Tie the legs with soft string. Brown the squabs slowly all over in 3 tablespoons of butter. Heat 3 tablespoons of brandy in a small pan, ignite and pour over the squabs. Remove squabs.

Blend into the pan juices, off the fire, ½ teaspoon of tomato paste, 1 teaspoon of meat glaze and 2 teaspoons of potato flour. Pour on ¾ cup of stock and ½ cup of white wine and stir over the fire until the mixture comes to a boil. Put back the squabs with a sprig of tarragon. Cover with waxed paper and a lid and simmer for 30 minutes.

To Serve: Place the squabs on a hot serving dish and spoon a little of the sauce over them. Serve the rest in a sauce bowl. Serves 2.

BROILED SQUAB

4 squabs	*8 thin slices bacon*
1 lemon	*1 loaf unsliced white bread*
salt, pepper	*fat for deep-fat frying*
3 tablespoons butter	*2 cups cooked strained chestnuts*
	1 bunch watercress

Split the squabs in half but do not cut them all the way through. Remove the backbones. Rub with a little lemon juice and season with salt and pepper. Brush with melted butter and wrap each one with 2 slices of bacon. Thread on long skewers, one for each squab. Broil until tender, about 30 minutes in all. Have the squabs at least 3 inches from the broiler flame so that they will not brown too much before they are sufficiently cooked. Baste several times with melted butter.

Cut 4 pieces of bread 3 inches thick. Scoop out a little of the center of the bread. Fry until golden brown in hot deep fat. Do this just before serving so that they will be hot and crisp.

To Serve: Add all the pan juices to 2 cups of hot strained chestnuts (this chestnut purée is obtainable in cans). Season and put into the bread cases. Arrange on a hot serving dish. Top each one with a squab on the skewer. Garnish with watercress. Serves 4.

GUINEA HEN

Guinea hens have a rather gamy flavor — in fact are sometimes classed as game — which is appealing to many people. It would have to be, since they are hard to get in many markets and quite costly. Buy a fairly large one, 3½ to 4 pounds, since the small ones have a lot of bone in proportion to meat, and serve it in rather special ways, although guinea hens are delicious just roasted with a simple bread stuffing.

GUINEA HEN WITH WILD RICE

1 guinea hen, 3½ to 4 pounds	1½ cups stock
6 tablespoons butter	¾ cup large white raisins
¼ cup brandy	½ cup white wine
1 apple, chopped	1 cup wild rice
1 stalk celery, thinly sliced	3 mushrooms, thinly sliced
1 small onion, thinly sliced	½ cup pine kernels
½ teaspoon tomato paste	1 cup sour cream
1 teaspoon meat glaze	½ cup heavy cream, whipped
3 tablespoons flour	2 truffles

Tie up the guinea hen. Heat 2 tablespoons of butter in a deep heavy saucepan and when the butter is on the point of turning color, put in the guinea hen (breast side down at first) and brown slowly all over, taking about 25 to 30 minutes in all. Heat ¼ cup brandy in a small pan, ignite and pour over the guinea hen. Remove the guinea hen. Put another tablespoon of butter in the pan. Add 1 chopped apple, a sliced stalk of celery and a small sliced onion; cook slowly for 5 minutes. Blend in, off the fire, ½ teaspoon of tomato paste, 1 teaspoon of meat glaze and 3 tablespoons of flour. Add 1½ cups of stock and stir over the fire until the mixture comes to a boil. Simmer for 10 minutes and then put through a strainer. Cut the guinea hen into serving pieces. Put it back into the sauce, skin side down, season and cook covered over a very slow fire until the guinea hen is tender, about 40 to 50 minutes.

Meanwhile soak ¾ cup large white raisins in ½ cup of white wine for ½ hour. Boil 1 cup of well-washed wild rice in plenty of liquid; chicken or veal stock is preferable but salted water will do. Sauté 3 thinly sliced mushrooms in 3 tablespoons of hot butter for 4 to 5 minutes. Drain the rice and drain the raisins (reserving the wine). Combine the rice, raisins, sautéed mushrooms with all the pan juices and ½ cup of pine kernels, using 2 forks to keep the kernels separate.

To Serve: Make a bed of the wild rice on a hot flat serving dish. Arrange the pieces of guinea hen on top of the rice. Add the drained wine to the sauce. Then beat in 1 cup of sour cream, a little at a time, using a wire whisk. Carefully add the whipped cream and 1 truffle, finely chopped. Spoon the sauce over the guinea hen and garnish with 1 sliced truffle. Serves 4.

BREAST OF GUINEA HEN WITH HAM

4 breasts of guinea hen	*3 tablespoons sherry*
6 to 7 tablespoons butter	*1½ cups heavy cream*
4 slices cooked smoked ham	*salt*
4 large mushroom caps	*4 rounds white bread*

Skin and bone 4 breasts of guinea hen. Cook slowly in 3 tablespoons of butter until tender and golden brown on both sides, about 30 minutes in all. Remove the guinea hen from the pan and keep warm. Put another tablespoon of butter in the same pan and lightly brown 4 slices of ham and 4 large mushroom caps. Remove and keep warm with the guinea hen. Pour 3 tablespoons of sherry into the pan and bring to a boil to lift the glaze. Add 1½ cups of cream and a little salt and simmer about 5 minutes.

Meanwhile cut 4 large rounds of firm white bread about ½ inch thick. Sauté until golden brown on both sides in 2 to 3 tablespoons of butter.

To Serve: Place the rounds of bread on a hot serving dish. Put a slice of ham on each one topped with a breast of guinea hen and a mushroom cap. Spoon the sauce over all and serve immediately while the bread is still crisp. Serves 4.

INDEX

INDEX

321